# CHOCOLATE

# SNOWBALL

A **ThreeForks** Book
Copyright 1999 Letty Halloran Flatt
Illustrations copyright 1999 Gregory S. Ragland

Published by Falcon® Publishing, Inc., Helena, Montana.
Printed in Singapore.
ThreeForks is an imprint of Falcon® Publishing, Inc.

Cover photos, clockwise from top left: Chocolate Snowball, Fresh
Nectarine Shortcake with Caramel Whipped Cream, Linzer Heart Cookies,
Chocolate Truffle Cake, by Michael Skarsten. Background photo by
Hughes Martin.

Library of Congress Cataloging-in-Publication Data
Flatt, Letty Halloran, 1952–
        Chocolate snowball and other fabulous pastries from Deer Valley
    Bakery / Letty Halloran Flatt ; photographs by Michael Skarsten ;
    photo styling by Susan Massey.
            p.   cm.
      ISBN 1-56044-828-8
      1. Baking.   2. Desserts.   3. Deer Valley Bakery.   I. Title.
    TX765.F64   1999
    641'.8"15—dc21
                                                    99-19569
                                                    CIP

For extra copies of this book and information about other Falcon
books, write Falcon, P.O. Box 1718, Helena, Montana 59624; or call
1-800-582-2665. To contact us by e-mail, visit our website at
http://www.falcon.com.

# CHOCOLATE

# SNOWBALL

AND OTHER FABULOUS PASTRIES FROM DEER VALLEY BAKERY

## LETTY HALLORAN FLATT

PHOTOGRAPHS BY MICHAEL SKARSTEN

PHOTO STYLING BY SUSAN MASSEY

ThreeForks

Helena, Montana

*To my husband, Robbie*

# Contents

# Foreword

By the mid-1970s the classical culinary rules, techniques and procedures were growing less and less important. A new thing was happening. There began a movement that dictated simplicity of procedure, freshness of ingredients and a sense for innovative presentations. The movement was a response to a new, surging demand by Americans for different dimensions in their dining experiences—better food, wholesome food, fresher food. There was an urge toward a better quality of health, thus a better quality of life.

Simultaneous with this culinary movement, the founders of Deer Valley conducted an extensive review of winter ski areas and resorts in North America. Their mission was to develop a resort that was better than any in existence. All facets of ski operations were studied including destination and site locations, mountain challenges, trail layouts, grooming, snowmaking, maintenance and a wide range of hospitality-related components: guest services, food preparation, and dining environments and design. What became increasingly clear to Deer Valley's founders was the dearth of attention devoted to guest-oriented hospitality issues. Mediocrity was evident everywhere!

Deer Valley found its raison d'être. No sense of service would be spared Deer Valley guests from the instant they arrived at the ski area through their entire on-mountain experience. Deer Valley would offer not only ski trails and downhill thrills, but also service competence and skilled food preparation at all outlets. The battle for quality and excellence would be unending, calling for vigorous programs and strenuous efforts at every stage of the resort's development.

Since its beginning in 1981, Deer Valley's organizational culture has provided a wide range of launching pads for individuals to perform unhindered, to find their métier and to distinguish themselves accordingly. One who recognized and grasped the opportunities at hand from the very outset is the author of this book, Letty Flatt. Through the profession she chose for herself, master baker and pâtissière, she personifies the Deer Valley mission. Although Letty had never baked professionally before coming to Deer Valley and did not receive formal instruction until she had spent two years in the resort's baking system, some fifteen years later she is publishing this fine cookbook, reflecting her intellectual ability as well as her superior baking skills.

Among those truths that never change is the tenet that conveys a powerful sentiment, "nothing is work unless you enjoy more doing something else." Letty, a woman of unbridled heart, passion, eloquence and imagination, enjoys everything that she does, be it skiing or baking. She has had to be a skilled baker, a product engineer, a labor expert, a cost manager and is now an accomplished cookbook author. For Letty, "pressure is a privilege," as Billie Jean King once said, "it comes only to those who earn it."

In context with the disappearing classical culinary rules with which this foreword opens you will find truly American recipes here that cut away from the time-honored traditions of home baking, yet fit comfortably with the skill and available equipment of the home baker.

Home bakers will benefit from the author's clarity of instructions and descriptions. Added bonuses in this book are twofold: the technical directions given for the unpredictable aspects of high altitude baking and the inclusion of timely recipes that are fat-free alternatives. As a good cookbook should, this one motivates and conveys trust. The author instills confidence as she guides you every step of the way, often with numerous pointers and trade secrets she includes as sidebars to a range of selected recipes.

To Letty, we should award ◆◆ for expertise and excellence in baking and a ● for the ease and simplicity with which she leads us into the world of her spirited recipes.

**James A. Nassikas**
*Former president of Deer Valley Resort*

# Acknowledgments

To my husband, Robbie: Thank you for sharing my goal in writing this cookbook, for giving it priority in our life and for our walks together along the creek path near our house.

I wish to thank Edgar and Polly Stern, whose brainchild Deer Valley is, for providing the work and the opportunities and for continuing to shape the resort with genteel polish.

Loving thanks to Julie Wilson, Deer Valley's food and beverage director, for her unerring sense of taste and complete support.

Thank you, Bob Wheaton, Deer Valley president and general manager, for encouragement and approval, and for every pat on the back.

To Deer Valley guests who have delighted in our pastries over the years—I appreciate every bite.

I could not do the task of running two pastry kitchens and guiding a crew of bakers by myself. I work closely with two talented pastry chefs who are in charge of bakery activities in each lodge. They keep me from being buried under an avalanche of pastries and paperwork. Thanks to pastry chef Wallace Rockwell for helping me write this book by overseeing Silver Lake Lodge's bakery and more and by allowing me the time away. I also thank pastry chef Steve Harty for managing the bakery at Snow Park and for his sacrifices on behalf of the book.

Deer Valley has always attracted energetic, creative and adept bakers. A standing ovation to previous pastry chefs Anne Voye Reynolds, Francy Royer and Susan Prieskorn, my cohorts, for bequeathing recipes and procedures. I acknowledge all Deer Valley bakers, past and present, for their contributions and hard work.

Antonia Allegra, friend and writing coach extraordinaire, is the angel looking over my shoulder. More than one aspect of this book reflects Toni's sensibilities, wisdom and subtle counsel.

I am filled with gratitude for all my teachers and mentors. Several I have had the fortune to study with, some have guided me through their cookbooks and others have become friends through the Bakers Dozen or by telephone, e-mail and fax machine. Thank you, Flo Braker, Shirley Corriher, Marion Cunningham, Carol Field, Bo Friberg, Maida Heatter, Madeleine Kamman, Nick Malgieri, Harold McGee, James McNair, Alice Medrich, Gayle and Joe Ortiz, Peter Reinhart, Lindsey Shere, Carole Walter and Anne Willan for your careful writing and generous natures. Thank you, Jim Dodge and Emily Luchetti, for encouraging me to write this cookbook when it was just a spark in my mind.

For help and assurance along the way, I am obliged to Wendy Faber, Annette Gooch, Virginia Rainey, Kristen Gould Case, Carla Williams, Jere Calmes, Bob O'Neill, Eric Witt and Ted Scheffler. I appreciate Abi Wright, Patricia Constable and Maura Mark for keeping me in shape, mentally and physically. Thank you, Steve Erickson, for the original ski recipe.

It was a pleasure collaborating with photographer Michael Skarsten and food stylist Susan Massey. Due to their professional patience, the photo shoots were almost relaxing instead of stressful. Thanks to Michael's wife, Melissa Skarsten, for adding her eye for detail and assistance. No Place Like Home in Park City and Williams-Sonoma in Salt Lake City generously donated props for the photos. Praises also to illustrator Greg Ragland for a job well done, and to Hughes Martin for providing the photo of "perfect snow."

Thank you to Megan Hiller, my editor, for the easy rapport and for encouraging a more personal style. For seeing the potential and for every suggestion, thank you to my agent, Julie Castiglia.

Special thanks and recognition go to all of my recipe testers. For ample and repeated testing at sea level and here in the mountains, kudos to Wallace Rockwell, Carolyn Weil, Shelly Southwick, Paula Rector, Terri Foley and Erika Foley as well as my sister, Katie Koziolek, who also tested more than a share. Other testers were Carol Agle, Mary Bernasconi, Patricia Constable, Jan DeMers, Sue Denkers, Mya Frantti, Jane Halloran, Leslie Halloran, Mary Halloran, Cynthia Howlett, Jeannie Lambert, Helene Maw, Andrea Nass, "Nipper" Noble, Lois Podolny, Susan Prieskorn, Alix Railton, Maria Spansk-McGrail and Priscilla Watts.

# Introduction

Welcome to a bustling day as a baker at Deer Valley Ski Resort. You'll find yourself in more than one place at a time, since Deer Valley has multiple lodges and two bakery kitchens. For your day, please dress in our uniform—white button-down jacket and black and white houndstooth check pants, apron, neckerchief and, to top it off, a tall, pleated white toque. Imagine arriving at Snow Park Lodge and punching the time clock at the stroke of midnight. During this graveyard shift, you will prepare five different varieties of bread—white and Seeded Whole Wheat Sourdough, plus baguettes, challah and a daily special for Snow Park's natural salad buffet. In addition, you will bake fresh muffins, croissants, scones, sweet bread and coffee cake for 5,000 skiers, as well as extra goodies for the 250 workers who eat breakfast every morning in the employee dining room.

At 4:00 a.m. you move halfway up the mountain as the early morning baker at Silver Lake Lodge. You bake the breakfast items that have been rising slowly since last evening—the Danish pastries, Whole Wheat Cinnamon Brioche Rolls and croissants. You mix two different batches of muffins as well as the daily-special bread for Silver Lake's natural salad buffet. You bake the buttery scones, prepare sweet bread and coffee cake and make pizza dough for Bald Mountain Pizza. You also whip up something extra for hungry Silver Lake–based employees. At daybreak, take a moment to watch the sun rise over Bald Mountain—greet the day.

Now imagine you are a day-shift baker. You arrive at 8:00 a.m. along with thirty cooks and a half-dozen other bakers. It's time to mix the cookie dough. Depending on the day's skier count estimate, you make one to four batches, for up to a thousand cookies. Your aim is to have the test cookies out of the oven and the dough set aside in huge plastic bins so restaurant attendants and cashiers can scoop them into balls before 10:30 a.m.

At each lodge, you take inventory of the freezer and refrigerator and fill out a production worksheet. You spread brownie batter into sheet pans, frost carrot cakes, roll pie dough and "blind bake" the shells, and make different sauces and garnishes—to name only a few of your projects. If you are a beginning baker, you are probably out front in the day restaurants, stocking the glass and brass shelves, greeting guests and baking cookies. If you are experienced, you could be assembling elaborate desserts or putting the finishing touches on a birthday cake.

Conclude your baker's day by imagining you are the evening shift baker. At Snow Park Lodge, you prepare for the prodigious Seafood Buffet dinner. You bake creamy custards in small ramekins and when they have cooled, you sprinkle sugar on top, torch the sugar into crunchy caramel and voilà—crème brûlée. You assemble Chocolate and Blueberry Bread Pudding. You cut and plate Honey Walnut Tart and bake Cappuccino Cheesecake for tomorrow night. Your day at Snow Park ends around 10:30 p.m., when the last guest has feasted from your dessert display.

Finish the day at Silver Lake Lodge by setting up for evening service at McHenry's and The Mariposa restaurants. You warm the Hot Fudge Sauce to go with ice cream sandwiches. You pipe the whipped cream on the Chocolate Snowball and assemble the Apple Phyllo Bundles. You prescoop the Maple Walnut Ice Cream and the Blood Orange Sorbet. Business is hopping at Silver Lake. Besides restaurant dish-up, you have a banquet for 150 people; you are serving Roasted Banana Panna Cotta for dessert. By the time the evening winds down, it is 11:00 p.m. That gives you an hour before you must be back at Snow Park Lodge to punch in for another day!

Now that you have completed your whirlwind tour of Deer Valley's bakeries, I invite you to bake your way through some of our best and time-tested recipes, modified for home bakers. Throughout this book, to augment your day in the bakery, look for anecdotes about Deer Valley and the bakery's inner workings. The first two chapters, "Breakfast Delights" and "Our Daily Breads," are from the early morning bakery shifts. The latter chapters, "Ice Creams and Sorbets" and "Odd Stuff: Distinctive Desserts, Puddings and Fruit Specialties," include recipes often prepared on the evening shifts. In between are "Cookies and Bars," "Cakes and Cheesecakes" and "Pies and Tarts"—recipes for items served throughout the day, from lunch to dinner. For the basic recipes, the building blocks of a baker's repertoire, the last recipe chapter is "Fundamental Formulas." Finally, "The Baker's Pantry: A Glossary of Ingredients, Tools, Terms, Techniques and Resources" is a reference for all bakers. If you live and bake above 3,000 feet above sea level, read the "Baking at Celestial Heights" chapter for guidance on the quirks and effects of high altitude baking. Although the recipes were written and tested for sea level, my suggestions for high altitude adjustments accompany each recipe.

Deer Valley hires new bakers every autumn to gear up for the busy ski season. The bakeries literally become a small pastry school with the lodge pastry chefs and me, as well as other returning bakers, teaching the uninitiated bakers as much as we can. We develop their skills, give them the reasons for certain procedures and show them what to look for when following baking techniques. We witness mistakes, answer questions and nurture them through the learning curve. In this book, I hope to be your baking mentor. I offer helpful hints throughout, guiding you through the recipes. You will find clarifying notes about ingredients or procedures, indicated by *. You'll also find my advice in the glossary, chapter introductions, and recipe headnotes and sidebars.

In the kitchen we use a French phrase, *mise en place*. It translates "put in its place," or have everything ready. It's about being organized. The first thing to do when you decide to make something is read through the recipe. As you read, imagine all the described steps. In your mind, get a feel for the methods, even if you've never done them. Then, assemble your ingredients, the necessary bowls, whisks and spatulas, and prepare your pans. Your thoughts as well as your tools should be organized, ready to bake, *mise en place*.

To keep beginning skiers from ending up on a steep hill, North American ski areas rate their trails according to difficulty. New skiers, awkward and timid, will choose an ● Easier gentle slope. After they acquire some skills and feel more confident, they might choose an ■ Intermediate run. The double black diamond ◆◆ trails are for experts who enjoy steep, challenging terrain. Just as a ski area rates its trails according to skier ability, the recipes in this book are rated according to ease of preparation. You'll see these guiding symbols on every recipe in this book.

- ● Easier recipes have fewer and simpler steps and can be used as learning recipes by novice bakers.
- ■ Intermediate recipes are more complicated and might require special equipment; you should be able to follow ■ Intermediate recipes if you have baking or kitchen experience.
- ◆ Advanced and ◆◆ Expert recipes have multiple steps and more difficult techniques—and they will take more time.

A beginner baker could tackle an ◆ Advanced recipe with success, just as beginning skiers have found themselves on ◆ Advanced runs and conquered the challenge triumphantly. Nonetheless, the symbols should be helpful in making recipe choices.

Because I am both a skier and a baker, to me the parallels between these pastimes run deeper than trail symbols and recipe ratings. As pastry chef at a ski resort, I am able to intertwine skiing and baking. I love to ski. I love the crisp, cool air and the way it tingles my face. I relish the freedom of gliding through powder snow, and the power in my legs as I carve turn after turn. I bask in the clear bright blue sky, the noble evergreen trees dusted with snowflakes, and the grandeur of panoramic mountain vistas.

I love to bake. I savor the warm kitchen with its nurturing aromas and the smell of chocolate cake as it wafts from the oven. When I knead and shape bread, I appreciate my strength, and I am grateful for a good whisking arm to make large batches of Vanilla Bean Pastry Cream. I get immediate satisfaction creating beautiful desserts; it's the same feeling I get standing at the bottom of a ski run and looking back up at my serpentine tracks.

Skiing and baking correlate in other ways. For example, you can't learn to ski in one day. You can acquire enough skills to get down the hill, but, right away you won't be able to race down a steep, tree-dotted slope. It's the same in baking. You can follow a recipe and have it come out well, but it takes time and experience to become a competent pastry cook. Both require learned techniques, yet offer tremendous enjoyment at the elementary level. Also, once you are proficient in either calling, there is always more to master, a higher skill level for which to aim.

The analogy continues: Skiing and baking can be religious experiences. You can know spirituality in nature, outdoors, at one with the snow and the mountain, or in the kitchen, creating beauty and nourishment with food. I am at peace in the peaks and I give thanks for the beauty that surrounds those who choose to live in the mountains. I offer goodness and sustenance through my pastries, breads and desserts.

Both skiing and baking offer sociability. Sharing a chairlift and the slopes with friends or family offers companionship. Mixing, tasting, and baking in the kitchen with others brings us together as we break bread. On the other hand, I appreciate the solitude of each. Imagine finding yourself on a freshly groomed trail, alone and lighthearted, feeling the snow beneath your moving body, with only the swish of your skis to keep you company. Or think about a quiet kitchen when no one is around. Content with your thoughts, you concentrate as you roll pastry or knead bread.

As I endeavor in skiing and baking, each continues to surprise me with life's lessons. I ponder how skiing and baking relate to life itself. I am not alone in my thinking. In 1843 Ralph Waldo Emerson wrote in his journal, "The sky is the daily bread of the eyes." Several authors philosophize about skiing and baking as metaphors for life. Allow me to share a few of my favorites with you.

In *Brother Juniper's Bread Book,* baker and author Peter Reinhart frequently likens breadmaking to life. Lyrically, he contemplates the fact that breadmaking illuminates and teaches us about life. He explains, "I have been trying to show that breadmaking does, silently, of its own accord . . . transmit love and goodness and that this energy works on us whether we are aware of it or not."

Delores LaChapelle, in her little-known vest-pocket *Deep Powder Snow: Forty Years of Ecstatic Skiing, Avalanches, and Earth Wisdom,* suggests the symbolism of skiing and life. Ms. LaChapelle tells us about the flowing interaction between a skier, the snow and the mountain. She reflects that skiing keeps us in tune with our existence, with life. "What we experience in powder is the original human self, which lies deeply inside each of us, still undamaged in spite of what our present culture tries to do to us."

*Becoming Bread* is a book of prayers in poetry. The author, Gunilla Norris, takes each step in the process of making bread and uses it as a metaphor. Meditatively, she explores how bread is analogous to love. "Here is the kitchen. Will you enter it with me? Let us share the heart of the house."

These writers know what I feel about baking and skiing—my life of skiing and baking rolled into one. The image is a chocolate snowball—my metaphor. This book is a symbol for my twin passions. Let it be. Let it snow. Let it dough.

# Breakfast Delights

● Deer Valley Granola

● Pumpkin Pecan Bread

● Cranberry Orange Bread

● Chocolate Zucchini Bread

● Sunshine Muffins

● Banana Raspberry Muffins

● Blueberry Corn Muffins

● Healthy Heart Muffins

● Banana Maple Nut Coffee Cake

● Raspberry Cream Cheese Coffee Cake

● Dried Cherry Scones

■ Oatmeal Rosemary Scones

■ Honey Sticky Buns

■ Good Friday Hot Cross Buns

◆ Beth's Tea Ring

◆ Whole Wheat Cinnamon Brioche Rolls

# Breakfast Delights

In the slumbering hours, while skiers dream of turns in soft powder snow, Deer Valley's bakers are busy making breakfast treats. In their white chef jackets, the denizens of the night kitchen have been baking up a floury storm. The night bakers are a talented crew, capable of juggling many tasks at once. Their timing must be just so to have everything ready before we open.

When they interviewed for the job, they took a baker's quiz—our 10-point questionnaire that helps assess an applicant's baking skills. The quiz is not a test—it even says to feel free to leave the space blank if you don't know the answer. One question asks applicants to name the ingredient that makes puff pastry, croissants, Danish dough and pie doughs flaky. Another asks for an explanation of the difference between pastry cream and crème anglaise. We include a math problem to help us discern multiplication, addition and subtraction competence—a baker is always converting recipes from one yield to another and a simple arithmetic error could lead to a disaster in the oven. We ask about the temperature for dissolving yeast and the proper method for melting chocolate. We even give the ingredients for chocolate chip cookies and ask for brief instructions on how to prepare the recipe. A question that relates to breakfast items is, "In most muffin recipes, the batter should be mixed very well, true or false?" Most applicants answer "false," which is correct. Throughout this book you will find the answers to the baker's quiz; in fact, you would pass with flying colors after baking your way through the chapters.

It's true, muffin batter should be mixed only until the dry ingredients are moistened; a few lumps or traces of flour are fine. In fact, if the batter is smooth, it is probably overmixed, and overmixed muffin batter makes tough, rubbery muffins full of tunnels or holes.

The muffin recipes in this chapter yield 12 large muffins. If your muffin cups hold less than ⅓ cup of liquid, or if you want smaller muffins, portion the batter into 16 cups. In order to produce the biggest muffin possible, you will need to fill the standard-size muffin cups almost to the top, even though it seems the batter will overflow in the oven. Be sure to grease the top surface around the cups so the tops of the muffins don't stick. We sell jumbo muffins at Deer Valley, baked in "Texas-size" pans. The muffin recipes will yield 6 mountainous muffins from these oversize pans. Reduce the baking time for smaller muffins; increase the time for giant ones.

A trick I learned from a baker who works in a grocery store bakery is to preheat the oven 50° hotter than the recipe requires. After placing the filled muffin tins in the oven to bake, lower to the regular temperature. Your muffins will have perfect, high, round tops, just as his do.

We use an ice cream scoop to fill muffin cups—it's an easy way to distribute the batter. It is the baker's choice to use paper cupcake liners or not; I like the look of a muffin without the paper wrapper, so I always coat muffin tins with cooking spray.

This chapter includes four sweet breads made with yeast. If you are not used to working with yeast or need a review, refer to the "Our Daily Breads" chapter. One of the ways the night bakers stay organized is to prepare yeast breakfast breads in large batches, keeping several days' worth of pre-cut cinnamon rolls and Danish pastries in the freezer. The last baker of the day does the "freezer pull" and arranges tomorrow's "bake-off" on baking sheets to thaw. The pans go on a rolling cart covered with a zippered plastic bag. The rolls and Danish and croissants are left to rise or "proof" in the bag, protected from drafts, making their own humidity. The night bakers monitor these yeasted breads proofing in the hours before dawn. When a batch of Banana Raspberry Muffins comes out of the oven, the Whole Wheat Cinnamon Brioche Rolls go in.

The night bakers at Silver Lake Lodge have a tradition of greeting the new day. They sneak away from the kitchen, scheduling their break between projects. Coffee or tea in hand, they watch the sun rise over the panoramic view from the Bald Mountain Room. Some mornings they even slip outside to feel the fresh air and say good-bye to the stars.

# • Deer Valley Granola

The milk powder gives this breakfast cereal uncommon flavor and extra nourishment.
Serve with milk or yogurt and sliced fresh fruit or berries.

3 cups old-fashioned rolled oats
1 cup instant nonfat dry milk powder
¾ cup shelled sunflower seeds
¾ cup sliced almonds
⅓ cup sesame seeds
⅓ cup pumpkin seeds
⅓ cup shredded coconut (page 245)
¼ cup canola oil
½ cup honey
½ teaspoon vanilla extract

Preheat oven to 300°. Mix the rolled oats, milk powder, sunflower seeds, almonds, sesame
seeds, pumpkin seeds and coconut in a large bowl. Measure the oil in a 1-cup measure.
Swish it to coat up to the ¾-cup mark, then add the honey to the mark. Add the vanilla.
Pour the liquids over the dry ingredients and mix everything together using your hands.
Spread onto a large baking sheet, about ½ inch deep. Bake 30 minutes or until golden
brown, stirring after 15 minutes so the granola in the middle of the pan will brown evenly
with the edges. Cool. Store in an airtight container.

*Makes about 8 cups.*

▲ High altitude: This recipe needs no adjustment.

# • Pumpkin Pecan Bread

My husband's family serves this bread with Thanksgiving dinner. At Deer Valley we offer it year-round, as part of our breakfast pastry assortment.

1¾ cups all-purpose flour
1⅓ cups sugar
1¼ teaspoons baking soda
¾ teaspoon salt
¾ teaspoon ground cinnamon
½ teaspoon ground nutmeg
¼ teaspoon ground ginger
2 eggs
½ cup canola oil
½ teaspoon apple cider vinegar
½ teaspoon vanilla extract
1¾ cups (15-ounce can) pumpkin purée
¾ cup old-fashioned rolled oats
¾ cup *plus* ¼ cup coarsely chopped pecans

Preheat the oven to 350°. Brush a 12x4-inch loaf pan (page 250) with melted butter and dust lightly with flour, or spray generously with cooking spray.

Sift the flour, sugar, baking soda, salt, cinnamon, nutmeg and ginger in a large bowl. In a second bowl, whisk the eggs, oil, vinegar, vanilla and pumpkin purée.

Using a wire whisk, mix the wet ingredients into the dry ingredients. Stir in the rolled oats and ¾ cup of the pecans. Spread into the prepared loaf pan and sprinkle with the remaining ¼ cup of nuts. Bake 60 to 70 minutes, until a toothpick inserted in the center comes out clean. Cool 30 minutes before removing from the pan.

*Makes 1 loaf, serves 12.*

▲ High altitude: Reduce sugar to 1¼ cups and reduce baking soda to 1 teaspoon.

# • Cranberry Orange Bread

The bits of cranberry add an alpenglow red color. I make this bread to give as Christmas presents, each loaf wrapped in cellophane and tied with a bright red bow.

8 tablespoons (1 stick) unsalted butter, room temperature
1⅓ cups sugar
1 teaspoon grated orange zest
2 eggs
3 cups all-purpose flour
2 teaspoons baking powder
¾ teaspoon baking soda
1 teaspoon salt
1 cup orange juice
1½ cups (6 ounces) cranberries, coarsely chopped ❋
¾ cup *plus* ¼ cup coarsely chopped walnuts (about 4 ounces total)

Preheat the oven to 350°. Brush a 12x4-inch loaf pan (page 250) with melted butter and dust lightly with flour, or spray generously with cooking spray.

With an electric mixer, cream together the butter, sugar and orange zest. Add the eggs one at a time. Scrape the sides and bottom of the bowl.

In a separate bowl, sift the flour, baking powder, baking soda and salt. Add half of the dry ingredients to the butter mixture; mix and scrape the bowl. Add the orange juice; mix. Blend in the remaining dry ingredients; scrape and mix well.

Fold in the cranberries and ¾ cup of the walnuts. Spread into the prepared pan and sprinkle with the remaining ¼ cup of nuts. Bake 60 to 75 minutes, until a toothpick inserted in the center comes out clean. Cool 30 minutes before removing from the pan.

*Makes 1 loaf, serves 12.*

▲ High altitude: Reduce sugar to 1¼ cups. Reduce baking powder to 1¾ teaspoons and baking soda to ½ teaspoon.

❋ Cranberries chop easily in a food processor. Turn the machine on and off with the pulse button, checking the cranberries after each pulse. If you are using frozen cranberries, let them thaw about 10 minutes, but chop them before they thaw completely.

*On clear days there is a warm reddish glow, called alpenglow, that reflects off mountain peaks. Alpenglow can occur twice a day, mirroring the rising sun or the late afternoon sunset. Whenever I see this alpine phenomenon, I remember to give thanks for another glorious day.*

# • Chocolate Zucchini Bread

If you have ever been blessed with an abundance of zucchini, you'll appreciate this unusual bread—it makes use of the garden's prosperity.

**1 (3-ounce) package cream cheese**
**1⅓ cups sugar**
**2 eggs**
**⅓ cup canola oil**
**1½ teaspoons vanilla extract**
**2 cups all-purpose flour**
**½ cup cocoa powder**
**1½ teaspoons ground cinnamon**
**1 teaspoon baking powder**
**1 teaspoon baking soda**
**¾ teaspoon salt**
**1½ cups grated zucchini**
**¾ cup *plus* ¼ cup sliced almonds**
**¾ cup semisweet chocolate morsels**

*If you prefer walnuts to almonds, or you have only cashews on hand, freely substitute one for another; nut varieties are mostly interchangeable.*

Preheat the oven to 350°. Brush a 12x4-inch loaf pan (page 250) with melted butter and dust lightly with flour, or spray generously with cooking spray.

With an electric mixer, beat the cream cheese and sugar. Add the eggs one at a time. Scrape the sides and bottom of the bowl. Mix in the oil and vanilla extract.

Sift the flour, cocoa powder, cinnamon, baking powder, baking soda and salt into another bowl. Add to the cream cheese mixture, blending well. Mix in the zucchini, ¾ cup of the almonds and the chocolate morsels. Spread into the prepared loaf pan and sprinkle with the remaining ¼ cup of nuts. Bake 60 to 75 minutes, until a toothpick inserted in the center comes out clean. Cool 30 minutes before removing from the pan.

*Makes 1 loaf, serves 12.*

▲ High altitude: Decrease sugar by 2 tablespoons. Reduce baking powder and baking soda to ¾ teaspoon each.

# • Sunshine Muffins

These muffins are like carrot cake but without the frosting. They're chock-full of goodies: Sunflower seeds provide crunch and nourishment, and fresh carrots and apples supply long-lasting moisture. Serve for breakfast, brunch or afternoon tea—they're guaranteed to brighten the day.

   3 eggs
   ⅔ cup canola oil
   2 teaspoons vanilla extract
   ½ cup dark raisins
   2 cups grated carrots
   2 cups grated apples
   ½ cup *plus* ⅓ cup shelled sunflower seeds
   2 cups all-purpose flour
   1 cup sugar
   2 teaspoons baking soda
   2 teaspoons ground cinnamon
   ½ teaspoon salt

Preheat the oven to 375°. Line 12 muffin cups with paper cupcake liners, or coat the muffin tins with melted butter and dust with flour, or spray generously with cooking spray. To make sure muffins release with ease, coat the top of the pan as well as the inside of the cups when you grease the tins.

Whisk the eggs, oil, vanilla and raisins together in a large bowl. Stir in the carrots, apples and ½ cup of the sunflower seeds. Sift the flour, sugar, baking soda, cinnamon and salt into another bowl, then mix into the carrot mixture. Divide into the prepared muffin tins. Sprinkle with the remaining ⅓ cup of sunflower seeds. Bake 25 to 30 minutes or until the tops of the muffins spring back when touched with a finger. Cool for about 5 minutes, then remove from the pan.

*Makes 12 muffins.*

▲ High altitude: Decrease sugar by 2 tablespoons. Reduce baking soda to 1½ teaspoons.

*In order to produce the biggest muffin possible, you will need to fill standard-size muffin cups almost to the top, even though it might seem the batter will overflow in the oven.*

# • Banana Raspberry Muffins

Slightly redolent of banana, these moist, berry-full treats are wonderful for Sunday brunch. Blackberries or blueberries can replace the raspberries in this recipe.

2½ cups all-purpose flour
2½ teaspoons baking powder
½ teaspoon baking soda
½ teaspoon salt
8 tablespoons (1 stick) unsalted butter, melted
⅔ cup firmly packed brown sugar
3 eggs
3 ripe bananas, mashed
⅔ cup whole milk
1 teaspoon vanilla extract
1½ cups raspberries, fresh or frozen
¼ cup Butter Streusel (page 210)

Preheat the oven to 375°. Line 12 muffin cups with paper cupcake liners, or coat the muffin tins with melted butter and dust with flour, or spray generously with cooking spray. To make sure muffins release with ease, coat the top of the pan as well as the inside of the cups when you grease the tins.

Sift together the flour, baking powder, baking soda and salt; set aside. Whisk the butter and brown sugar in a large bowl, then whisk in the eggs. Add the bananas, milk and vanilla. Add the dry ingredients all at once, stirring just until blended. Quickly fold in the berries. Divide into prepared muffin cups and sprinkle with Butter Streusel. Bake 25 to 30 minutes or until the tops of the muffins are golden brown and they spring back when touched with a finger. Cool for about 5 minutes, then remove from the pan.

*Makes 12 muffins.*

▲ High altitude: Reduce baking powder to 1¾ teaspoons.

*When bananas turn brown and almost too soft to eat, peel and freeze them in a plastic bag. They'll be ready and waiting for you to make muffins or breads that call for ripe bananas; thaw until mashable.*

*Opposite: Banana Raspberry Muffins*

# • Blueberry Corn Muffins

Applesauce enriches these muffins, keeping them moist and replacing some of the fat. As with the Banana Raspberry Muffins, the blueberries can be replaced with raspberries or blackberries.

**3 cups unsweetened applesauce**
**¾ cup sugar**
**½ cup canola oil**
**1 egg**
**1 teaspoon grated lemon zest**
**½ teaspoon vanilla extract**
**½ teaspoon orange or lemon extract**
**1½ cups all-purpose flour**
**1½ cups yellow cornmeal**
**2¼ teaspoons baking soda**
**¾ teaspoon salt**
**2 cups blueberries, fresh or frozen**❄
**¼ cup Butter Streusel (page 210)**

❄ If you use frozen berries, keep them in the freezer until just before folding. You don't want them to thaw too soon or their juice will color the muffins an undesirable purple.

Preheat the oven to 375°. Line 12 muffin cups with paper cupcake liners, or coat the muffin tins with melted butter and dust with flour, or spray generously with cooking spray. To make sure muffins release with ease, coat the top of the pan as well as the inside of the cups when you grease the tins.

Whisk the applesauce, sugar, oil, egg, lemon zest, vanilla and orange or lemon extracts together in a large bowl. In another bowl, sift the flour, cornmeal, baking soda and salt. Stir the dry ingredients into the wet ingredients, blending just until mixed. Quickly fold in the blueberries.

Divide into prepared muffin cups and sprinkle with Butter Streusel. Bake 30 to 35 minutes or until the tops of the muffins are golden brown and they spring back when touched with a finger. Cool for about 5 minutes, then remove from the pan.

*Makes 12 muffins.*

▲ High altitude: Reduce baking soda to 1½ teaspoons.

# • Healthy Heart Muffins

On winter mornings I make the rounds of the bakery, checking out the pastries and spot-tasting for quality control. I could test these muffins every day. They're fat-free and inherently healthful, made with whole grains, laced with fruit and sweetened with honey.

¼ cup pitted prunes, tightly packed
2 tablespoons hot water
1½ cups unsweetened applesauce
⅓ cup orange juice
3 egg whites or ⅓ cup liquid egg substitute
⅓ cup honey
⅓ cup dark raisins
2 teaspoons vanilla extract
¾ teaspoon orange extract
1 teaspoon grated orange zest, optional
1½ cups whole wheat flour
2 teaspoons baking soda
¾ teaspoon baking powder
¾ teaspoon salt
¾ teaspoon ground cinnamon
¼ teaspoon ground nutmeg
¾ cup oat bran❋
¼ cup old-fashioned rolled oats, for garnish

❋ Oat bran is sold in most natural food stores. If unavailable, substitute old-fashioned rolled oats that have been ground in a food processor.

Preheat the oven to 375°. Line 12 muffin cups with paper cupcake liners, or coat the muffin tins with melted butter and dust with flour, or spray generously with cooking spray. To make sure muffins release with ease, coat the top of the pan as well as the inside of the cups when you grease the tins.

Soak the prunes in the hot water for 10 minutes. Purée in a food processor until quite smooth and no large chunks remain. Transfer to a large bowl. Whisk in the applesauce, orange juice, egg whites, honey, raisins, vanilla and orange extracts and orange zest, if using. Sift the flour, baking soda, baking powder, salt, cinnamon and nutmeg into another bowl. Stir in the oat bran. Add the dry ingredients to the wet, mixing just to moisten. Divide into the prepared muffin cups and sprinkle with the rolled oats. Bake 25 to 30 minutes or until the tops of the muffins spring back when touched with a finger. Cool for about 5 minutes, then remove from the pan.

*Makes 12 muffins.*

▲ High altitude: Reduce honey to ¼ cup and reduce baking soda to 1½ teaspoons.

# • Banana Maple Nut Coffee Cake

Maple syrup, with its rich, natural flavor, is by far my favorite sweetener. You can substitute honey, if that's what you have on hand. At home, I replace the walnuts with roasted sunflower seeds. They are high in calcium—nutritious and delicious.

Topping:
**2 tablespoons unsalted butter, room temperature**
**⅓ cup firmly packed brown sugar**
**½ teaspoon ground cinnamon**
**⅓ cup coarsely chopped walnuts**

Batter:
**4 tablespoons unsalted butter, room temperature**
**½ cup sugar**
**½ cup maple syrup**
**2 eggs**
**3 ripe bananas, mashed**
**1⅔ cups all-purpose flour**
**¾ teaspoon baking soda**
**½ teaspoon salt**
**½ cup coarsely chopped walnuts**

❉ To make this coffee cake for a crowd, double the recipe and bake it in a 9x13-inch pan.

**To make the topping:**
Blend the butter with the brown sugar and cinnamon using your fingers or a wooden spoon. Mix in the nuts.

**To make the batter:**
Preheat the oven to 350°. Brush an 8x8-inch square or a 9x2-inch round pan❉ with melted butter and dust lightly with flour, or spray generously with cooking spray.

Beat the butter, sugar and maple syrup with an electric mixer. Add the eggs one at a time. Scrape the sides and bottom of the bowl. Mix in the bananas.

Sift the flour, baking soda and salt; add to the banana mixture, blending well. Stir in the walnuts. Spread into the prepared pan. Drop the topping in small dollops onto the banana batter. Bake 45 to 50 minutes or until the coffee cake is a deep golden brown and a toothpick inserted into the center comes out clean. Cool in the pan for 30 minutes. Invert onto a plate, then invert again so coffee cake is right-side up on a serving plate.

*Makes 1 coffee cake, serves 8 to 12.*

▲ High altitude: Decrease sugar in batter by 2 tablespoons. Reduce baking soda to ½ teaspoon.

# • Raspberry Cream Cheese Coffee Cake

This coffee cake can sit in our pastry window almost all day without drying out, which is particularly remarkable considering Utah's low average humidity. My advertisement would say, "Ski the light and dry powder snow, then enjoy this rich and moist coffee cake."

8 tablespoons (1 stick) unsalted butter, softened
1 (8-ounce) package cream cheese
¾ cup sugar
2 eggs
¾ teaspoon vanilla extract
2 cups all-purpose flour
1 teaspoon baking powder
¾ teaspoon baking soda
½ teaspoon salt
⅓ cup whole milk
½ cup raspberry preserves or spreadable fruit
⅓ cup Butter Streusel (page 210)

Preheat the oven to 350°. Brush a 9- or 10-inch round cake pan with melted butter and dust lightly with flour, or spray generously with cooking spray. The raspberry preserves sink and stick to the bottom of the pan; line the bottom with a circle of parchment or waxed paper so the coffee cake removes easily.

Beat the butter, cream cheese and sugar with an electric mixer. Add the eggs one at a time. Scrape the sides and bottom of the bowl. Mix in the vanilla.

Sift the flour, baking powder, baking soda and salt; add to the cream cheese mixture, blending well. Add the milk; mix and scrape. Spread into the prepared pan. Dollop the raspberry preserves onto the batter, then swirl a knife through it to marble the batter and preserves. Sprinkle evenly with the Butter Streusel. Bake 60 to 70 minutes or until the coffee cake is a deep golden brown and the top springs back when touched with a finger. Cool 30 minutes in the pan. Invert onto a plate and remove the parchment paper, then invert again so the coffee cake is right-side up on a serving plate.

*Makes 1 coffee cake, serves 12.*

▲ High altitude: Decrease sugar by 1 tablespoon. Reduce baking powder to ¾ teaspoon and baking soda to ½ teaspoon.

# • Dried Cherry Scones

In parts of Utah, scones are prepared as deep-fried puffs of dough, much like the Mexican *sopaipilla*. Utah natives are sometimes surprised by Deer Valley's biscuitlike, baked scones, which are more like those traditional in the British Isles. Serve these scones with fruit preserves for afternoon tea as well as breakfast. This is a very adaptable recipe; I often add nuts to the dough or use dried fruit other than cherries, such as apricots.

> 3 cups cake flour<sup>❊</sup>
> ½ cup sugar
> 1 tablespoon baking powder
> 1 teaspoon salt
> 2 teaspoons grated orange zest
> 12 tablespoons (1½ sticks) cold unsalted butter, cut in ½-inch pieces
> ¾ cup buttermilk
> ½ cup chopped dried cherries
> 2 tablespoons milk or heavy cream, optional
> 1 tablespoon crystal or granulated sugar (pages 255–256)

❊ Cake flour makes the scones more tender. You can substitute all-purpose flour, but use ⅓ cup less.

Sift flour, sugar, baking powder and salt into a large bowl. Stir in the zest. Cut the butter into the dry ingredients, using your fingers or a pastry blender, until the mixture resembles coarse meal. With a fork, stir in the buttermilk and cherries, and mix until the dough comes together. It will be quite sticky. To form this soft dough into a round, line a 9-inch round cake pan with plastic wrap. Put the dough into the pan and fold the plastic wrap over to completely cover the dough. Form the dough into an even round disk, about ½ inch thick, by pushing the dough around under the plastic wrap. Refrigerate or freeze about 1 hour, or until cold enough to cut.

Preheat oven to 375°. Line a large baking sheet with parchment paper, or coat lightly with butter or cooking spray. Cut the scone dough round into 10 pie-shaped wedges. Arrange on the prepared pan at least 1 inch apart. Brush with milk or cream, if using, and sprinkle with sugar. Bake 15 to 20 minutes or until the bottoms are light golden brown and your finger doesn't leave an indentation when you touch the tops.

*Makes 10 scones.*

▲ High altitude: Decrease sugar by 1 tablespoon. Reduce baking powder to 2 teaspoons.

# ■ Oatmeal Rosemary Scones

The first step of this recipe—steeping rosemary in hot cream—imparts the herb's fragrance to the cream. When the rosemary infusion is cold, mix it into the dry ingredients. Fresh rosemary is important to this recipe; I do not recommend dried rosemary as a substitute.

    1½ teaspoons finely chopped fresh rosemary
    ¾ cup half-and-half cream
    1½ cups all-purpose flour
    ⅓ cup sugar
    1½ teaspoons salt
    1 tablespoon baking powder
    1½ cups old-fashioned rolled oats
    12 tablespoons (1½ sticks) cold unsalted butter, cut in ½-inch pieces
    ¾ cup golden raisins
    2 tablespoons milk or heavy cream, optional
    1 tablespoon crystal or granulated sugar (pages 255–256)

Heat the rosemary and the cream in a small saucepan over medium heat until very hot but not boiling. Refrigerate until the cream is cold, about 30 minutes.

Sift the flour, sugar, salt and baking powder into a large bowl, and stir in the rolled oats. Cut the butter into the dry ingredients, using your fingers or a pastry blender, until the mixture resembles coarse meal. With a fork, stir in the cold rosemary cream and the raisins, and mix until the dough comes together. It will be quite sticky. To form this soft dough into a round, line a 9-inch round cake pan with plastic wrap. Put the dough into the pan and fold the plastic wrap over to completely cover the dough. Form the dough into an even round disk, about ½ inch thick, by pushing the dough around under the plastic wrap. Refrigerate or freeze about 1 hour, or until cold enough to cut.

Preheat oven to 375°. Line a large baking sheet with parchment paper, or coat lightly with butter or cooking spray. Cut the scone dough round into 10 pie-shaped wedges. Arrange on the prepared pan at least 1 inch apart. Brush with milk or cream, if using, and sprinkle with sugar. Bake 15 to 20 minutes or until the bottoms are light golden brown and your finger doesn't leave an indentation when you touch the tops.

*Makes 10 scones.*

▲ High altitude: Decrease sugar by 1 tablespoon. Reduce baking powder to 2 teaspoons.

*Rosemary is a lovely aromatic herb, a member of the mint family, with dark gray-green leaves that resemble small pine needles. It has a fairly strong and distinct flavor— pungent, lemony and slightly piney. An evergreen shrub native to the Mediterranean, it was used by the ancient Greeks and Romans as a culinary and medicinal herb. Rosemary is the symbol of fidelity, friendship and remembrance; brides wore garlands of it in their hair, as did Greek students during their examinations.*

# ■ Honey Sticky Buns

Honey keeps the caramel topping softer than when made with just butter and sugar. If you wish, make these rolls without the pecans—they will be just as gorgeous and gooey.

Dough:
**2¼ teaspoons (1 package) active dry yeast**
**1 tablespoon honey**
**⅔ cup warm water (105° to 115°)**
**3 eggs, lightly beaten**
**1 (5-ounce) can evaporated milk**
**4½ to 5 cups all-purpose flour**
**¾ teaspoon salt**
**8 tablespoons (1 stick) unsalted butter, softened**
**¼ cup firmly packed brown sugar**
**½ teaspoon cinnamon**

Sticky goo:
**8 tablespoons (1 stick) unsalted butter, softened**
**½ cup honey**
**¼ cup firmly packed brown sugar**
**¾ cup pecan halves or chopped pecans, optional**

**To make the dough:**
In the work bowl of a heavy-duty electric mixer or in a large bowl, whisk the yeast and the honey into the warm water. Let stand about 5 minutes, until the mixture bubbles. Add the eggs, milk, the 4½ cups of flour, salt and butter. If using a machine, fit the bowl with a dough hook, and knead on a low speed. Otherwise, use a wooden spoon and stir to blend, then turn it out onto a lightly floured surface and knead by hand. Knead about 5 minutes, adding the remaining ½ cup of flour if necessary, until the dough is soft, smooth and elastic.

Place the dough in an oiled bowl, cover, and allow to rise at room temperature until doubled, about 1 hour. Mix the brown sugar and cinnamon in a small bowl; set aside.

**To prepare the sticky goo:**
Mix the butter, honey and brown sugar until smooth. Brush a 9 x 13-inch pan✱ with butter or spray with cooking spray. Spread the sticky goo into the pan. Sprinkle with the pecans, if using.

**To assemble and bake:**
Deflate the dough with your fist. On a lightly floured work surface, roll into a 16 x 11-inch rectangle, about ½-inch thick. Sprinkle evenly with the brown sugar and cinnamon mixture. With a long edge of the rectangle facing you, roll it into a tight, long cylinder, like

✱ I use a glass pan so I can see the color of the dough as it bakes. The buns should bake to a golden brown on the bottoms as well as the tops.

a jelly roll. Pinch the top edge to seal so it can't unroll. Cut into 12 slices. Arrange evenly, cut side down, in the goo-prepared pan; they should be almost touching. Cover with plastic wrap and allow to rise at room temperature for about 30 minutes. Preheat oven to 375°.

Place the pan of buns on a baking sheet to catch any overflowing goo. Bake 40 to 45 minutes or until the tops of the rolls are light golden brown. Immediately invert onto a clean tray or serving platter, taking care not to spatter yourself with hot goo. If there is goo left in the pan, scrape and spread it back onto the buns.

*Makes 12 buns.*

▲ High altitude: The dough will rise faster; check sooner for doubling. Put the rolls in the oven just before they double in size. This allows for more oven spring (the immediate rising of the dough in the hot oven, before it begins to brown).

# ■ Good Friday Hot Cross Buns

These buns predate Christianity. In ancient times they were made in spring to celebrate the renewal of life; the cross represented the four seasons. Now the cross is a symbol of Good Friday and Holy Week. In keeping with tradition, I bake Hot Cross Buns every spring for the Easter holidays.

Dough:
2¼ teaspoons (1 package) active dry yeast
⅔ cup warm water (105° to 115°)
1 (5-ounce) can evaporated milk
4 tablespoons (½ stick) unsalted butter, melted
1 egg, lightly beaten
3½ to 4 cups all-purpose flour
¼ cup firmly packed brown sugar
¾ teaspoon salt
¾ teaspoon ground cinnamon
¼ teaspoon ground cardamom
¼ teaspoon ground mace
¼ cup chopped dried apricots
¼ cup golden raisins
¼ cup chopped dried cherries
¼ cup chopped pitted dates
1 egg beaten with 1 tablespoon milk or water, for glaze

Cross:
1 cup confectioners' sugar
2 teaspoons lemon juice
2 teaspoons water

**To make the dough:**
In the work bowl of a heavy-duty electric mixer or in a large bowl, sprinkle the yeast over the warm water, stirring to dissolve; let stand about 5 minutes.

Add the milk, the melted butter and the egg, the 3½ cups of flour, brown sugar, salt, cinnamon, cardamom and mace. If using a machine, fit the bowl with a dough hook, and knead on a low speed. Otherwise, use a wooden spoon and stir to blend, then turn it out onto a lightly floured surface and knead by hand. Knead about 5 minutes, adding the remaining ½ cup of flour if necessary, until the dough is soft, smooth and elastic. During the last minute, mix in the apricots, raisins, cherries and dates.

Place the dough in an oiled bowl. Cover with plastic wrap and allow to rise at room temperature until doubled in size, about 45 minutes. Deflate the dough with your fist. Divide into 12 portions and shape into smooth balls, tucking the fruit pieces inside.

Brush a 9 x 13-inch pan with butter or spray with cooking spray. Arrange the rolls evenly in the pan; there will be about ½ inch of space between the rolls. Cover with plastic wrap and allow to rise at room temperature for about 1 hour. Preheat oven to 375°.

Brush egg glaze on top of the buns. Bake 25 to 30 minutes or until they are light golden brown. Cool.

**To make the cross:**
Mix the confectioners' sugar, lemon juice and water to a smooth frosting. Spoon into a pastry bag fitted with a small (¼ inch) plain tip and pipe a cross on the top of each bun. (Or drizzle the crosses using a spoon.)

*Makes 12 buns.*

▲ High altitude: The dough will rise faster; check sooner for doubling. Put the rolls in the oven just before they double in size. This allows for more oven spring (the immediate rising of the dough in the hot oven, before it begins to brown).

*Hot-cross buns! Hot-cross buns! One a penny, two a penny, hot-cross buns. If you have no daughters, give them to your sons. Hot-cross buns! Hot-cross buns!*
*—Old Nursery Rhyme*

# ◆ Beth's Tea Ring

Beth is Deer Valley's executive assistant, who orders this yeasted coffee cake, a traditional Scandinavian pastry, every Christmas Eve. She asked if we'd create something less calorific and not too butter-rich—this is the result. To lower the fat even more, replace the egg with 2 egg whites and omit the butter in the filling. This recipe can be doubled to make a larger ring.

Dough:
**2¼ teaspoons (1 package) active dry yeast**
**1 tablespoon honey**
**½ cup warm water (105° to 115°)**
**1 egg, lightly beaten**
**1 tablespoon canola oil**
**1¾ to 2 cups all-purpose flour**
**¼ cup wheat germ**
**¼ cup nonfat dry milk powder**
**2 tablespoons cornmeal**
**1 teaspoon vanilla extract**
**¼ teaspoon ground cardamom**
**½ teaspoon salt**

Filling:
**2 tablespoons unsalted butter, softened**
**2 tablespoons brown sugar**
**¾ teaspoon ground cinnamon**
**½ cup chopped dried fruit, such as cherries, cranberries,**
   **apricots or golden raisins or pre-cut dried fruit bits**
**2 tablespoons Apricot Glaze, warm (page 208)**
**¼ cup Simple Vanilla Glaze (page 208)**

**To make the dough:**
In the work bowl of a heavy-duty electric mixer or in a large bowl, whisk the yeast and the honey into the warm water. Let stand about 5 minutes, until the mixture bubbles.

Add the egg and oil, the 1¾ cups of flour, wheat germ, milk powder, cornmeal, vanilla, cardamom and salt. If using a machine, fit the bowl with a dough hook and knead on a low speed. Otherwise, use a wooden spoon and stir to blend, then turn it out onto a lightly floured surface and knead by hand. Knead 8 to 10 minutes, adding the remaining ¼ cup of flour if necessary, until the dough is soft, smooth and elastic.

Place in an oiled bowl at least twice the volume of the dough. Cover with plastic wrap and let rise at room temperature until doubled in size, about 1 hour.

*Opposite: Beth's Tea Ring*

**To make the filling:**
Mix the butter, sugar and cinnamon until smooth and spreadable.

**To assemble and bake:**
Line a large baking sheet with parchment paper, or lightly coat it with butter, or spray it with cooking spray. Deflate the dough with your fist. On a lightly floured surface, roll it into a 9x11-inch rectangle, about ⅜ inch thick. Spread evenly with the butter-cinnamon mixture, leaving a ½-inch border at the top. Sprinkle with the dried fruit. With a long edge of the rectangle facing you, roll it into a tight, long cylinder, like a jelly roll. Pinch the top edge to seal so it can't unroll. Bring the 2 ends of the log together, pinching again. The center opening should be about 3 inches in diameter.

Lift the ring gently and place, seam side down, on the prepared baking sheet. With scissors, cut slashes in the roll every 1½ inches, cutting three-quarters of the way through the roll. Lift and turn each partially cut section on its side so the filling is visible. Cover loosely with plastic wrap and let rise until almost doubled in size, 45 minutes to an hour. Preheat oven to 350°.

Bake 30 to 35 minutes, until the ring is golden brown. Brush with warm Apricot Glaze and drizzle with Simple Vanilla Glaze.

*Makes 1 (9-inch) ring, serves 6 to 8.*

▲ High altitude: The dough will rise faster; check sooner for doubling. Put the coffee cake in the oven a little earlier to allow for more oven spring (the immediate rising of the dough in the hot oven, before it begins to brown).

*Cardamom grows in pods on a flowering bush in the coastal hills of western India, each outer pod containing tiny inner seeds. Prized for its flavor, it is a fairly expensive, wonderfully aromatic spice; it blends into curries and chutney as well as delicate baked goods. Former Deer Valley chef Chuck Wiley likes to chew on a cardamom pod when he skis; in India, cardamom is offered at the end of the meal to aid digestion and to freshen the breath.*

# ◆ Whole Wheat Cinnamon Brioche Rolls

Made with a great deal of eggs and butter, brioche is the richest of breads. With a little whole wheat flour and cinnamon, raisins and walnuts, it turns into the ultimate cinnamon bun. Prepare the dough in the evening, and let it cool-rise overnight; it will be ready to shape, proof and bake the next morning.

Dough:
2¼ teaspoons (1 package) active dry yeast
3 tablespoons warm water (105° to 115°)
2½ cups all-purpose flour
1 cup whole wheat flour
6 eggs
2 tablespoons sugar
1½ teaspoons salt
12 tablespoons (1½ sticks) unsalted butter, softened

Filling:
4 tablespoons (½ stick) unsalted butter, softened
1½ teaspoons ground cinnamon
¼ cup firmly packed brown sugar
¾ cup dark raisins
½ cup coarsely chopped walnuts, optional
½ cup Simple Vanilla Glaze (page 208)

**To make the dough:**
In the work bowl of a heavy-duty electric mixer or in a large bowl, sprinkle the yeast over the water, stirring to dissolve. Add a tablespoon of the measured all-purpose flour, mix well and allow to sponge for 20 minutes.

Add the remaining flours, eggs, sugar and salt to the yeast sponge. If using a machine, fit the bowl with a paddle attachment and beat. Otherwise, use a wooden spoon and beat for a minute, then turn it out onto a clean surface, and use a scraper to gather the dough up, then slap it down, scraping and slapping to beat the soft and sticky dough. Beat the dough about 5 minutes, stopping to scrape the sides and bottom of the bowl if you are using a machine. After 5 minutes, remove the paddle attachment and fit the machine with a dough hook. Add the soft butter, 2 tablespoons at a time, kneading or slapping, incorporating each portion of butter into the dough before adding more. This will take at least another 5 minutes. The dough will be very soft and sticky and seem too wet, but after it chills and the butter is cold, it will be easy to work with.

Place in an oiled bowl at least twice the volume of the dough. Cover with plastic wrap and let rise at room temperature until double, 45 minutes to an hour. Deflate with your fist, cover again, and refrigerate overnight, or until the dough is very cold.

**To make the filling and assemble:**

Mix the butter, cinnamon and brown sugar into a smooth spread. Deflate the cold dough with your fist. On a lightly floured surface, roll it into a 12×16-inch rectangle about ¼ inch thick. Spread the filling all the way to the short edges, but leave a ½-inch border on the longer edges. Sprinkle with the raisins, and then the walnuts, if using. With a long edge of the rectangle facing you, roll it into a tight long cylinder, like a jelly roll. Pinch the top edge to seal so it can't unroll. If the brioche is soft, refrigerate until firm, so it cuts easily. Cut the cylinder into 16 slices.

Line 2 large baking sheets with parchment paper or coat lightly with butter or cooking spray. Arrange the rolls cut side down about 2 inches apart, leaving room for them to double in size. Cover with plastic wrap and allow to rise at room temperature for about 1 hour. Preheat oven to 375°.

Bake 20 to 25 minutes, until the rolls are light golden brown. Drizzle Simple Vanilla Glaze on each warm roll.

*Makes 16 rolls, about 3½ inches in diameter.*

▲ High altitude: The dough will rise faster; check sooner for doubling. Put the rolls in the oven just before they double in size. This allows for more oven spring (the immediate rising of the dough in the hot oven, before it begins to brown).

# Our Daily Breads

● 

Green Chili and Cheese Cornbread

●

Sun-Dried Tomato Anadama Bread

●

Buttermilk Raisin Bread

■

Roquefort Gougères

■

Oatmeal Walnut Bread

■

Red Pepper Cheddar Cheese Bread

■

Potato Focaccia with Red Onions and Basil

■

Four Grain Poppy Seed Bread

■

Onion Curry Bread

■

Stanford Court Sourdough Bread

■

Seeded Whole Wheat Sourdough Bread

■

Dark Chocolate Bread

■

Holiday Stollen

# Our Daily Breads

Before I became a baker at Deer Valley, I was a "ski bum." I skied my way through college; upon graduation I hung my diploma in a ski locker. I worked as a waitress and a caterer, arranging my schedule so I could ski every day. My first job at Deer Valley was on the ski patrol, allowing me plenty of ski time. Then I parked my skis at the lodge door and traded my red wool ski patroller's hat for a white chef's toque.

I hadn't lost my appetite for skiing. As a Deer Valley baker, two days a week, I started work at 4:00 in the morning—which allowed me to punch out at lunchtime and ski the rest of the day. My first season in the bakery, I skied four days a week.

When I look back on that year, breadmaking comes to my mind as much as the skiing. As the early morning baker, I made the specialty bread for the natural salad buffet, our lavish, overflowing array of fresh foods. I loved it. It was my job to research and develop a daily bread. My breads featured whole grains, natural sweeteners and various nuts. Often I would add flavored oils or herbs and spices. I even had a condiment series: mustard bread, olive bread, pickle bread and tomato bread. I had a chance to experiment and learn and mostly my breads were successful. I must admit there were some failures—one time I added too much flour to my rye bread and the finished loaves resembled heavy bricks. Another time the bread never rose; I had killed the yeast with overheated water.

This chapter offers recipes for some of the imaginative and tasty breads developed over the years by Deer Valley bakers, including some I made that first year. Early morning bakers still create a specialty whole-grain bread for the natural buffet, and I encourage them to discover different combinations.

In all but one yeast recipe, I use the traditional method of separately dissolving the yeast in warm water before adding it to the remaining ingredients. In the Buttermilk Raisin Bread, the yeast is mixed with the dry ingredients without dissolving it first, and the heated buttermilk warms the dough and yeast at the same time. Both methods work, but I think the traditional method is reassuring; you can see the yeast become active as it dissolves.

I use an instant-read thermometer to determine liquid temperatures (page 256). Since body temperature is about 99° and a perfect hot tub is about 104°, you can make an educated guess and dissolve yeast without a thermometer.

Many of these recipes call for bread flour, which has a higher gluten content than all-purpose flour and produces better volume and texture. Dough made with bread flour usually feels more elastic during kneading. If you substitute all-purpose flour, you may need to use a little more flour in the recipe.

At Deer Valley we mix 25 loaves of bread at a time in our 60-quart floor-model mixer. At home I use a dough hook attachment on a much smaller 5-quart free-standing mixer to knead bread on low speed. This saves me time—while the machine is kneading I can wash the dishes. But I always turn the dough out and knead it by hand, just a little, before placing it in the bowl to rise. It's important to sense the dough's resilience and elasticity to make sure you've kneaded it enough. Besides, there is tranquillity in handling smooth dough and working it around on the table.

The temperature of the room will make a difference in the rising times. If your kitchen is cool, below 72°, the dough will take longer to double in size. If warm, the dough will rise faster. I often put the rising dough in my water heater closet since my Park City house is almost always cool.

To check whether the dough has doubled in size, press the tip of your finger 1 inch into the dough, then quickly remove it. If your finger indentation remains, the dough has doubled; if it fills in quickly, let it rise longer. After the first rising, the dough needs to be deflated. This gets rid of excess carbon dioxide and contributes to the bread's flavor. To do this, make a fist and push it into the center of the dough. Pull the sides up and in toward the center before turning the dough out of the bowl.

If a yeast dough rises quickly and has doubled in bulk before you are ready to shape it, punch it down and let it rise an extra time. It is better to punch down the dough early than to let it rise so far that it collapses on its own.

Even though I may specify in a recipe one form or another, yeast breads can be shaped into rectangular or round loaves. You can place rectangular loaves in bread pans or, as with rounds, on baking sheets, to rise and bake. For rectangular loaves, either freeform or panned, use a rolling pin to roll the deflated dough into a flat rectangle on an unfloured work surface. Shape the loaf by rolling it up jelly roll fashion, then pinch the seam and loaf ends with your fingers to seal. The important thing is to roll tightly. Bring it into a uniform shape using both hands, gently massaging the dough against the table.

To make round loaves, roll or pat the dough flat on an unfloured work surface, then fold the outside edges into the middle. Turn the dough over so the seams are against the table. Use your hands to cup the dough, letting your little fingers almost meet underneath the ball. Rotate the dough as you cup it against the table, tucking and shaping it into a tight ball.

The slashes cut in the top of a loaf of bread just before baking are more than decoration. They allow the loaves to expand rapidly in the hot oven without bursting any which way they might. The slashes are also a place for moisture to escape. Most rectangular loaves get diagonal slashes across the top; round loaves can have diagonals, crosses and other designs. Some bakers use different slash designs so they can easily tell several bread varieties apart—just as chocolatiers distinguish the tops of chocolate candy with various swirls and garnishes.

There is true joy in the hands-on process of breadmaking. May you delight in it as much as I do, which is so fully that I forget I am not skiing—well, almost.

# ● Green Chili and Cheese Cornbread

Green chilies, also called Anaheim chilies, provide moisture and pungent, mild flavor.
For spicier cornbread, replace the regular Monterey Jack with jalapeño pepper jack cheese.
If you wish, make 12 muffins instead of one square pan; baking time will be less, about
20 minutes.

**1 cup all-purpose flour**
**¼ cup sugar**
**2½ teaspoons baking powder**
**½ teaspoon salt**
**⅔ cup yellow cornmeal**
**1 cup buttermilk❋**
**2 tablespoons olive oil**
**1 egg, lightly beaten**
**4 ounces (1 small can) diced roasted green chilies, drained**
**½ cup (about 2 ounces) grated Monterey Jack cheese**
**⅓ cup diced red onion**

Preheat the oven to 375°. Brush an 8 x 8-inch baking pan with melted butter or spray
generously with cooking spray.

   Sift the flour, sugar, baking powder and salt into a large mixing bowl. Stir in the
cornmeal.

   In a separate bowl, whisk together the buttermilk, oil and egg. Stir the wet ingredients into the flour mixture, just enough to combine; avoid overmixing. Fold in the green
chilies, cheese and onions. Scrape into the prepared pan and bake 30 to 35 minutes, until
the top is a very light golden brown. Cool at least 10 minutes before cutting.

*Makes 12 (2-inch) squares.*

▲ High altitude: Reduce baking powder to 1½ teaspoons.

❋ I keep "cultured buttermilk blend" in my pantry,
so I always have butter-
milk on hand. To use this
powdered equivalent,
whisk it in with the dry
ingredients and replace
the liquid buttermilk with
water, following the directions on the can.

# ● Sun-Dried Tomato Anadama Bread

Sun-dried tomatoes give flavorful glitter to traditional anadama bread, and the tang of the tomatoes is wonderful against the subtle molasses sweetness. Polenta has more texture, but you can use all cornmeal instead.

**2¼ teaspoons (1 package) active dry yeast**
**1 cup warm water (105° to 115°)**
**1½ cups all-purpose flour**
**1½ to 2 cups bread flour**
**¼ cup polenta grits**
**¼ cup yellow cornmeal *plus* 1 teaspoon for garnish**
**2 tablespoons olive oil**
**¼ cup unsulphured mild molasses**
**1 teaspoon salt**
**½ cup chopped (¼-inch pieces) sun-dried tomatoes**❈
**1 egg beaten with 1 tablespoon milk or water, for glaze**

❈ If dried tomatoes are not soft enough to cut, place them in a small bowl and cover with hot water for 10 minutes. Drain before chopping.

In the work bowl of a heavy-duty electric mixer, or in a large bowl, sprinkle the yeast over the warm water, stirring to dissolve; let stand about 5 minutes.

Add the all-purpose flour, the 1½ cups of bread flour, the polenta and ¼ cup of the cornmeal, olive oil, molasses and salt. If using a machine, fit the bowl with a dough hook and knead on a low speed. Otherwise, use a wooden spoon and stir to blend, then turn it out onto a lightly floured surface and knead by hand. Knead 8 to 10 minutes, adding the remaining ½ cup of bread flour if necessary, until the dough is soft, smooth and elastic. Add the dried tomatoes during the last minute of kneading.

Place in an oiled bowl at least twice the volume of the dough. Cover with plastic wrap and let rise at room temperature until doubled in size, about 1 hour.

Brush a 9 x 5 x 3-inch loaf pan with oil or spray with cooking spray. Deflate the dough with your fist. Flatten into a rectangle the length of the bread pan. Roll up tightly, pinch the seams and ends to seal, and place in the pan, seam side down. Cover and allow to rise until almost doubled in size, 45 to 60 minutes. Preheat the oven to 375°.

Brush the loaf with egg glaze. Sprinkle with the extra teaspoon of cornmeal. With a sharp knife, make 4 or 5 diagonal slashes (¼ to ½ inch deep) across the top. Bake until rich golden brown, and the bottom of the loaf sounds hollow when tapped, 35 to 45 minutes. Remove to a rack to cool completely before serving.

*Makes 1 loaf, about 2 pounds.*

▲ High altitude: The dough will rise faster; check sooner for doubling. Deflate the dough twice before shaping so the total rising time is not shortened. Put the bread in the oven just before it doubles in size. This allows for more oven spring (the immediate rising of the dough in the hot oven, before it begins to brown).

*There is a story about how anadama bread got its name that I tell to new bread bakers—I am not sure anyone believes the story but it's always good for a chuckle at my corny humor. It goes like this: In New England there lived a toiling wife named Anna and her grouchy husband. She prepared all their meals and all he would do was complain. She grew tired of her thankless life and one day deserted him, leaving only molasses and cornmeal in the cupboard. For supper, he made bread using those ingredients, all the while cursing, "Anna damn her."*

*Opposite: Sun-Dried Tomato Anadama Bread (sliced) and Four Grain Poppy Seed Bread (page 45)*

# • Buttermilk Raisin Bread

I am not particularly fond of caraway seeds and sometimes I eliminate them from recipes, but in this bread the caraway seeds have a lovely symbiosis with the sweet raisins. This is a yeasted Irish soda bread; we serve it on March 17, to celebrate St. Patrick's Day.

> 1¼ cups buttermilk or plain yogurt
> 3 tablespoons unsalted butter, cut into chunks
> 3½ to 4 cups all-purpose flour
> 3 tablespoons sugar
> ¾ teaspoon salt
> 1 tablespoon caraway seeds
> 1 teaspoon baking soda
> 2¼ teaspoons (1 package) active dry yeast
> 1 cup dark raisins

Heat the buttermilk and butter in a saucepan to about 120°. The butter may not melt completely—that's all right.

In the work bowl of a heavy-duty electric mixer, or in a large bowl, mix the 3½ cups of flour, sugar, salt, caraway seeds, baking soda and yeast. With a wooden spoon, stir to blend in the warm buttermilk mixture. If using a machine, fit the bowl with a dough hook and knead on a low speed. Otherwise, turn it out onto a lightly floured surface and knead by hand. Knead 8 to 10 minutes, adding the remaining ½ cup of flour if necessary, until the dough is soft, smooth and elastic. Add the raisins during the last minute of kneading.

Place in an oiled bowl at least twice the volume of the dough. Cover with plastic wrap and let rise at room temperature until doubled in size, about 1 hour.

Brush a baking sheet with oil or spray with cooking spray. Deflate the dough with your fist. Shape it into a round ball and place on the pan. Cover and allow to rise at room temperature until doubled in size, about 1 hour. Preheat the oven to 375°.

Lightly dust the top of the loaf with flour and with a sharp knife, make a crisscross slash (¼ to ½ inch deep). Bake until rich golden brown, 35 to 45 minutes. Remove to a rack to cool completely before serving.

*Makes 1 loaf, about 2 pounds.*

▲ High altitude: The dough will rise faster; check sooner for doubling. Deflate the dough twice before shaping so the total rising time is not shortened. Put the bread in the oven just before it doubles in size. This allows for more oven spring (the immediate rising of the dough in the hot oven, before it begins to brown).

# ■ Roquefort Gougères

These are savory cream puffs with cheese, French pop-in-your-mouth snacks, traditionally served with red wine. They aren't really a bread, but the recipe fits better in this chapter than anywhere else in the book. Gougères (goo-ZHAIR) are usually made with Gruyère cheese; Roquefort cheese is the Deer Valley twist. They make a delicious hors d'oeuvre filled with a mixture of cream cheese, diced tart apples and toasted walnuts.

**1 cup water**
**¼ pound (1 stick) unsalted butter, cut into pieces**
**¼ teaspoon salt**
**1 cup and 2 tablespoons bread flour**
**3 eggs *plus* 1 egg**
**1 cup (about 4 ounces) crumbled Roquefort cheese**
**⅛ teaspoon ground white pepper**

Preheat the oven to 375°. Line 3 baking sheets with parchment paper, or butter them lightly, or lightly spray them with cooking spray.❋

In a heavy-bottomed saucepan bring to a boil the water, butter and salt. As soon as it reaches a boil, remove from the heat to prevent evaporation through simmering.

Immediately add the flour all at once, stirring with a wooden spoon until the flour is incorporated. Return to medium heat and continue stirring until the dough comes together in a mass and there is a thin skin on the bottom of the pan.

Transfer the hot paste to a mixing bowl. Using an electric mixer or a wooden spoon, beat about a minute to dissipate some of the heat. Then, one at a time, beat in 3 of the eggs, incorporating each egg before adding the next. In a small bowl, stir the remaining egg with a fork. Beat about half of this egg into the batter. If the dough is still stiff, beat in the rest of the beaten egg; if the dough can barely hold a shape, don't add the remaining egg. Beat in the cheese and white pepper.

Using a spoon or a tiny ice cream scoop (page 250), drop the mixture into small (1 inch) balls, leaving 2 inches between each mound. Or scrape the batter into a pastry bag fitted with a ½-inch plain tip and pipe out the mounds.

Bake for 15 minutes, resisting the urge to open the oven during this time to check the gougères, as this could lower the temperature enough that the puffs fall before they have a chance to set. (Once the gougères have a little color and are set, it's okay to open the oven to check for browning.) Bake 5 to 15 more minutes, for a total of 20 to 30 minutes, until the gougères are rich golden brown. Serve warm. They can be made ahead and frozen, then reheated just before serving.

*Makes 40 to 60 gougères.*

▲ High altitude: Bake 20 minutes before checking. The gougères may take longer to bake to a golden brown.

❋ This recipe makes enough dough to fill 3 baking sheets, but air circulation in the oven will be better if you bake only 2 sheets at a time.

# ■ Oatmeal Walnut Bread

The day you make this bread, treat yourself to a bowl of hot oatmeal for breakfast; just cook a little more so there is some left over. This bread's rustic appeal comes not only from the oatmeal, but from the walnuts and their skins, which often dye the dough an earthy purple-brown.

> 2¼ teaspoons (1 package) active dry yeast
> ½ cup warm water (105° to 115°)
> 2 cups cooked oatmeal, room temperature
> ¼ cup walnut oil or olive oil ✳
> 2 tablespoons honey
> 2 cups whole wheat flour
> 2 to 2½ cups bread flour
> 2 teaspoons salt
> 1 cup chopped walnuts, toasted (page 256)
> 1 egg beaten with 1 tablespoon milk or water, for glaze
> 2 tablespoons old-fashioned rolled oats

✳ Walnut oil is found near other cooking oils in well-stocked supermarkets. There is a first-pressed virgin walnut oil with an exceptionally intense flavor and aroma available by mail. It is extracted and distributed by The California Press in the Napa Valley (page 258).

In the work bowl of a heavy-duty electric mixer, or in a large bowl, sprinkle the yeast over the warm water, stirring to dissolve; let stand about 5 minutes.

Add the oatmeal, oil, honey, whole wheat flour, 2 cups of the bread flour, salt and walnuts. If using a machine, fit the bowl with a dough hook and knead on a low speed. Otherwise, use a wooden spoon and stir to blend, then turn it out onto a lightly floured surface and knead by hand. Knead 8 to 10 minutes, adding the remaining ½ cup of bread flour if necessary, until the dough is smooth and elastic.

Place in an oiled bowl at least twice the volume of the dough. Cover with plastic wrap and let rise at room temperature until doubled in size, about 1 hour.

Brush 1 large baking sheet or 2 (9 x 5 x 3-inch) loaf pans with oil or spray with cooking spray. Deflate the dough with your fist and divide into 2 equal portions. Flatten the dough into rectangles about 14 inches long for freeform loaves, or 8 inches long for bread pans. Roll up tightly, pinch the seams and ends to seal, and place on or in the pans, seam side down. Cover and allow to rise until almost doubled in size, about 1 hour. Preheat the oven to 375°.

Brush the loaves with the egg glaze and sprinkle with rolled oats. With a sharp knife, make 4 or 5 diagonal slashes (¼ to ½ inch deep) across the top of each loaf. Bake until rich golden brown and the bottom of each loaf sounds hollow when tapped, 35 to 45 minutes. Remove to a rack to cool completely before serving.

*Makes 2 loaves, about 1½ pounds each.*

▲ High altitude: The dough will rise faster; check sooner for doubling. Deflate the dough twice before shaping so the total rising time is not shortened. Put the bread in the oven just before it doubles in size. This allows for more oven spring (the immediate rising of the dough in the hot oven, before it begins to brown).

# ■ Red Pepper Cheddar Cheese Bread

Purchased roasted red peppers will give this bread a deeper orange color than home-roasted red peppers will. The hot pepper sauce provides just a hint of fire—if you like more heat, as my husband does, use double the amount.

⅓ cup warm water (105° to 115°)
2¼ teaspoons (1 package) active dry yeast
1 cup whole milk
1 tablespoon olive oil
2 cups whole wheat flour
1¾ to 2¼ cups bread flour
½ cup diced, roasted and peeled red peppers*
1 teaspoon Louisiana hot pepper sauce
1 teaspoon salt
1½ cups (about 6 ounces) grated sharp Cheddar cheese
1 egg beaten with 1 tablespoon milk or water, for glaze
Grated Parmesan cheese or sesame seeds, for garnish

In the work bowl of a heavy-duty electric mixer, or in a large bowl, sprinkle the yeast over the warm water, stirring to dissolve; let stand about 5 minutes.

Add the milk, oil, whole wheat flour, the 1¾ cups of bread flour, the peppers, hot pepper sauce and salt. If using a machine, fit the bowl with a dough hook and knead on a low speed. Otherwise, use a wooden spoon and stir to blend, then turn it out onto a lightly floured surface and knead by hand. Knead 8 to 10 minutes, until the dough is soft, smooth and elastic, adding the remaining ½ cup of bread flour, if necessary. Mix in the Cheddar cheese during the last minute of kneading.

Place in an oiled bowl at least twice the volume of the dough. Cover with plastic wrap and let rise at room temperature until doubled in size, about 1 hour.

Brush 1 large or 2 small baking sheets with oil or spray with cooking spray.

Deflate the dough with your fist and divide into 2 equal portions. Shape each into a tight, round loaf. Arrange on the prepared pan(s). Cover and allow to rise until almost doubled in size, about 1 hour. Preheat the oven to 375°.

Brush the loaves with the egg glaze and sprinkle with Parmesan cheese or sesame seeds. With a sharp knife, make a crisscross slash (¼ to ½ inch deep) into the top. Bake until golden brown and the bottom of each loaf sounds hollow when tapped, 30 to 40 minutes. Remove to a rack to cool completely before serving.

*Makes 2 loaves, about 1 pound, 5 ounces each.*

▲ High altitude: The dough will rise faster; check sooner for doubling. Deflate the dough twice before shaping so the total rising time is not shortened. Put the bread in the oven just before it doubles in size. This allows for more oven spring (the immediate rising of the dough in the hot oven, before it begins to brown).

※ Use roasted red peppers from a jar or can, or roast fresh peppers on a grill or stovetop burner or under a broiler.

# ■ Potato Focaccia with Red Onions and Basil

Focaccia is Italian flatbread, a cousin of pizza. Bake in rounds and serve in wedges as an appetizer or with salad, or bake in a rectangular pan and cut into squares for sandwich buns. The potato adds moisture for keeping fresh and contributes to this bread's light and chewy texture. Other topping possibilities include sun-dried tomatoes, walnuts, fresh herbs, prosciutto—really anything you wish.

Dough:
**2 medium russet potatoes (about ¾ pound)**
**2¼ teaspoons (1 package) active dry yeast**
**¾ cup warm water (105° to 115°)**
**1 cup *plus* 3¼ cups all-purpose flour**
**2 tablespoons olive oil**
**¼ cup finely chopped red onion**
**2 teaspoons dried basil**
**1 teaspoon minced garlic**
**1 tablespoon kosher salt**
**Olive oil, as needed**
**Cornmeal, as needed**

Topping:
**2 tablespoons olive oil**
**1 teaspoon kosher salt**
**½ teaspoon coarsely ground black pepper**
**1 teaspoon dried basil leaves**
**½ cup finely chopped red onion**
**¼ cup grated Parmesan cheese**

**To make the dough:**
Peel and cut the potatoes into ½-inch chunks. Put in a saucepan with about 2 cups of water; cover and boil until tender. Drain, reserving 1½ cups of the water for the dough. Mash the potatoes until smooth. You may use some of the 1½ cups of reserved water to mash the potatoes, if desired. Set aside.

In the work bowl of a heavy-duty electric mixer, or in a large bowl, sprinkle the yeast over the ¾ cup of warm water, stirring to dissolve; let stand about 5 minutes. Add the cup of flour and mix well with a wooden spoon. Allow to rise until doubled in size, 15 to 20 minutes.

Add the reserved 1½ cups of potato cooking water (or less if you used some of it to mash the potatoes), the remaining 3¼ cups of flour, the mashed potatoes, oil, onion, basil, garlic and salt. If using a machine, fit the bowl with a dough hook and mix on a low speed. Otherwise, use a wooden spoon and mix by hand. Mix for about 5 minutes.

If you are using the dough hook, stop to scrape the bottom of the bowl to make sure all the flour is incorporated. The dough will be very soft and sticky. Transfer to a large oiled bowl at least twice the volume of the dough. Cover with plastic wrap and refrigerate. Allow to cool rise at least 4 hours or overnight.

**To shape, top and bake:**
Preheat the oven to 375°. Brush 2 (9-inch) round cake pans or 1 (11 x 17-inch) baking sheet with olive oil. Sprinkle with cornmeal. Scrape the dough into the pan(s.) Coat your hands with oil and spread the dough to fit into the corners. Drizzle on the 2 tablespoons of oil. Sprinkle evenly with the salt, pepper, basil and onion, and finally with the cheese. Let rest uncovered at room temperature about 15 minutes. Bake until golden brown, 45 to 50 minutes. Cool 5 minutes, then remove from the pan(s).

*Makes 2 (9-inch) rounds or 1 large rectangle of focaccia.*

▲ High altitude: This recipe needs no adjustment.

# ■ Four Grain Poppy Seed Bread

*(See photo on page 36)*

This is a richly textured loaf with millet polka dots. Though you'll miss its golden dazzle and crunch, you can replace the millet with bulgur or cracked wheat.

1¼ cups whole milk
⅓ cup olive oil
¼ cup honey
⅓ cup millet<sup>❈</sup>
4½ teaspoons (2 packages) active dry yeast
⅔ cup warm water (105° to 115°)
2 eggs, lightly beaten
4 to 4½ cups bread flour
1 cup whole wheat flour
½ cup wheat germ
½ cup old-fashioned rolled oats
½ cup yellow cornmeal
2½ teaspoons salt
1 tablespoon *plus* 1 teaspoon poppy seeds
1 egg beaten with 1 tablespoon milk or water, for glaze

❈ Millet is a small, round, yellow grain, high in vitamins and minerals—the hulled culinary version of what we know as birdseed. It is available in natural food stores. For extra flavor, toast the millet by cooking and stirring several minutes in a skillet on medium heat before adding it to the milk.

Heat the milk, olive oil and honey in a saucepan to about 120°. Add the millet, and set aside to soften.

In the work bowl of a heavy-duty electric mixer, or in a large bowl, sprinkle the yeast over the warm water, stirring to dissolve; let stand about 5 minutes.

Add the eggs, the 4 cups of bread flour, the whole wheat flour, wheat germ, rolled oats, cornmeal, the milk mixture, salt and 1 tablespoon of the poppy seeds. If using a machine, fit the bowl with a dough hook and knead on a low speed. Otherwise, use a wooden spoon and stir to blend, then turn it out onto a lightly floured surface and knead by hand. Knead 8 to 10 minutes, adding the remaining ½ cup of bread flour if necessary, until the dough is soft, smooth and elastic.

Place in an oiled bowl at least twice the volume of the dough. Cover with plastic wrap and let rise at room temperature until doubled in size, about 1 hour.

Brush 1 large baking sheet or 2 (9 x 5 x 3-inch) loaf pans with oil or spray with cooking spray. If you wish, sprinkle the pans lightly with cornmeal.

Deflate the dough with your fist and divide into 2 equal portions. Flatten the dough into rectangles about 14 inches long for freeform loaves, or 8 inches long for bread pans. Roll up tightly, pinch the seams and ends to seal, and place on or in the pans, seam side down. Cover and allow to rise until almost doubled in size, about 1 hour. Preheat the oven to 375°.

Brush the egg glaze over the loaves and sprinkle with the remaining teaspoon of poppy seeds. With a sharp knife, make 4 or 5 diagonal slashes (¼ to ½ inch deep) on each loaf. Bake until golden brown, 35 to 40 minutes. Remove to a rack to cool completely before serving.

*Makes 2 loaves, about 2 pounds each.*

▲ High altitude: The dough will rise faster; check sooner for doubling. Deflate the dough twice before shaping so the total rising time is not shortened. Put the bread in the oven just before it doubles in size. This allows for more oven spring (the immediate rising of the dough in the hot oven, before it begins to brown).

# ■ Onion Curry Bread

Serve this tantalizing and unusual bread along with lentil or vegetable soup, or make into sandwiches with turkey, Cheddar cheese and chutney.

1½ cups (12 ounces) beer
¼ cup olive oil
2 tablespoons honey
2¼ teaspoons (1 package) active dry yeast
½ cup warm water (105° to 115°)
3½ to 4 cups bread flour
3 cups whole wheat flour
1 tablespoon curry powder
2 teaspoons salt
1 cup, ¼-inch dice, yellow or red onion
¾ cup shelled sunflower seeds, raw or toasted
1 egg beaten with 1 tablespoon milk or water, for glaze
½ teaspoon kosher salt, for garnish

Heat the beer, oil and honey in a saucepan to about 115°. Set aside.

In the work bowl of a heavy-duty electric mixer, or in a large bowl, sprinkle the yeast over the warm water, stirring to dissolve; let stand about 5 minutes.

Add the 3½ cups of bread flour, the whole wheat flour, curry powder and salt. Stir in the warm beer mixture. If using a machine, fit the bowl with a dough hook and knead on a low speed. Otherwise, use a wooden spoon and stir to blend, then turn it out onto a lightly floured surface and knead by hand. Knead 8 to 10 minutes, adding the remaining ½ cup of bread flour if necessary, until the dough is soft, smooth and elastic. Add the onions and sunflower seeds during the last minutes of kneading.

Place in an oiled bowl at least twice the volume of the dough. Cover with plastic wrap and let rise at room temperature until doubled in size, about 1 hour.

Brush 1 large baking sheet or 2 (9 x 5 x 3-inch) loaf pans with oil or spray with cooking spray.

Deflate the dough with your fist and divide into 2 equal portions. Flatten the dough into rectangles about 14 inches long for free-form loaves, or 8 inches long for bread pans. Roll up tightly, pinch the seams and ends to seal, and place on or in the pans, seam side down. Cover and allow to rise until almost doubled in size, about 1 hour. Preheat the oven to 375°.

Brush the loaves with the egg glaze. With a sharp knife, make 4 or 5 diagonal slashes (¼ to ½ inch deep) across the top of each loaf. Sprinkle with kosher salt. Bake until rich golden brown and the bottom of each loaf sounds hollow when tapped, 35 to 45 minutes. Remove to a rack to cool completely before serving.

*Makes 2 loaves, about 1¾ pounds each.*

▲ High altitude: The dough will rise faster; check sooner for doubling. Deflate the dough twice before shaping so the total rising time is not shortened. Put the bread in the oven just before it doubles in size. This allows for more oven spring (the immediate rising of the dough in the hot oven, before it begins to brown).

# ■ Stanford Court Sourdough Bread

Deer Valley's sourdough starter comes from San Francisco's Stanford Court Hotel bakery. It was hand-carried to Utah by Jim Nassikas, who was at one time the president of Stanford Court Hotel and of Deer Valley Resort, and who greatly influenced Deer Valley's ideal of excellence. We've been nurturing and feeding the starter in our dry Utah climate since 1985, and I'm sure it has taken on its own characteristics from the wild yeasts in our atmosphere. Your bread, too, will be unique to the starter you obtain. The yeast in this recipe ensures consistency; you could eliminate the yeast and let the natural sourdough leaven the bread, although the rising would take more time.

1¾ cups Basic Sourdough Starter (page 215)
1 cup *plus* ½ cup warm water (105° to 115°)
2 cups *plus* 3½ to 4 cups bread flour
1 teaspoon active dry yeast
1 tablespoon kosher salt
About 2 tablespoons cornmeal, optional
1 egg white, beaten with 1 tablespoon water, for glaze

Using a wooden spoon, mix the Basic Sourdough Starter, 1 cup of the warm water and 2 cups of the flour in the work bowl of a heavy-duty electric mixer or in a large bowl. Allow to rest for 20 minutes. (If you fed your starter the day before, the starter will be at room temperature. You can use cold starter directly from the refrigerator if it has been fed recently, but know that the kneaded dough may take longer to double in size. Remember to feed your Basic Sourdough Starter, since you used 1¾ cups in this recipe.)

In a small bowl, sprinkle the yeast over the remaining ½ cup of water, stirring to dissolve; let stand for about 5 minutes.

To the sourdough mixture, add the dissolved yeast, 3½ cups of the remaining flour, and the salt. If using a machine, fit the bowl with a dough hook and knead on a low speed. Otherwise, use a wooden spoon and stir to blend, then turn it out onto a lightly floured surface and knead by hand. Knead about 10 minutes, adding the remaining ½ cup of flour if necessary, until the dough is soft, smooth and elastic. It should be as moist as possible without being too sticky.

Place in an oiled bowl at least twice the volume of the dough. Cover with plastic wrap and let rise at room temperature until doubled in size, 1½ to 2 hours, depending on the temperature of the dough and the room.

Deflate the dough with your fist and divide into 2 equal portions. Form each into a loose ball, cover and let rest on a floured work table 15 minutes.

Line 1 large or 2 small baking sheets with parchment paper, or brush them lightly with oil, or spray with cooking spray. Sprinkle lightly with cornmeal, if desired.

Flatten the resting balls and shape each into a tight round loaf.❊ Place them on the prepared pan(s). Cover and allow to rise at room temperature until doubled in size, 1 to 1½ hours. Preheat the oven to 450°.

❊ To make round loaves, roll or pat the dough flat, then fold the outside edges into the middle. Turn the dough over so the seams are against the table. Use your hands to cup the dough, letting your little fingers almost meet underneath the ball. Rotate the dough as you cup it against the table, tucking and shaping it into a tight ball.

*Edgar and Polly Stern are the founders of Deer Valley Resort. They also developed and owned the Stanford Court Hotel in San Francisco in the 1970s and 1980s; at that time, the Stanford Court was considered one of the finest hotels in the world. When Deer Valley and the Stanford Court were sister properties, I had the opportunity to work at the San Francisco hotel as an intern baker. My housing was a luxurious suite, with a view of the Bay. It was an easy commute by elevator to my 4:00 a.m. bread shift.*

Toward the end of the rising period, place a pan of hot water on the oven floor.❋❋ Brush the loaves with the egg white glaze. With a sharp knife, make a tic-tac-toe pattern of 4 diagonal slashes and 4 horizontal slashes (¼ to ½ inch deep) across the top of each loaf. Bake the bread until it is a rich golden brown and the bottom of each loaf sounds hollow when tapped, 25 to 35 minutes. Remove to a rack to cool completely before serving.

*Makes 2 loaves, about 1¾ pounds each.*

▲ High altitude: The dough will rise faster; check sooner for doubling. Deflate the dough twice before shaping so the total rising time is not shortened. Put the bread in the oven just before it doubles in size. This allows for more oven spring (the immediate rising of the dough in the hot oven, before it begins to brown).

❋❋ We have a steam injection system in Deer Valley's bread ovens—it gives the bread extra lift and a crackly crust. The pan of hot water on the oven floor is the home version for steam. You can also spritz the oven with water from a spray bottle just before putting in the loaves.

# ■ Seeded Whole Wheat Sourdough Bread

We embellish the Stanford Court Sourdough Bread with whole wheat flour and pumpkin and sunflower seeds. In order to easily tell the two breads apart, this one has a cross cut on top, different from the tic-tac-toe pattern on the Stanford Court Sourdough Bread. Both breads are staples of The Mariposa restaurant, and we bake them every day during the ski season.

1¾ cups Basic Sourdough Starter (page 215)
1 cup *plus* ½ cup warm water (105° to 115°)
2 cups *plus* 1 to 1½ cups bread flour
3 cups whole wheat flour
1 teaspoon active dry yeast
1 tablespoon kosher salt
¼ cup shelled pumpkin seeds
¼ cup shelled sunflower seeds
About 2 tablespoons cornmeal, optional
1 egg white beaten with 1 tablespoon water, for glaze

Using a wooden spoon, mix the Basic Sourdough Starter, 1 cup of the warm water and the 2 cups of bread flour in the work bowl of a heavy-duty electric mixer or in a large bowl. Allow to rest for 20 minutes. (If you fed your starter the day before, the starter will be at room temperature. You can use cold starter directly from the refrigerator if it has been fed recently, but know that the kneaded dough may take longer to double in size. Remember to feed your Basic Sourdough Starter, since you used 1¾ cups in this recipe.)

In a small bowl, sprinkle the yeast over the remaining ½ cup of water, stirring to dissolve; let stand for about 5 minutes.

To the sourdough mixture, add the dissolved yeast, 1 cup of the remaining bread flour, the whole wheat flour, and the salt. If using a machine, fit the bowl with a dough hook and knead on a low speed. Otherwise, use a wooden spoon and stir to blend, then turn it out onto a lightly floured surface and knead by hand. Knead about 10 minutes, adding the remaining ½ cup of bread flour if necessary, until the dough is soft, smooth and elastic. It should be as moist as possible without being too sticky. Mix in the pumpkin and sunflower seeds during the last minute of kneading.

Place in an oiled bowl at least twice the volume of the dough. Cover with plastic wrap and let rise at room temperature until doubled in size, 1½ to 2 hours, depending on the temperature of the dough and the room.

Deflate the dough with your fist and divide into 2 equal portions. Form each into a loose ball, cover and let rest on a floured work table 15 minutes.

Line 1 large or 2 small baking sheets with parchment paper, or brush them lightly with oil, or spray with cooking spray. Sprinkle with cornmeal, if desired.

Flatten the resting balls and shape each into a tight round loaf.❋ Place on the

❋ To make round loaves, roll or pat the dough flat, then fold the outside edges into the middle. Turn the dough over so the seams are against the table. Use your hands to cup the dough, letting your little fingers almost meet underneath the ball. Rotate the dough as you cup it against the table, tucking and shaping it into a tight ball.

*Dormant, refrigerated sourdough starter may have a layer of clear liquid on top; this is normal, just stir it back into the starter.*

prepared pan(s). Cover and allow to rise at room temperature until doubled in size, 1 to 1½ hours. Preheat the oven to 450°.

Toward the end of the rising period, place a pan of hot water on the oven floor.❋❋ Brush the loaves with the egg white glaze. With a sharp knife, make a large cross (¼ to ½ inch deep) on top of each loaf. Bake the bread until it is a rich golden brown and the bottom of each loaf sounds hollow when tapped, 25 to 35 minutes. Remove to a rack to cool completely before serving.

*Makes 2 loaves, about 1¾ pounds each.*

▲ High altitude: The dough will rise faster; check sooner for doubling. Deflate the dough twice before shaping so the total rising time is not shortened. Put the bread in the oven just before it doubles in size. This allows for more oven spring (the immediate rising of the dough in the hot oven, before it begins to brown).

❋❋ We have a steam injection system in Deer Valley's bread ovens—it gives the bread extra lift and a crackly crust. The pan of hot water on the oven floor is the home version for steam. You can also spritz the oven with water from a spray bottle just before putting in the loaves.

*Sometimes when I make both Stanford Court Sourdough and Seeded Whole Wheat Sourdough Breads on the same day, I make swirl loaves out of the two doughs. I flatten equal half-portions of each and lay one on top of the other and then roll them into one rectangular loaf. When sliced, the finished loaf shows a beautiful light and dark swirl.*

# ■ Dark Chocolate Bread

My college chum Paula chooses this bread over chocolate brownies. It has a wonderful bitter chocolate flavor, and it is not too sweet. I use it in Chocolate and Blueberry Bread Pudding, adding a quality not achieved using white bread. You only need one loaf for the pudding; give the extras as gifts, or eat this toothsome bread yourself with cream cheese and fruit preserves. For added pleasure, mix chopped nuts or dried fruit—like pistachios or walnuts, cherries or apricots—into the dough.

> 6 ounces bittersweet chocolate, chopped in ½-inch pieces
> 2 tablespoons unsalted butter, cut into pieces
> 2 tablespoons and ¾ teaspoon (3 packages) active dry yeast
> 1½ cups warm water (105° to 115°)
> ½ cup honey
> ¼ cup unsulphured mild molasses
> 1 teaspoon instant espresso coffee powder
> 1 teaspoon vanilla extract
> ⅓ cup cocoa powder
> 2 cups *plus* 2½ to 3 cups all-purpose flour
> 2 teaspoons salt
> 1 cup chopped nuts or dried fruit, optional
> 1 egg beaten with 1 tablespoon milk or water, for glaze, optional

Melt the chocolate and the butter in the top of a double boiler, over gently boiling water; the upper pan should not touch the water. Set aside.

In a large bowl, or in the work bowl of a heavy-duty electric mixer, sprinkle the yeast over the warm water, stirring to dissolve. Add the honey, molasses, espresso powder, vanilla, cocoa powder and 2 cups of the flour. Beat until the ingredients are well mixed. Cover and let sponge 20 minutes.

To the sponge, add the melted chocolate and butter and salt. Add 2½ cups of the remaining flour. If using a machine, fit the bowl with a dough hook and knead on a low speed. Otherwise, use a wooden spoon and stir to blend, then turn it out onto a lightly floured surface and knead by hand. Knead 8 to 10 minutes, until the dough is soft, smooth and elastic. To keep the dough from sticking, add the remaining ½ cup of flour a little at a time, if necessary. During the last minute of kneading, add the chopped nuts or dried fruit, if using.

Place in an oiled bowl. Cover with plastic wrap and let rise at room temperature, about 1¼ hours. This is a relatively dense dough and will not double in size during the rising.

Brush a large baking sheet with oil or spray with cooking spray.

Deflate the dough with your fist. Divide into 3 equal parts, and shape each into a small round loaf, about 5 inches wide.❈ Place on the pan, staggering the loaves for optimum spacing. Cover and allow to rise at room temperature, about 1¼ hours. Preheat the oven to 375°.

❈ The dough can also be shaped into 3 rectangular loaves, about 6 inches long, and placed in small (7½ x 3¾ x 2¼-inch) loaf pans. Or, for larger loaves, divide the dough into 2 equal parts, and shape each into a round or rectangular loaf.

For a shiny finish, brush the tops of the loaves with the egg glaze. Otherwise, brush with water. With a sharp knife, make a large cross (¼ to ½ inch deep) on the top of each loaf. Though the dough is sluggish when rising in the bowl and after shaping, it has good oven spring, which is the immediate rising of the dough in the hot oven. Bake 30 to 35 minutes, until the bottom of each loaf sounds hollow when tapped. Remove to a rack to cool completely before serving.

*Makes 3 loaves, about 1 pound each.*

▲ High altitude: The dough will rise faster, although it will never double in size.

# ■ Holiday Stollen

We always try to serve this bread on Christmas Eve or Christmas Day; the fruit and nuts are so festive. Though rich, the bread is not too sweet to serve for lunch on the natural salad buffet. The simple folded-over shape is said to symbolize the swaddling blankets of the infant Jesus. Francy Royer, previous Deer Valley pastry chef, puts chocolate chips in her stollen—and serves it toasted. Beware: If you make stollen with chocolate chips, toast the slices on a pan in a broiler or toaster oven because the chips melt and fall to the bottom of an upright toaster.

½ cup dark raisins
½ cup golden raisins
⅓ cup dried cranberries
⅓ cup dried cherries
⅓ cup chopped dried apricots
⅓ cup chopped pitted dates
⅓ cup dark rum
1¼ cups whole milk
½ cup honey
2¼ teaspoons (1 package) active dry yeast
⅓ cup warm water (105° to 115°)
4 to 4½ cups bread flour
1 cup whole wheat flour
2 eggs, lightly beaten
1 teaspoon grated lemon zest
1 teaspoon grated orange zest
4 tablespoons unsalted butter, softened
1 teaspoon salt
¾ cup coarsely chopped or slivered almonds
½ cup semisweet chocolate chips, optional
2 tablespoons unsalted butter, melted
1 teaspoon granulated sugar

Place the dried fruit in a bowl; the chopped pieces should all be about the size of the raisins. Pour the rum over the fruit and let it macerate while you prepare the dough.

Heat the milk and honey in a saucepan to about 120°. Set aside.

In the work bowl of a heavy-duty mixer, or in a large bowl, sprinkle the yeast over the warm water, stirring to dissolve; let stand about 5 minutes. Add 2 cups of the bread flour, the whole wheat flour, eggs, grated lemon and orange zests, butter and salt. Pour in the milk and honey mixture and mix well with a wooden spoon.

Add 2 more cups of bread flour. If using a machine, fit the bowl with a dough hook and knead on a low speed. Otherwise, use a wooden spoon and stir to blend, then turn it out onto a lightly floured surface and knead by hand. Knead 8 to 10 minutes, until the dough is soft, smooth and elastic. During the last 3 minutes of kneading, mix in the fruit with rum, almonds and chocolate chips, if using. To keep the dough from sticking, add the remaining ½ cup of flour a little at a time, if necessary.

Place in a large oiled bowl. Cover with plastic wrap and let rise at room temperature about 1½ hours. The dough won't double in bulk because more than half of its weight is fruit and nuts; it has risen enough if you poke a finger in and the indentation remains. Deflate the dough with your fist and let rise again, about 1 hour.

Brush a large baking sheet with oil or spray generously with cooking spray.

Deflate the dough again, and divide into 2 equal portions. Roll or pat each portion into a 12 x 9-inch oval. Fold each over lengthwise, not quite in half, so the top sits back 1 inch from the bottom edge; pinch to seal. Place on the baking sheet, cover and let rise at room temperature about 1 hour. Preheat the oven to 350°.

Bake until golden brown, 35 to 45 minutes. Immediately brush with melted butter and sprinkle with sugar. Remove to a rack to cool completely before serving.

*Makes 2 loaves, about 2 pounds each.*

▲ High altitude: The dough will rise faster; test for ample rising by poking with a finger. When the indentation remains in the first rising, the dough is ready to be shaped. When the indentation remains in a shaped loaf, it is ready to be put in the oven.

# Cookies and Bars

- Jumbo Chocolate Chip Cookies
- Jumbo Double Chocolate Chip Cookies
- Jumbo Oatmeal Raisin Cookies
- Macadamia Nut Cookies
- Chocolate Almond Macaroons
- Chocolate Espresso Slice and Bakes
- Chocolate Walnut Brownies
- Peanut Butter Truffles
- Low-Fat Honey Jumbo Cookies
- Snowshoe Tommy Bars
- World's Best Almond Biscotti
- Raspberry Granola Bars
- Almost Sinless Brownies
- Linzer Heart Cookies
- Orange Blossom Brownies
- Fat-Free McHenergy Bars

# Cookies and Bars

I could recite the recipe in my sleep. . . Put 9 pounds of butter into a 60-quart mixer. Add 16 pounds of sugar, some brown, some white, and start creaming. Meanwhile, crack 40 eggs into a large bowl and sift 18 pounds of flour with baking soda and salt into an even larger bowl. Have ready ½ cup of pure vanilla extract and 20 cups of Hershey's chocolate chips. Mix it all together and what have you got? Deer Valley Jumbo Cookies, 4 inches across, 250 to a batch. We make about 28 batches a week all winter long; that's more than 126,000 cookies a season.

The aroma of these baking cookies wafts throughout the lodges. Guests can watch bakers place the raw dough scoops—bigger than golf balls, smaller than tennis balls—on the 2-foot baking sheets. Eight cookie balls to a pan, ten pans at a time, the front baker loads and reloads the oven all day long. There are days we can barely keep up with demand. Fresh from the oven, warm and enormous, these cookies are an irresistible temptation to hungry skiers.

This chapter includes the formulas for all our jumbo cookies, with reduced quantities for home bakers. There are also recipes for little "gourmet" cookies to accompany ice cream, the ultra-best biscotti and bar cookies, including a fat-free energy bar made with dried fruits and honey.

At Deer Valley one of the first procedures rookie bakers learn is how to make jumbo cookies. Each new baker shadows a more experienced pastry cook, learning where ingredients and tools are kept and how to operate the mixer. For you beginning bakers, I suggest starting with cookies and bars since these are some of the ● Easier recipes of the book. More so, just as a skier will find the ■ Intermediate runs less challenging at Deer Valley than at Snowbird, the difficulty ratings in this chapter are easier than others in the book. If you are a confident, experienced baker already capable of ◆ Advanced recipes, consider these recipes indispensable—the ones to use for all the cookie baking times of your life.

# • Jumbo Chocolate Chip Cookies

After we mix a huge batch of cookie dough, we put a test cookie in the oven. By the time all the raw cookie balls are scooped and wrapped—if you are a fast scooper—the warm tester is ready to eat. You can make your cookies smaller than we do at Deer Valley; just scoop the dough by teaspoons or tablespoons or use a miniature ice cream scoop. Be on the watch, though: The smaller the cookie, the shorter the baking time.

½ pound (2 sticks) unsalted butter, softened
1 cup sugar
¾ cup firmly packed brown sugar
2 eggs
1¼ teaspoons vanilla extract
3 cups all-purpose flour
1 teaspoon baking soda
1 teaspoon salt
1 cup semisweet chocolate morsels

Preheat oven to 325°. In a large bowl, using an electric mixer, cream the butter, sugar and brown sugar until light and fluffy. Add the eggs and vanilla. Mix well and scrape the sides and bottom of the bowl. Sift together the flour, baking soda and salt. Mix into the creamed butter, scraping again. Stir in the chocolate morsels.

Line 3 large baking sheets with parchment paper or oil them lightly with canola oil. Scoop the cookie dough into 12 large (⅓ cup) mounds, arranging them, 4 to a sheet, about 3 inches apart. Bake until cookies are flat and very light golden brown, 20 to 25 minutes.

*Makes 12 jumbo or 24 medium cookies.*

▲ High altitude: Reduce sugar to ¾ cup.

*Opposite: Jumbo Chocolate Chip Cookies with*
*Jumbo Double Chocolate Chip Cookies (page 62)*

# • Jumbo Double Chocolate Chip Cookies

*(See photo on page 60)*

This is my favorite of our jumbos. My willpower is vulnerable whenever these chocolate temptations are nearby—especially one that's warm out of the oven.

½ pound (2 sticks) unsalted butter, softened
1 cup sugar
¾ cup firmly packed brown sugar
2 eggs
1 teaspoon vanilla extract
½ teaspoon instant espresso coffee powder
2 cups all-purpose flour
⅔ cup cocoa powder
1 teaspoon baking soda
1 teaspoon salt
¾ cup white chocolate morsels
½ cup semisweet chocolate morsels

Preheat oven to 325°. In a large bowl, using an electric mixer, cream the butter, sugar and brown sugar until light and fluffy. Add the eggs, vanilla and espresso powder. Mix well and scrape the sides and bottom of the bowl. Sift together the flour, cocoa powder, baking soda and salt. Mix into the creamed butter, scraping again. Stir in the white and semisweet chocolate morsels.

Line 3 large baking sheets with parchment paper or oil them lightly with canola oil. Scoop the cookie dough into 12 large (⅓ cup) mounds, arranging them, 4 to a sheet, at least 3 inches apart. Bake until cookies are flat, 20 to 25 minutes.

*Makes 12 jumbo or 24 smaller cookies.*

▲ High altitude: Reduce sugar to ¾ cup.

*It's hard to tell when dark chocolate cookies are done; by the time they have color, they are overbaked. My trick is to lift the baking sheet and bang it on the oven rack; if the cookies still have a dome, leave them in; if they flatten, remove from the oven.*

# Jumbo Oatmeal Raisin Cookies

These have a pleasing cinnamon flavor and the wholesomeness of oats and raisins. I think one of the secrets to our jumbo cookies is the lower baking temperature—the large dough balls have time to flatten, yet stay soft and chewy. Resist baking the cookies longer once they have flattened; remember that they continue to cook on the hot baking sheet.

**½ pound (2 sticks) unsalted butter, softened**
**1 cup sugar**
**¾ cup firmly packed brown sugar**
**2 eggs**
**2 cups all-purpose flour**
**1 teaspoon baking soda**
**1 teaspoon salt**
**1 teaspoon ground cinnamon**
**1¾ cups old-fashioned rolled oats**
**1 cup dark raisins**

Preheat oven to 325°. In a large bowl, using an electric mixer, cream the butter, sugar and brown sugar until light and fluffy. Add the eggs. Mix well and scrape the sides and bottom of the bowl. Sift together the flour, baking soda, salt and cinnamon. Mix into the creamed butter, scraping again. Add the oats and raisins. Mix and scrape.

Line 3 large baking sheets with parchment paper or oil them lightly with canola oil. Scoop the cookie dough into 12 large (⅓ cup) mounds, arranging them, 4 to a sheet, about 3 inches apart. Bake until cookies are flat and very light golden brown, 20 to 25 minutes.

*Makes 12 jumbo or 24 smaller cookies.*

▲ High altitude: Reduce sugar to ¾ cup.

# • Macadamia Nut Cookies

To me, these delicate and buttery cookies look like miniature sombreros, the broad-rimmed hats from Mexico. Pair with tropical fruits, such as coconut, mango or banana, to complement the nut's light flavor and tender crunch.

½ pound (2 sticks) unsalted butter, softened
½ cup *plus* ½ cup sugar
1 egg
½ teaspoon vanilla extract
1 teaspoon dark rum, optional
2½ cups all-purpose flour
½ teaspoon baking powder
½ teaspoon baking soda
¼ teaspoon salt
1 cup *plus* 120 (about ⅔ cup) unsalted macadamia nut halves❀

❀ I use raw unsalted macadamia nuts, purchased in bulk. If you can only find them roasted and salted, rinse and dry the nuts thoroughly before using.

In a large bowl, using an electric mixer, cream the butter and the first ½ cup of sugar until light and fluffy. Add the egg, vanilla and rum, if using, and mix well. Scrape the sides and bottom of the bowl. Sift together the flour, baking powder, baking soda and salt. Mix into the creamed butter, scraping the bowl again. Grind 1 cup of the nuts with the remaining ½ cup of sugar in a food processor. Mix into the dough; scrape.

Divide the dough into 2 equal portions. On a piece of parchment or waxed paper, pat each portion into a 12-inch log. Use the parchment to roll smooth, even logs, about 1½ inches in diameter. Refrigerate 2 hours or freeze 45 minutes, until firm.

Preheat oven to 325°. Line 3 large baking sheets with parchment paper, or oil them lightly with canola oil. Slice each log into ½-inch rounds and arrange on the baking sheets ½ inch apart. Gently press a nut half into the center of each cookie. Bake 15 to 18 minutes, until the cookies are slightly golden brown.

*Makes about 10 dozen cookies.*

▲ High altitude: Reduce the first ½ cup of sugar by 2 tablespoons. Reduce the baking powder and baking soda to ¼ teaspoon each.

# • Chocolate Almond Macaroons

I worked my way through college eating almond macaroons. They were offered with the guest check where I waitressed and I ate more than my share—the chef would have killed me had he known how many. I still love them, both the regular and chocolate varieties. You can turn these into plain almond macaroons by simply eliminating the cocoa and espresso powders.

> **1 cup (about 8 ounces) almond paste**
> **⅔ cup sugar**
> **¼ cup cocoa powder**
> **¼ teaspoon instant espresso coffee powder**
> **1 egg white**
> **About 40 whole almonds**

Preheat the oven to 325°. Line 2 large baking sheets with parchment paper or aluminum foil.

Put the almond paste and sugar into a food processor work bowl and process until the almond paste has broken down and mixed with the sugar. Add the cocoa and espresso powders. Mix in the egg white until well blended. Drop by rounded spoonfuls or with a small ice cream scoop (page 250), about 1 inch apart, onto the prepared baking sheets. Press a whole almond on top of each mound. Bake 15 to 18 minutes, just until you can slide a macaroon on the baking sheet and it will move without losing shape. Cool. Store in an airtight container.

*Makes about 40 small cookies.*

▲ High altitude: Decrease the sugar by 1 tablespoon.

# • Chocolate Espresso Slice and Bakes

*(See photo on page 166)*

Serve these crisp cookies on a beautiful plate for a casually elegant dessert. Or offer them for afternoon tea with other small treats. This is a variation of a recipe I got from Jim Dodge when he was pastry chef at the Stanford Court Hotel in San Francisco.

½ pound (2 sticks) unsalted butter, softened
½ cup and 1 tablespoon sugar
½ cup firmly packed brown sugar
1 egg
2 teaspoons instant espresso coffee powder
1 teaspoon vanilla extract
2 cups all-purpose flour
1 tablespoon cocoa powder
1 teaspoon ground cinnamon
¾ teaspoon salt
4 ounces bittersweet chocolate, grated❊

❊ I use the grater attachment of a food processor to grate chocolate. Otherwise, my warm hands melt it before it's all grated and I (literally) have a gooey mess on my hands.

In a large bowl, using an electric mixer, cream the butter, sugar and brown sugar until light and fluffy. In a small bowl, whisk the egg with the espresso powder and vanilla. Add to the butter mixture; scrape the sides and bottom of the bowl. Sift together the flour, cocoa powder, cinnamon and salt. Mix into the creamed butter, scraping again. Stir in the grated chocolate.

Divide the dough in half. On a piece of parchment or waxed paper, form each portion of dough into a 1¼-inch-square log, 11 inches long. Wrap the parchment around the log and use it to square up the corners. Refrigerate for 2 hours or freeze for 45 minutes, until firm enough to slice.

Preheat the oven to 325°. Line 3 large baking sheets with parchment paper or oil them lightly with canola oil. Slice ⅛-inch squares and arrange on baking sheets ½ inch apart. Bake 12 to 15 minutes, until the cookies have lost their wet shine and you can slide a cookie on the baking sheet and it will move without losing shape.

*Makes about 9 dozen cookies.*

▲ High altitude: Eliminate the extra tablespoon of sugar. Reduce the brown sugar to ⅓ cup.

# • Chocolate Walnut Brownies

A cross between chocolate fudge and chocolate cake, this is my idea of the perfect brownie. These are delicious served with Vanilla Bean Ice Cream and Hot Fudge Sauce.

   **5 (1-ounce) squares unsweetened chocolate**
   **10 tablespoons (1¼ sticks) unsalted butter**
   **1¾ cups sugar**
   **4 eggs**
   **1 teaspoon vanilla extract**
   **1¼ cups all-purpose flour**
   **1 teaspoon baking powder**
   **¾ cup *plus* ¼ cup finely chopped walnuts**

Preheat the oven to 350°. Brush a 9 x 13-inch baking pan with melted butter and dust the sides lightly with flour or spray generously with cooking spray.

Melt the chocolate and the butter in the top of a double boiler over gently boiling water; the upper pan should not touch the water.

In a large bowl, beat the sugar, eggs and vanilla until well blended. Mix in the melted chocolate and butter.

Sift the flour and baking powder together. Add to the chocolate batter. Mix well and scrape the sides and bottom of the bowl. Stir in ¾ cup of the walnuts. Spread into the prepared pan. Sprinkle with the remaining ¼ cup of walnuts.

Bake until the brownies are set but still moist in the center, 25 to 30 minutes. Cool completely before cutting.

*Makes 12 (3-inch square) or 24 (2-inch square) bar cookies.*

▲ High altitude: Reduce sugar by 3 tablespoons. Reduce baking powder to ¾ teaspoon.

# ■ Peanut Butter Truffles

These look like the French candy truffles, especially when dusted with cocoa, but they are definitely an American treat, given our fondness for peanut butter. Take pleasure in getting chocolate all over your hands when you coat the peanut butter balls—it's fun, and you'll feel like a real chocolatier.

  **4 tablespoons unsalted butter, softened**
  **½ cup creamy peanut butter**
  **¾ cup sifted confectioners' sugar**
  **½ teaspoon vanilla extract**
  **½ pound bittersweet chocolate, chopped**
  **About ½ cup cocoa powder, optional**

With an electric mixer, beat the butter, peanut butter, sugar and vanilla until creamy and smooth. Refrigerate for at least an hour, until firm enough to form into balls.

Scoop the dough into 1-inch mounds using a teaspoon or a small ice cream scoop and place on a parchment-lined baking sheet. You may need to briefly roll the mounds between your hands to form smooth, round balls. Freeze until very firm, at least 2 hours.

Melt the chocolate in the top of a double boiler, over gently boiling water; the upper pan should not touch the water.

Pour about 3 tablespoons of melted chocolate into the cupped palm of your less-dominant hand—if you are right-handed, put the chocolate in your cupped left hand. Pick up a peanut butter ball with your other hand and drop it into your cupped palm. Roll it in the chocolate, coating evenly. Place the candy back on the sheet pan using your "clean" fingers, shaking off excess chocolate into your cupped "chocolatey" hand. Continue rolling each ball in chocolate, adding more melted chocolate to your cupped hand as needed. Refrigerate. If desired, put the cocoa powder on a plate and roll the cold truffles in the cocoa powder until they are lightly coated.

*Makes about 30 candies.*

▲ High altitude: This recipe needs no adjustment.

# ■ Low-Fat Honey Jumbo Cookies

These cookies may not taste as decadent as one of our regular jumbo cookies, but they do satisfy a sweet tooth—like mine—seeking a healthier choice. Honey Jumbos are soft cookies, before and after baking; the dough will be stickier than one with butter and is easier to scoop when cold. My friend Patricia tempers the cookie's austerity by substituting chocolate chips for the raisins.

¾ cup pitted prunes, tightly packed
⅓ cup hot water
¼ cup canola oil
¾ cup honey
¼ cup unsulphured molasses
¾ cup apple juice concentrate (page 241)
1¼ teaspoons vanilla extract
3 cups whole wheat flour
1 teaspoon baking soda
1 teaspoon baking powder
1 tablespoon ground cinnamon
1 teaspoon ground ginger
1 teaspoon salt
½ cup golden raisins
½ cup shelled sunflower seeds

Soak the prunes in the hot water for 10 minutes. Purée in a food processor until quite smooth and no large chunks remain. In a large bowl, using an electric mixer, beat the prune purée, oil, honey, molasses, apple juice concentrate and vanilla until well blended, 3 to 5 minutes. Sift the flour, baking soda, baking powder, cinnamon, ginger and salt together into another bowl. Add the dry ingredients to the wet ingredients and mix well, stopping to scrape the sides and bottom of the bowl. Mix in the raisins and sunflower seeds. Cover and refrigerate until cold, about 1 hour.

Preheat the oven to 325°. Line 3 large baking sheets with parchment paper, or oil them lightly with canola oil, or spray them with cooking spray. Drop the cookie dough onto the baking sheets in large balls, about ⅓ cup dough each, about 3 inches apart. Gently flatten the balls, using the bottom of a drinking glass that has been dipped in water. Bake until the tops of the cookies spring back when touched with a finger, about 20 minutes.

*Makes 16 to 18 large cookies.*

▲ High altitude: Reduce baking soda and baking powder to ½ teaspoon each.

# ■ Snowshoe Tommy Bars

Tommy Thompson was an early Deer Valley local, a miner who traipsed around Bald Mountain long before chairlifts and skiers, carving his name or initials into more than one aspen tree. Deer Valley named a mountaintop hut as well as these chewy "blond" brownies after Snowshoe Tommy and the vestigial tree trunks.

12 tablespoons (1½ sticks) unsalted butter, softened
1½ cups firmly packed brown sugar
3 eggs
2 teaspoons vanilla extract
1½ cups all-purpose flour
½ teaspoon salt
1½ teaspoons baking powder
1 cup semisweet chocolate morsels
1 cup shredded coconut
1 cup old-fashioned rolled oats
½ cup dark raisins
½ cup chopped pitted dates
½ cup chopped walnuts

Preheat the oven to 325°. Brush a 9 x 13-inch baking pan with melted butter and dust lightly with flour or spray generously with cooking spray.

In a large bowl, using an electric mixer, cream the butter and brown sugar until light and fluffy. Add the eggs one at a time, beating and scraping the bowl after each addition. Mix in the vanilla.

Sift the flour, salt and baking powder together. Mix into the butter and scrape the sides and bottoms of the bowl. Stir in the chocolate morsels, coconut, oats, raisins, dates and walnuts. Spread the batter into the prepared pan.

Bake until the bars are set, moist but not raw in the center, 40 to 45 minutes. Cool completely before cutting.

*Makes 12 (3-inch square) or 24 (2-inch square) bar cookies.*

▲ High altitude: Reduce brown sugar to 1¼ cups. Reduce baking powder to 1 teaspoon.

# ■ World's Best Almond Biscotti

*(See photo on page 162)*

Biscotti are the long cookies sold in jars at espresso coffee stands. Typically, they are a bit hard and dry, good for dipping into cappuccino or dessert wine, but these are deliciously buttery, like shortbread. The Italian word *biscotti* means "twice cooked"; they are first baked in a log shape, then sliced and baked again.

**½ pound (2 sticks) unsalted butter, softened**
**1 cup sugar**
**1 teaspoon grated orange zest**
**1 teaspoon grated lemon zest**
**2 eggs**
**1½ teaspoons vanilla extract**
**2 cups all-purpose flour**
**1½ teaspoons salt**
**1½ cups finely ground almonds**❈
**½ cup coarsely chopped whole almonds**

In a large bowl, using an electric mixer, cream the butter, sugar and citrus zests until light and fluffy. Add the eggs and vanilla. Mix well and scrape the sides and bottom of the bowl. Stir the flour and salt together, then mix into the creamed butter. Scrape. Add both the ground and the chopped almonds; mix, scrape and mix again.

On a piece of parchment or waxed paper, shape the dough into a 16-inch log, about 2 inches in diameter, using the parchment to roll an even, round log. Chill the log for at least an hour, so it won't spread too quickly when it bakes.

Preheat the oven to 325°. Line a large baking sheet with parchment paper or oil it lightly with canola oil. Place a whole biscotti log in the center of the baking sheet and bake 30 to 35 minutes, until the dough at the top of the log no longer feels raw and is just beginning to turn light brown on the edges. Cool 20 minutes.❈❈

Carefully move the log to a cutting board and cut into ¾-inch slices. Lay the slices on their sides and bake again, about 15 minutes, until the cookies are light golden brown.

To make "mini" biscotti, divide the dough in half and shape each portion into 16-inch logs, about 1¼ inches in diameter. Chill, bake and cool as for the large biscotti, but cut into ½-inch slices for baking the second time.

*Makes about 20 large biscotti or about 55 mini biscotti.*

▲ High altitude: Decrease sugar by 2 tablespoons.

❈ A food processor is the perfect tool for grinding nuts. You may grind whole almonds, or slivers, or slices; just be sure to measure the 1½ cups of nuts after they have been ground.

❈❈ Make sure to let the first-baked log cool before cutting, until it is firm enough to move, so you don't smash or break more biscotti than you make.

# ■ Raspberry Granola Bars

I call these granola bars because they contain granola ingredients such as rolled oats and nuts, though the butter makes them less wholesome than the word granola might imply.

> 1⅓ cups all-purpose flour
> 1¼ cups old-fashioned rolled oats
> ¾ cup firmly packed brown sugar
> ⅔ cup shredded coconut
> ⅔ cup finely ground walnuts
> 12 tablespoons (1½ sticks) cold unsalted butter, cut into pieces
> 1 apple (any variety), cored and grated
> 1 cup (10-ounce jar) raspberry preserves or spreadable fruit

Preheat the oven to 325°. Brush a 9 x 13-inch baking pan with melted butter and dust lightly with flour or spray generously with cooking spray.

Mix the flour, oats, brown sugar, coconut and walnuts in a large bowl. Using your fingers or an electric mixer, work in the butter until it resembles a coarse meal, being careful not to overmix it into a dough.❋ Pat a little more than half of this mixture (about 3 cups) into the bottom of the prepared pan. Bake 10 to 15 minutes, until the crust just begins to turn brown. Cool.

Stir the grated apple into the preserves. Spread onto the pre-baked crust. Sprinkle evenly with the remaining flour and nut mixture. Bake 30 to 35 minutes, until the top crust is a light golden brown. Cool completely before cutting.

*Makes 12 (3-inch square) or 24 (2-inch square) bar cookies.*

▲High altitude: The bars may require longer baking, as the crust may take 5 to 7 minutes longer to turn golden brown.

**Variation:**
*Date, Apricot or Cherry Granola Bars:* Cook 1½ cups of dried fruit with 1½ cups of orange juice on low heat for about 15 minutes, until the fruit is soft and the liquid reduces by half. Cool. Purée in a food processor. Substitute for the raspberry and apple spread. Bake as directed.

❋ You can also use a food processor: Put the flour, oats, brown sugar, coconut, walnuts and butter pieces in the work bowl and pulse 4 or 5 times.

# ■ Almost Sinless Brownies

Many people are concerned about their fat intake; these brownies prove it—at Deer Valley they outsell our regular, gratifyingly rich Chocolate Walnut Brownies. Even though these brownies are fat-free, they are sweetened with sugar, so we call them "almost" sinless.

**1 cup pitted prunes, tightly packed**
**½ cup hot water**
**1 cup firmly packed brown sugar**
**¼ cup *plus* ½ cup sugar**
**2 egg whites (about ¼ cup) *plus* 4 egg whites (about ½ cup)**
**1½ teaspoons apple cider vinegar**
**1 teaspoon vanilla extract**
**¾ teaspoon instant espresso coffee powder**
**1½ cups all-purpose flour**
**¾ cup cocoa powder**
**1½ teaspoons baking powder**
**½ teaspoon baking soda**
**½ teaspoon salt**
**½ teaspoon ground cinnamon**
**Confectioners' sugar, as needed to dust the top**

Preheat the oven to 325°. Brush a 9 x 13-inch baking pan with melted butter and dust lightly with flour or spray generously with cooking spray.

Soak the prunes in the water for 10 minutes. Purée in a food processor until quite smooth and no large chunks remain. In a large bowl, mix the prune purée, brown sugar, the ¼ cup of sugar, 2 of the egg whites, vinegar, vanilla and espresso powder. Set aside. In another bowl, sift the flour, cocoa powder, baking powder, baking soda, salt and cinnamon. Set aside.

Using an electric mixer with a clean bowl and whisks, whip the remaining 4 egg whites and ½ cup sugar until they form soft peaks.

Stir the flour mixture and half of the whipped egg whites into the prune and sugar mixture. Mix well, then fold in the remaining whipped egg whites, blending until there are no white streaks of meringue left. Pour into the prepared pan. Bake 40 to 50 minutes. When the brownies are done, the top around the sides will spring back and the top center will leave a slight indentation when touched with a finger. Cool completely before cutting. Dust with confectioners' sugar before serving.

*Makes 12 (3-inch square) or 24 (2-inch square) bar cookies.*

▲ High altitude: Reduce second sugar by 1 tablespoon. Reduce baking powder to 1 teaspoon.

# ■ Linzer Heart Cookies

These are beautiful sandwich cookies, filled with raspberry jam that peeks through a hole in the sugar-dusted top. Cinnamon spicy and almond nutty, they make wonderful valentines—and are perfect for weddings as well. At Christmas, use round fluted cutters and the Linzer cookies will resemble miniature wreaths.

**1 recipe cold Linzertorte dough (page 135)**
**All-purpose flour, as needed, for rolling the dough**
**About ⅓ cup good-quality raspberry preserves**
**Confectioners' sugar for dusting the top cookie**

Preheat the oven to 325°. Line 3 large baking sheets with parchment paper or oil them lightly with canola oil. Divide the dough into 4 portions. Roll one portion at a time, keeping the others refrigerated while you work.

Flatten one of the portions into a round disk, using your hands. On a lightly floured surface, roll it less than ⅛ inch thick, using short, coaxing strokes of the rolling pin. Lift and turn the dough frequently, dusting the work surface and the rolling pin with flour as needed to keep the dough from sticking. With a 2-inch heart-shaped cutter, cut out about 10 hearts. Arrange them about ½ inch apart on 1 of the baking sheets. Roll 10 more hearts out of another dough portion and arrange on the baking sheet. These will be the bottoms of the cookie sandwich. Gather the scraps and refrigerate.

Roll and cut the third portion of dough as you did the first two. Using a ½-inch round cutter, cut out a hole in the center of these hearts and arrange them on the other baking sheet; they will be the tops of the cookie sandwich. Repeat with the last portion. Roll and cut all the leftover dough scraps into an equal number of tops and bottoms.

Bake for 12 to 14 minutes, or until the cookies no longer appear raw and you can slide a cookie on the baking sheet and it will move without losing shape. Cool.

To assemble, spread about ½ teaspoon of raspberry preserves in the center of each cookie bottom. Sprinkle the cookie tops with confectioners' sugar. Gently press a "dusted" heart on top of each "jammed" bottom.

*Makes 24 to 30 cookies.*

▲ High altitude: Reduce the baking powder as suggested when making the Linzertorte dough.

*Opposite: Linzer Heart Cookies*

# ■ Orange Blossom Brownies

These bar cookies have a pre-baked chocolate layer underneath a tangy-sweet orange filling. When they bake together, the citrus melds into the chocolate for a dense, rich brownie. The optional orange flower water adds a bouquet above and beyond the familiar fruit. Just a whiff triggers memories of walking through endless rows of orange trees, drinking in the delicate white blossoms' heady fragrance. It is one of my most vivid recollections of growing up in Southern California.

Chocolate layer:
¼ pound (1 stick) unsalted butter, cut in small pieces
3 (1-ounce) squares unsweetened chocolate
1 cup all-purpose flour
¼ teaspoon baking powder
¼ teaspoon salt
3 eggs
1 cup sugar
1 teaspoon grated orange zest
¼ teaspoon orange extract
¼ teaspoon vanilla extract

Orange layer:
1¾ cups sugar
¼ cup all-purpose flour
½ teaspoon baking powder
4 teaspoons grated orange zest
½ cup fresh-squeezed orange juice
¼ cup fresh-squeezed lemon juice
1 teaspoon orange flower water, optional❈
½ teaspoon orange extract
4 eggs, lightly beaten

**Confectioners' sugar, optional topping**

**To make the chocolate layer:**
Melt the butter and chocolate in the top of a double boiler, over gently boiling water; the upper pan should not touch the water.

Preheat the oven to 325°. Brush a 9 x 13-inch baking pan with melted butter and dust lightly with flour or spray generously with cooking spray.

Stir the flour, baking powder and salt together; set aside. In a medium bowl, whisk the eggs, sugar and orange zest until well blended. Add the orange and vanilla extracts to the melted butter and chocolate, and stir into the egg mixture. Add the dry ingredients and mix well, scraping the sides and bottom of the bowl. Spread the batter in the prepared pan. Bake 25 to 30 minutes, until the filling is set, but not dry. Cool about 10 minutes.

❈ Orange flower water is an extraction of the aromatic flowers of the oldest known orange, the bitter Seville, imported to Spain by the Arabs. It is available in specialty stores and some large supermarkets.

**To make the orange layer:**

Sift the sugar, flour and baking powder into a large bowl. Whisk in the orange zest, the orange and lemon juices, the orange flower water, if using, and the orange extract. Whisk in the eggs, stirring until smooth. Pour over the pre-baked bottom and bake another 40 to 50 minutes, until the filling puffs up. The top should be light golden brown and the filling set. Cool completely. Refrigerate until cold before cutting. You will need to wipe the knife between cuts, as necessary. To serve, dust with confectioners' sugar, if desired.

*Makes 24 (2-inch square) bar cookies.*

▲ High altitude: Reduce the sugar in the filling to 1½ cups.

# ◆ Fat-Free McHenergy Bars

These are sports and fitness energy bars named after McHenry's restaurant in Silver Lake Lodge. I wrap each bar separately and freeze them. When I ski, bike or hike, I grab one for my pocket—a healthy energizing snack.

1 cup unsweetened applesauce
⅔ cup honey
¾ cup apple juice concentrate (page 241)
1 cup grated carrots
½ cup golden raisins
½ cup dried apricots
½ cup (about 6) dried figs, stems removed
1 teaspoon vanilla extract
½ teaspoon orange extract
2¼ cups whole wheat flour
1 cup old-fashioned rolled oats
¼ cup yellow cornmeal
1 tablespoon cocoa powder
1 teaspoon baking soda
1¼ teaspoons ground cinnamon
¼ teaspoon ground mace
¼ teaspoon salt
1 cup puffed millet cereal❊
⅓ cup pitted, chopped dates

❊ Puffed millet is a ready-to-eat version of the millet grain. Look for bags of the cereal in health food stores.

*McHenergy bars have less than 150 calories, about 34 grams of carbohydrates, 3 grams of protein and less than 1 gram of fat.*

Lightly coat a 9 x 13-inch baking pan with canola oil or spray with cooking spray.

Put the applesauce, honey, apple concentrate and carrots in a stainless steel saucepan. Cook on very low heat, stirring occasionally to prevent scorching, until the mixture is almost boiling. Remove from heat. Stir in the raisins, apricots and figs; allow the dried fruit to soften at least 10 minutes. Add the vanilla and orange extracts.

Preheat the oven to 325°. Put the flour, oats, cornmeal, cocoa powder, baking soda, cinnamon, mace and salt into a food processor work bowl. Process until the oats are finely ground and the dry ingredients are well mixed. Transfer to a large bowl.

Pour the applesauce and fruit mixture into the food processor work bowl and process until smooth. Stir into the bowl of dry ingredients. Add the millet and the dates. Mix with a rubber spatula until all the dry ingredients are moistened and the millet and dates are well distributed; the batter will be fairly stiff. Spread evenly into the prepared pan. Bake 55 to 60 minutes, until a finger indentation does not remain when touched. Cool completely. Invert the bars onto a cutting board. Trim ⅛ inch off the sides, then cut into individual bars.

Makes 24 (1⅜ x3-inch) bars.

▲ High altitude: Reduce baking soda to ¾ teaspoon.

# Cakes and Cheesecakes

● 

Chocolate Snowball

● 

Chocolate Cranberry Cheesecake Cupcakes

■ 

Deep Powder Carrot Cake

■ 

Deer Valley Cheesecake with Strawberry Sauce

■ 

Chameleon Cheesecake

■ 

Milk Chocolate Cheesecake with Caramel Sauce
and Peanut Brittle

■ 

Mango Cinnamon Trifle

■ 

Peanut Butter Lover's Cake

■ 

Chocolate Truffle Cake

■ 

Stein's Favorite Marzipan Cake

■ 

Low-Fat Black Forest Mousse Cake

◆ 

Tiramisù Yule Log

◆ 

Lemon and Strawberry Dacquoise

◆ 

Gâteau Opéra

◆◆ 

Orange Almond Wedding Cake

# Cakes and Cheesecakes

One winter season we had a couple of young, fun-loving women in the bakery. They always came to work with a mischievous twinkle in their eyes, and sometimes their hilarious sense of humor would have me almost rolling on the floor with laughter. After work, these two would patronize Park City's drinking establishments. They liked sweet liqueur cocktails with names like Kamikaze, Black Russian, and Harvey Wallbanger. They were happy to sample the new and exotic, and I'm certain the local bartenders enjoyed coaching them.

I knew they were investigating new possibilities for cheesecake flavors, because the mornings after their tasting forays they would arrive at work bubbling with ideas. "Let's make a B-52 with Kahlúa, Baileys, and Grand Marnier." "How about a Fuzzy Navel with orange juice and peach schnapps?" Even now, some of our dessert offerings echo their evening escapades.

The Chameleon Cheesecake is a basic recipe for your own cheesecake fantasies. You can also mix and match the different cakes, fillings and frostings from any of the recipes; the possibilities are innumerable. I encourage you to create new personal combinations once you are comfortable with the techniques and the separate parts of the recipes. Follow your imagination.

Many of the recipes in this chapter have three and more components to the final assembly. Don't let yourself be overwhelmed or discouraged; the trick is to divide the work over several days (or weeks, using the freezer), then put everything together on the momentous day. We certainly do this at Deer Valley; in a busy kitchen, we don't have time for last-minute undertakings. We keep cake rounds and sheets in the freezer, and simple syrups, fillings and buttercream in the refrigerator, preparing ahead so we're ready for the crazy times.

When you preheat the oven for cakes, position the oven rack in the lower third of the oven. That way the cake itself will be in the center of the oven with room for air to circulate between the pans. If you are baking more than 3 pans at a time or your oven is of small capacity, turn the pans halfway through baking to prevent uneven baking from reduced air circulation. At Deer Valley, we make large batches of cake but we have convection ovens to help with the air circulation.

I always give directions for lining cake pans with parchment (or waxed) paper, besides coating the pan with butter and flour or cooking spray. This is insurance to prevent the baked and cooled cake from sticking to the pan when inverted. The parchment circle lining also keeps cakes moist. For cheesecakes, I often line the sides of the springform pan too, so I don't have to worry about the cheesecake sticking to the ring when I remove it. I cut strips of parchment about 2 inches high to fit inside the ring. I brush the sides of the pan with butter to adhere the parchment strips to the sides of the pan.

Cool cakes at least 10 minutes before turning them out of the pan. If you have wire cooling racks, place hot cake pans on them, so air can circulate underneath. Otherwise, put the pans on a heatproof surface to cool. After 10 minutes you can invert the cakes onto a wire rack or a cardboard circle to cool completely. At Deer Valley, we just leave the cakes in the pan and turn them out when they are completely cool. Always be sure to remove the parchment paper liner before re-inverting the cake right-side up.

Use a serrated knife to trim cake layers. To give the frosted cake a more professional, elegant appearance—flat, not rounded—I trim the dome from the top of cake rounds. Hold the knife level and parallel to the bottom of the cake when trimming the rounded dome. Rest your other hand gently on top of the cake while slicing. Also, hold the knife level and parallel to the bottom of the cake to split cake layers evenly in half or in thirds. Start by slicing into the cake only 1 inch, rotating the cake on a turntable or on a cardboard circle on a work surface, until you have cut around the circumference of the cake.

Continue to rotate the cake and keep your knife level, slicing into the cake an inch at a time, until you can feel that the knife has sliced the cake layer all the way across. To keep the knife in the same horizontal plane without wavering, it helps to hold your elbow close to your torso. If the sides of the cake seem dry, or if it is a light-colored cake, carefully trim ⅛ inch off the sides to remove the dry, darker edge. I slide cardboard circles underneath each split cake layer so I can move them around easily.

I almost always moisten cake layers with flavored simple syrup before filling and frosting. The syrup adds flavor while it ensures the cake stays moist. Moistening cake layers is especially beneficial in the non-humid air of high altitudes. Use a pastry brush to put the syrup on the trimmed layers.

Use a cake turntable (page 243) to make it easier to frost cakes with buttercream, ganache, whipped cream or any frosting. First apply the frosting to the sides of the cake. Using an icing spatula, apply the frosting with one hand and rotate the turntable with the other, holding the icing spatula at a right angle to the table. To frost the top, rotate the turntable and apply the frosting with the icing spatula, this time holding the spatula parallel to the table. Use gentle pressure to spread the frosting, and to remove the excess. For right-angled edges, always keep the spatula square to the surface. Try to keep about ¼ inch of frosting in front of the spatula as you spread the frosting, until the cake is completely covered—this will help prevent cake crumbs from mixing with the frosting.

To cut finished cakes, dip a long, thin-bladed knife into a pitcher of very hot water and wipe the knife dry before slicing. Dip and wipe before each cut for clean, professional-looking portions. At home I have an instant hot water faucet. I run my knife under the tap and wipe it dry before cutting each slice of cake.

Just as learning to ski takes time and perseverance, it takes practice to make beautiful cakes. With experience, you gain the skills to tackle the most elaborate recipe. Remember to bring a sense of fun to your baking. Who knows? You might end up rolling on the floor with laughter.

# • Chocolate Snowball

Doesn't it seem fitting that a ski area should serve snowballs for dessert? This is the taste chocoholics dream about—opulent chocolate, smooth and creamy on the tongue. Bake the batter in a bowl to give the cake its round shape. Chill and invert the dome, then pipe whipped cream stars all over. For this flourless chocolate cake, edible pansies, violas or Johnny-jump-ups are a perfect garnish.

Cake:
**12 ounces semisweet chocolate, chopped in ½-inch pieces**
**1 cup strong coffee, hot**
**1 cup sugar**
**¾ pound (3 sticks) unsalted butter, softened**
**6 eggs, lightly beaten**

Frosting:
**1½ cups heavy cream**
**2 tablespoons sugar**
**½ teaspoon vanilla extract**
**15 to 20 fresh, edible purple flowers, for garnish**

**To make the cake:**
Preheat the oven to 350°. Line a medium (5- to 6-cup, about 8-inch diameter) stainless steel bowl with aluminum foil so the foil overlaps the bowl 3 or 4 inches.

Put the chocolate in a saucepan. Pour the coffee over, which will melt some of the chocolate. Place over medium-low heat; add the sugar and stir with a wire whisk to dissolve the sugar and any unmelted chocolate. Add the butter gradually, a dollop at a time, whisking until the butter is incorporated before adding the next dollop. This should take about 10 minutes. Remove from the heat.

Slowly whisk the beaten eggs into the chocolate mixture. Pour through a strainer into the foil-lined bowl. Discard any firm bits of egg that remain in the strainer. Bake 50 to 55 minutes, until the batter rises and a cracked top crust forms. The mixture will still jiggle, like molded gelatin. Resist the urge to bake it a little more; the butter and chocolate set up when chilled.

Let the cake cool. Fold the overlapping foil over the top and refrigerate at least 8 hours, keeping the cake in the bowl. It will keep for up to a week if refrigerated and well wrapped in plastic wrap. (It is best to store the cake in the bowl, but, once it is cold, you can invert the dome onto a cardboard circle—but do not remove the foil wrapper. Wrap the foil-enclosed dome in plastic wrap.) The cake can also be frozen for up to a month; thaw in the refrigerator before frosting.

**To frost and serve:**
Remove the plastic wrap from the bowl. (If you have taken the cake out of the bowl for storage, invert it back into the bowl.) Pull the overlapping foil away from the cake. The

*The Snowball has been served from The Mariposa pastry table since opening day in 1981. It is from Anne Willan, founder and president of La Varenne, the prestigious French cooking school. Our food and beverage director, Julie Wilson, is a graduate of La Varenne and brought us the recipe.*

*Opposite: Chocolate Snowball*

cake will have fallen in the center; to make the top (or what will be the bottom of the cake) flat and even, press the raised outer edges down, or trim the extra height with a knife, reserving the scraps for indulgent snacks. Place a flat serving plate or cardboard circle over the bowl and invert. Gently remove the foil.

Whip the cream with the sugar and the vanilla until the cream comes to soft peaks that hold their shape. Put the cream into a pastry bag fitted with a large star tip. Pipe stars, covering the dome completely. If you wish, decorate with edible flowers or another garnish such as chocolate shavings or crystallized flowers.

*Makes 1 (8-inch) cake, serves 10 to 12.*

▲ High altitude: Reduce the sugar in the cake by 2 tablespoons.

*We often serve individual "plated" Snowballs for Deer Valley banquets as well as Mariposa desserts. We use an ice cream scoop to portion the cold baked chocolate out of the larger Snowball. We place one scoop in the middle of a chocolate-drizzled plate, pipe on the whipped cream stars and scatter flower petals over all. You can bake the batter in a regular 9- or 10-inch foil-lined cake pan instead of the bowl if you plan to serve individual Snowballs.*

# Chocolate Cranberry Cheesecake Cupcakes

These are yummy, tender chocolate muffins with a cream cheese and cranberry filling—potentially addictive snacks. We used to make them with chocolate chips in the filling, but I like the dried cranberries, which brighten the flavor immensely. If you wish, substitute dried cherries for the cranberries.

Filling:
1 (8-ounce) package cream cheese, softened
3 tablespoons sugar
1 egg
1 cup dried cranberries or cherries

Cupcakes:
1¾ cups all-purpose flour
1 cup sugar
¼ cup cocoa powder
1 teaspoon baking soda
½ teaspoon salt
1 cup water
⅓ cup canola oil
1 tablespoon apple cider vinegar
1 teaspoon vanilla extract

**To make the filling:**
In a small bowl or food processor, beat the cream cheese with the sugar until it is smooth. Mix in the egg completely, scraping the bowl as needed. If using a food processor, transfer the mixture to a bowl. By hand, stir in the cranberries, and set aside.

**To make the cupcakes:**
Preheat the oven to 375°. Line 12 muffin tins with paper cupcake liners or coat the tins with melted butter and dust with flour or spray generously with cooking spray.

Sift the flour, sugar, cocoa powder, baking soda and salt into a medium bowl. In another bowl, mix the water, oil, vinegar and vanilla. Pour the wet ingredients into the dry ingredients; mix until well blended. Divide the batter evenly into the prepared tins. Spoon about 2 tablespoons of the cream cheese filling into the center of each cupcake. The chocolate batter will rise around the filling as it bakes.

Lower the oven temperature to 350°. Bake 25 to 30 minutes, until the cake part of the cupcake springs back when touched with a finger. Cool. Remove from the pan and serve.

*Makes 12 cupcakes.*

▲ High altitude: Reduce the sugar in the cupcakes by 2 tablespoons. Reduce the baking soda to ¾ teaspoon.

*A baker in a silly mood named these cupcakes Deer Valley Ding Dongs. I admit, they are reminiscent of those lunch box desserts my mother refused to buy—only better. I've also heard them called Two-Tones and Black Bottom Muffins.*

# ■ Deep Powder Carrot Cake

An inviting cinnamon aroma pervades the lodge when we bake this moist cake. The frosting is smooth and rich, with less sugar and more cream cheese than most other cream cheese icings. For a unique turnabout, try the Pineapple Upside-Down Cake variation. Rather than fruit in the batter, the inverted cake has a topping of glazed pineapple rings.

Cake:
**4 eggs**
**1½ cups sugar**
**½ cup canola oil**
**2 cups all-purpose flour**
**1½ teaspoons ground cinnamon**
**½ teaspoon baking powder**
**1 teaspoon baking soda**
**½ teaspoon salt**
**1 pound carrots, grated (about 4 cups)**
**⅔ cup walnuts, coarsely chopped**

Frosting:
**¼ pound (1 stick) unsalted butter, softened**
**2 (8-ounce) packages cream cheese**
**½ teaspoon vanilla extract**
**Pinch salt**
**2 cups sifted confectioners' sugar**
**½ cup finely chopped or ground walnuts**

*Carrot cake is our most popular cake, and I notice that guests usually choose the piece with the most generous frosting. This recipe comes from Anne Voye Reynolds, Deer Valley's first pastry chef.*

**To make the cake:**
Preheat the oven to 350°. Brush 2 (9-inch) round pans with melted butter and dust lightly with flour or spray generously with cooking spray. Line the bottoms with circles of parchment or waxed paper.

Whip the eggs and sugar with an electric mixer for about 5 minutes, until the mixture is very thick and pale yellow. Add the oil, whipping until it is incorporated.

Sift together the flour, cinnamon, baking powder, baking soda and salt. Add to the egg mixture and mix on low speed until well mixed, stopping to scrape the sides and bottom of the bowl. Add the carrots and walnuts and mix well. Pour into the prepared pans. Bake until the centers of the cakes spring back when touched with a finger, 45 to 50 minutes. Cool completely.

**To make the frosting:**
Beat the butter with an electric mixer until it is smooth. Scrape the sides and bottom of the bowl to make sure there are no lumps. Add the cream cheese and mix well, scraping the bowl again. Add the vanilla, salt and confectioners' sugar and mix 30 seconds on low

speed. Scrape. Mix on medium speed for another 30 seconds; scrape again. Be careful not to mix too much, before or after adding the sugar, or the frosting will be runny.

**To assemble:**
Trim any dome off the top so the cakes are flat, keeping your knife level and parallel to the bottom of the cake.

Place one of the cake layers on a flat serving plate or a cardboard circle. Spread with a layer of frosting, ⅜ inch thick. Place the second layer on top and frost it and the sides of the cake. Press the walnuts onto the sides. If desired, spoon the remaining frosting into a pastry bag fitted with a medium star tip, and decorate with a shell border.

*Makes 1 (9x3-inch) cake, serves 12.*

▲ High altitude: Reduce the sugar in the cake by 3 tablespoons and reduce the baking soda to ½ teaspoon.

**Variation:**
*Pineapple Upside-Down Carrot Cake:* Preheat oven to 350°. Melt 4 tablespoons unsalted butter and ½ cup firmly packed brown sugar in a small saucepan, then pour into a buttered and parchment-lined 9-inch cake pan. Arrange rings of fresh or canned pineapple on top of the sugar mixture. Place dried cherries in the center of each pineapple ring. Prepare a half-recipe of Deep Powder Carrot Cake. Pour the batter into the pan, over the pineapple and sugar. Bake 45 to 50 minutes, until the center of the cake springs back when touched with a finger. Using a knife, loosen the sides of the pan and invert immediately onto a serving platter. Serve warm or at room temperature.

*Makes 1 (9-inch) cake, serves 8 to 10.*

*When you frost a cake, don't fret and fuss too much over untidy sides. As one of our chefs used to say, "Nuts will cover a multitude of sins."*

## ■ Deer Valley Cheesecake with Strawberry Sauce

Sometimes cheesecakes develop a crack in the top during baking even though you followed the instructions to the letter. You don't have to worry about cracks with this recipe—the sour cream topping fills in and hides them. The strawberries are a crowning touch, but feel free to serve this cheesecake with any other fruit or simply unadorned.

Crust:
1½ cups graham cracker crumbs (about 11 whole crackers)
¼ cup sugar
4 tablespoons (½ stick) unsalted butter, melted

Filling:
4 (8-ounce) packages cream cheese, softened
1 cup sugar
4 eggs
1 teaspoon vanilla extract
¼ teaspoon almond extract, optional

Topping:
2 cups (1 pint) sour cream
¼ cup sugar
¼ teaspoon vanilla extract
¼ cup Apricot Glaze (page 208)
12 to 16 fresh strawberries, stems removed, for garnish

1½ cups Strawberry Sauce (page 210)

**To make the crust:**
Preheat the oven to 325°. Wrap a 12 x 12-inch square of parchment or waxed paper over the metal bottom of a 10-inch springform pan. Include the parchment when you close the metal ring around the pan bottom; the parchment will become an easy-to-remove lining. Mix the crumbs, sugar and butter, and press evenly into the bottom of the pan. Bake 5 minutes to set the crust.

**To make the filling:**
Beat the cream cheese and sugar with an electric mixer until smooth and well blended, stopping to scrape the sides and bottom several times. Add the eggs one at a time, scraping and beating well after each addition. Do not beat too much. Mix in the vanilla and almond extract, if using. Pour into the prepared crust. Bake 60 to 75 minutes, until the cake rises slightly, loses its shine and is not liquid in the center when you jiggle the pan. Cool at least 30 minutes so the filling does not displace when you spread the topping over it.

**To make the topping:**

Preheat the oven again to 350°. Whisk the sour cream and sugar in a small bowl. Spread evenly over the cooled cheesecake and bake 10 minutes. Remove promptly from the oven; the topping will set as it cools. Let the cheesecake cool completely, then refrigerate at least 8 hours.

**To serve:**

Carefully unclamp and remove the sides of the pan. To loosen the cake, slide a knife between the bottom crust of the cheesecake and the parchment lining. Carefully slide a cardboard circle or a flat serving plate underneath the cheesecake. Heat the Apricot Glaze in a small saucepan. Lightly brush each strawberry with glaze. Place the whole strawberries on top around the edge, tapered side up. Serve with Strawberry Sauce.

*Makes 1 cheesecake, serves 12 to 20.*

▲ High altitude: Decrease the sugar in the filling by 2 tablespoons. Increase baking time of the filling by 10 to 15 minutes, or until the cake is done as described in the recipe.

*I remember being offered cheesecake when I was 10 years old. I turned up my nose—I couldn't imagine a cake with cheese tasting good. My Aunt Jan and my cousin looked at me funny and said, "Oh well, more for us!" I later realized how satisfying a slice of cheesecake can be, creamy in the mouth, with a gentle tartness.*

# ■ Chameleon Cheesecake

Called "Chameleon" not because it looks like a lizard, but because the recipe is so changeable; you can flavor it many, many ways. Start with the base formula and add various ingredients to the crust and filling—my list of possibilities follows. Balance the anise flavor of Galliano liqueur with succulent blueberries or marry almonds and sultry amaretto.

Crust:
**1½ cups graham cracker crumbs (about 11 whole crackers) or 1½ cups chocolate wafer crumbs (about 30 wafers)**
**¼ cup sugar**
**4 tablespoons (½ stick) unsalted butter, melted**

Filling:
**4 (8-ounce) packages cream cheese, softened**
**1 cup sugar**
**4 eggs**
**2 cups (1 pint) sour cream**
**Baker's choice of flavoring**

**To make the crust:**
Preheat the oven to 300°. Wrap a 12 x 12-inch square of parchment or waxed paper over the metal bottom of a 10-inch springform pan. Include the parchment when you close the metal ring around the pan bottom; the parchment will become an easy-to-remove lining. Mix the crumbs, sugar and butter, and press evenly into the bottom of the pan. Bake 5 minutes to set the crust.

**To make the filling:**
Beat the cream cheese and sugar with an electric mixer until smooth and well blended, stopping to scrape the sides and bottom several times. Add the eggs one at a time, scraping and beating well after each addition. Do not beat too much. Mix in the sour cream and your choice of flavoring.

Pour into the prepared crust. Bake 60 to 75 minutes, until the cake rises slightly, loses its shine and is not liquid in the center when you jiggle the pan. Cool. Refrigerate at least 8 hours.

**To serve:**
Carefully unclamp and remove the sides of the pan. To loosen the cake, slide a knife between the bottom crust of the cheesecake and the parchment lining. Carefully slide a cardboard circle or a flat serving plate underneath the cheesecake. Garnish with a complementary fresh fruit, if desired.

*Makes 1 cheesecake, serves 12 to 20.*

▲ High altitude: Decrease the sugar in the filling by 2 tablespoons. Increase baking time of the filling by 10 to 15 minutes, or until the cake is done as described in the recipe.

**Flavoring options:**

*B-52 Cheesecake:* Use chocolate crust. Divide the filling evenly into three bowls. Whisk 2 tablespoons coffee-flavored liqueur into one bowl, 2 tablespoons of Irish cream liqueur into a second bowl and 2 tablespoons orange-flavored brandy into the third bowl. Pour the 3 flavored fillings into the crust, one on top of the other. Swirl a small spatula or table knife gently through the filling to intermix or marble the flavors.

*Lime Cheesecake:* Add 1 teaspoon grated lime zest and ⅔ cup fresh or bottled lime juice to the filling.

*Grasshopper Cheesecake:* Use chocolate crust. Add 3 tablespoons each crème de menthe and crème de cacao liqueur to the filling. If desired, lightly tint the batter using green crème de menthe or a little food coloring.

*Fuzzy Navel Cheesecake:* Add 1 tablespoon grated orange zest, 2 tablespoons orange juice concentrate and 2 tablespoons peach-flavored liqueur to the filling.

*Almond Cheesecake:* Add ¼ cup finely ground almonds to graham cracker crust. Add 1 teaspoon vanilla extract, ½ teaspoon almond extract and 3 tablespoons amaretto liqueur to the filling.

*Blueberry Galliano Cheesecake:* Sprinkle 2 cups fresh blueberries over graham cracker crust and add ½ cup Galliano liqueur to the filling.

*Cappuccino Cheesecake:* Use chocolate crust. Divide the filling evenly into three bowls. Sift ¼ cup cocoa powder into one of the bowls, then pour it into the prepared crust. Place the pan in the freezer for about an hour, until it freezes enough to hold another layer of filling without sinking. Whisk 1 tablespoon instant espresso coffee powder dissolved in 1 tablespoon hot water into the second bowl of filling, spread on top of the cocoa layer, and freeze again. Add 1 teaspoon grated orange zest to the last bowl and spread onto the coffee layer. (Because of the frozen layers, this cheesecake may take longer to bake; look for the visual indications of doneness as described in the main recipe.)

# ■ Milk Chocolate Cheesecake with Caramel Sauce and Peanut Brittle

This cheesecake has a melt-in-your-mouth quality—it tastes like a malted milkshake. Served with the Caramel Sauce and Peanut Brittle, it reminds me of a Snickers candy bar. Make the Peanut Brittle ahead—it will last for months in an airtight container. If you prefer, make it with whole peeled almonds—or with pecans, for a delicious pecan brittle.

Crust:
**1½ cups chocolate wafer crumbs (about 30 wafers)**❋
**¼ cup sugar**
**2 tablespoons (¼ stick) unsalted butter, melted**

Filling:
**6 tablespoons unsalted butter, softened**
**3 (8-ounce) packages cream cheese, softened**
**⅓ cup sugar**
**3 eggs**
**12 ounces milk chocolate, melted (page 244)**
**2 tablespoons coffee-flavored liqueur**
**Pinch salt**

Topping:
**2 tablespoons heavy cream**
**2 ounces milk chocolate, chopped in ½-inch pieces**
**¾ cup (1 recipe) Peanut Brittle, broken into 2-inch pieces (page 223)**
**1 cup (1 recipe) Caramel Sauce, warm (page 222)**

❋ Chocolate wafer crumbs are available in supermarkets, usually in the same aisle as cake mixes.

**To make the crust:**
Preheat the oven to 300°. Wrap a 12 x 12-inch square of parchment or waxed paper over the metal bottom of a 10-inch springform pan. Include the parchment when you close the metal ring around the pan bottom; the parchment will become an easy-to-remove lining. Mix the crumbs, sugar and butter, and press evenly into the bottom of the pan. Bake 5 minutes to set the crust.

**To make the filling:**
Beat the butter with an electric mixer until it is smooth. Add the cream cheese and sugar; beat well, stopping to scrape the sides and bottom several times. Add the eggs one at a time, scraping and beating well after each addition. Do not beat too much. Mix in the melted chocolate, scraping one more time than you think you need to. Mix in the liqueur and salt. Pour into the prepared pan. Bake 60 to 75 minutes, until the cake loses its shine and is not liquid in the center when you jiggle the pan. Cool. Refrigerate at least 8 hours.

**To make the topping:**

Put the cream and the chocolate in the top of a double boiler. Place over gently boiling water; the upper pan should not touch the water. Stir occasionally, until the chocolate melts and the mixture is smooth. Pour over the middle of the chilled cheesecake, leaving about 1 inch of edge without topping. Refrigerate about 30 minutes to set the topping.

Unclamp and carefully remove the sides of the pan. To loosen the cake, slide a knife between the bottom crust of the cheesecake and the parchment lining. Carefully slide a cardboard circle or a flat serving plate underneath the cheesecake. Sprinkle the Peanut Brittle pieces over the cake as garnish. Serve with warm Caramel Sauce.

*Makes 1 cheesecake, serves 12 to 20.*

▲ High altitude: Increase baking time of the filling by 10 to 15 minutes, or until the cake is done as described in the recipe.

**Variation:**

*White Chocolate Cheesecake:* Substitute white chocolate for the milk chocolate and crème de cacao liqueur for the coffee-flavored liqueur. Serve with fresh raspberries and raspberry sauce instead of Peanut Brittle and Caramel Sauce.

# ■ Mango Cinnamon Trifle

A harmonious blend of fragrant mango, vanilla custard, almond spice cake and dark rum. This would be a sublime finale for a Southwestern theme dinner.

Cake:
¼ cup (about 2 ounces) almond paste
¼ cup *plus* ¼ cup sugar
10 tablespoons (1¼ sticks) unsalted butter, softened
5 eggs, separated
⅛ teaspoon cream of tartar
¾ cup cake flour
½ teaspoon ground cinnamon
¼ teaspoon ground cloves
1 tablespoon cocoa powder

Assembly:
4 ripe mangoes
¼ cup dark rum
1¼ cups (1 recipe) Vanilla Bean Pastry Cream, cold (page 218)
1 cup heavy cream
¼ cup toasted sliced almonds (page 256)

**To make the cake:**
Preheat the oven to 350°. Brush a 9-inch round pan with melted butter and dust lightly with flour or spray generously with cooking spray. Line the bottom with a circle of parchment or waxed paper.

Put the almond paste and ¼ cup of the sugar into a food processor work bowl; process until the almond paste has broken down and mixed with the sugar. With the processor running, drop in the butter, 2 tablespoons at a time; mix well. If you don't have a food processor, cream the almond paste, sugar and butter in a bowl using an electric mixer until the mixture is very light and aerated. Add the egg yolks one at a time and process until the batter is very smooth, stopping to scrape the bowl. Transfer to a large bowl.

Whip the egg whites and cream of tartar in a clean bowl, using an electric mixer. When the whites are frothy, gradually add the remaining ¼ cup of sugar, whipping until soft peaks form. Fold the whites into the yolk mixture.

Sift together the flour, cinnamon, cloves and cocoa powder. Sift again directly onto the batter and gently fold in. Spread evenly into the prepared pan. Bake 25 to 30 minutes, until the cake is light golden brown and the center springs back when touched with a finger. Cool.

**To assemble the trifle:**

With a serrated knife, slice the cinnamon cake into 3 thin layers, keeping the knife level and parallel to the bottom of the cake. Cut the layers into 10 wedges each. Arrange a third of the cake wedges in the bottom of a 2-quart glass bowl or soufflé dish. Peel, pit and dice the mangoes into ½-inch pieces. If the mangoes are juicy, add the juice to the rum. Sprinkle with about a tablespoon of the rum and a fourth of the diced mango.

Whisk the Vanilla Bean Pastry Cream with 2 tablespoons of rum. Whip the cream until it comes to soft peaks that hold their shape. Fold into the pastry cream and rum. Spread a third of this custard over the cake and mango.

Arrange another layer of the cake wedges, sprinkle with another tablespoon of rum and another fourth of the fruit; cover with another third of the custard. Repeat the assembly one more time, ending with the last of the mango pieces. Cover and refrigerate for at least 3 hours to let the flavors meld.

**To serve:**

Garnish with toasted almonds. Spoon the trifle from the bowl.

*Serves 12 to 16.*

▲ High altitude: For the cake, use extra care when whipping the egg whites to soft peaks—as at sea level, they should just fold over; do not beat until stiff and dry.

*Kitchen and gourmet stores sell footed glass bowls made specially to show off the layers in trifle, a classic English dessert. At Seafood Buffet, we make and serve individual trifles in wine goblets.*

# ■ Peanut Butter Lover's Cake

This deep cocoa batter mixes up almost as fast as a boxed cake mix. It's the same recipe as the Chocolate Cranberry Cheesecake Cupcakes but baked in a round pan. The filling is sweet, creamy and peanut-buttery, and reminds me of chocolate-covered peanut butter cups. Especially if you keep all the ingredients in your pantry, this is a good choice for a last-minute birthday cake.

Cake:
**1¾ cups all-purpose flour**
**1 cup sugar**
**¼ cup cocoa powder**
**½ teaspoon salt**
**1 teaspoon baking soda**
**1 tablespoon apple cider vinegar**
**⅓ cup canola oil**
**1 teaspoon vanilla extract**
**1 cup cold water**

Frosting:
**1 (5-ounce) can evaporated milk**
**8 ounces semisweet chocolate, chopped in ½-inch pieces**
**3 tablespoons creamy peanut butter**
**1 tablespoon honey**

Filling:
**6 tablespoons unsalted butter, softened**
**1 cup creamy peanut butter**
**1⅓ cups sifted confectioners' sugar**
**¾ teaspoon vanilla extract**

Assembly:
**⅓ cup Coffee Simple Syrup (page 209)**
**¾ cup Peanut Brittle, optional (page 223)**

**To make the cake:**
Preheat the oven to 350°. Brush a 9-inch round pan with melted butter and dust lightly with flour or spray generously with cooking spray. Line the bottom with a circle of parchment or waxed paper.

Sift the flour, sugar, cocoa powder, salt and baking soda into a mixing bowl. In a separate bowl, whisk the vinegar, oil, vanilla and water; then add to the dry ingredients. Mix for 2 minutes with a hand whisk or with an electric mixer on low speed. Pour into the prepared pan. Bake 30 to 35 minutes, until the center of the cake springs back when touched with a finger. Cool completely.

**To make the frosting:**

Place the evaporated milk and the chocolate in the top of a double boiler. Place over gently boiling water; the upper pan should not touch the water. Stir occasionally, until the chocolate melts and the mixture is smooth. Remove from heat. Whisk in the peanut butter and honey and set aside. (This becomes more spreadable as it cools. If I'm in a hurry, I place the top of the double boiler in a bowl of ice and stir just until the frosting is spreadable, removing it from the ice bath before it becomes too hard.)

**To make the filling:**

With an electric mixer, beat the butter, peanut butter, sugar and vanilla until creamy and smooth. Scrape onto a sheet of waxed or parchment paper. Using your fingers, pat the filling into a 9-inch circle, about ¾ inch thick. Wrap in plastic wrap and set aside.

**To assemble:**

With a serrated knife, trim the dome from the top of the cake if you want it to be flat, not rounded. Split the cake in half, keeping the knife level and parallel to the bottom of the cake. Trim the sides of the cake if they seem dry. Reserve the cake trimmings to grind and put on the sides of the frosted cake if you are not using Peanut Brittle.

Put the bottom cake layer on a cardboard circle or a flat serving plate. Moisten it with half of the Coffee Simple Syrup. Unwrap the disk of peanut butter filling and invert it on the cake. Use a frosting spatula to smooth out the filling, spreading it to meet the edge of the cake. Place the second cake layer on top, pressing gently to flatten. Brush with the remaining coffee syrup.

Frost the sides and top of the cake with the chocolate frosting. You can be generous; the recipe makes more than enough. Or, reserve ½ to ¾ cup of the frosting for a decorative border, if desired. If you are using Peanut Brittle, crush half of it into small bits in a food processor or between sheets of waxed paper. Press the crushed Peanut Brittle onto the sides of the cake. (Or grind the reserved cake trimmings and press them onto the sides of the frosted cake.)

If desired, spoon the remaining frosting into a pastry bag fitted with a medium star tip and decorate with a shell border. Arrange the remaining Peanut Brittle, if using, on top of the cake as garnish.

*Makes 1 (9 x 2-inch) round cake, serves 10 to 12.*

▲ High altitude: For the cake, reduce the sugar by 2 tablespoons. Reduce the baking soda to ¾ teaspoon.

# ■ Chocolate Truffle Cake

You may be familiar with truffles as a decadent chocolate candy—little cocoa-dusted gems redolent of liqueur. They are made of ganache, an all-purpose frosting and filling made from chocolate and cream. This recipe features ganache in three different ways: beaten with whipping cream to make a luscious filling, as the frosting and glaze, and finally, scooped into little balls for the ornamental truffles. At Deer Valley we serve this cake with Vanilla Bean Crème Anglaise (page 224). It's also delicious with store-bought or homemade raspberry sauce.

Cake:
**10 tablespoons (1¼ sticks) unsalted butter, cut in pieces**
**4 (1-ounce) squares unsweetened chocolate, chopped in ½-inch pieces**
**1½ cups sugar**
**2 cups all-purpose flour**
**2 teaspoons baking powder**
**¾ teaspoon baking soda**
**1 teaspoon salt**
**4 eggs**
**1 teaspoon vanilla extract**
**1 cup cold water**

Truffles, filling and frosting:
**2¾ cups Chocolate Ganache, room temperature (page 211)**
**¼ cup cocoa powder**
**1 cup heavy cream**

Moistening syrup:
**2 tablespoons coffee-flavored liqueur, optional**
**⅓ cup Coffee Simple Syrup (page 209)**

**To make the cake:**
Preheat oven to 350°. Brush 2 (9-inch) round pans with melted butter and dust lightly with flour or spray generously with cooking spray. Line the bottoms with circles of parchment or waxed paper.

Melt the butter and chocolate in the top of a double boiler, over gently boiling water; the upper pan should not touch the water. Stir in the sugar; set aside. Sift the dry ingredients together and set aside.

With an electric mixer or with a wire whisk, beat the eggs and vanilla until smooth. Add the chocolate mixture and beat until homogenous. Add half of the dry ingredients to this batter. Mix well, scraping the bottom and sides of the bowl. Add the remaining dry ingredients; mix well and scrape again. Slowly add the water; mix and scrape.

*Opposite: Chocolate Truffle Cake*

Divide the batter evenly into the prepared pans. Bake 25 to 30 minutes or until the center of the cake springs back when touched with a finger. Cool completely.

**To make the truffles:**
Refrigerate ½ cup of the Chocolate Ganache until it is cold. Put the cocoa powder on a plate. Scoop the cold ganache with a teaspoon and shape into twelve small balls. Drop the truffle balls into the cocoa powder and roll them around until they are lightly coated. Refrigerate.

**To make the filling:**
Put ¾ cup of Chocolate Ganache in a medium bowl and whisk to lighten, about 10 strokes. Add one quarter of the cream, gently whisking until smooth. Add the remaining cream and whisk by hand until the chocolate cream holds a soft shape. Be careful; if the ganache is too warm or if you overwhip the ganache and cream, the chocolate cream will curdle. Refrigerate until you are ready to assemble the cake.

**To assemble:**
If using, add the coffee-flavored liqueur to the Coffee Simple Syrup.  With a serrated knife, trim the dome from both cakes so they are flat, not rounded. Trim the sides of the cake if they seem dry. If you wish, grind the cake trimmings in a food processor and reserve them for the sides of the cake.

Put one of the cake layers on a cardboard circle or a flat serving plate. Moisten it with half of the syrup. Spread on the chocolate cream filling. Gently flatten the second cake layer on top and brush it with the remaining syrup.

Frost the sides and top of the cake with 1 cup of room temperature Chocolate Ganache. Refrigerate the cake for 10 minutes. Meanwhile, place the remaining ½ cup of Chocolate Ganache in the top of a double boiler. Place over gently boiling water; the upper pan should not touch the water. Stir while heating, just until the ganache becomes a runny glaze. Pour it evenly over the top of the cake; use a spatula to smooth out any glaze that runs down the side.

If desired, press some of the reserved cake crumbs onto the sides of the cake. Shake the excess cocoa powder off the truffles. Arrange them around the top edge of the cake, evenly spaced, pressing each gently into the fresh glaze.

*Makes 1 (9 x 3-inch) round cake, serves 12 to 20.*

▲ High altitude: Reduce sugar by 3 tablespoons. Reduce baking powder to 1 teaspoon and baking soda to ½ teaspoon.

*Dessert truffles got their name because they resemble, in size and shape, the European black truffle—the rare and pungent fungus unearthed by trained pigs in Provence and prized by gourmet chefs.*

# ■ Stein's Favorite Marzipan Cake

This is my version of the Scandinavian favorite. The almond-flavored cake is tender and moist and accented with a thin layer of raspberry jam. You can make the cake in advance and keep it well-wrapped at room temperature for a day or in the freezer for up to a month. The marzipan can also be made well ahead—it keeps in the refrigerator several weeks. Frost with fresh whipped cream and press toasted sliced almonds on the side—you will have a gold medal–winning favorite.

Cake:
¼ cup (about 2 ounces) almond paste
¼ cup *plus* ¼ cup sugar
10 tablespoons (1¼ sticks) unsalted butter, softened
5 eggs, separated
⅛ teaspoon cream of tartar
¾ cup cake flour

Marzipan:
¾ cup (about 6 ounces) almond paste
1 cup sifted confectioners' sugar
1 tablespoon corn syrup

Frosting:
1½ cups heavy cream
1 tablespoon sugar
½ teaspoon vanilla extract

Assembly:
½ teaspoon vanilla extract
⅓ cup Simple Syrup (page 209)
⅓ cup raspberry preserves
½ cup sliced almonds, toasted and cooled

**To make the cake:**
Preheat the oven to 350°. Brush a 9-inch round cake pan with melted butter and dust lightly with flour or spray generously with cooking spray. Line the bottom with a circle of parchment or waxed paper.

Put the almond paste and ¼ cup of the sugar into a food processor work bowl; process until the almond paste has broken down and mixed with the sugar. With the motor running, drop in the butter, 2 tablespoons at a time; mix well. If you don't have a food processor, cream the almond paste, sugar and butter in a bowl using an electric mixer, until the mixture is very light and aerated. Add the egg yolks one at a time and process until the batter is very smooth, stopping to scrape the bowl several times. Transfer to a large bowl.

Whip the egg whites and cream of tartar in a clean bowl, using an electric mixer.

When they are frothy, gradually add the remaining ¼ cup of sugar, whipping until soft peaks form. Fold the whites into the yolk mixture.

Sift the flour onto the batter and gently fold it in. Spread evenly into the prepared pan. Bake 25 to 30 minutes, until the cake is light golden brown and the center springs back when touched with a finger. Cool.

### To make the marzipan:

With an electric mixer, or in a food processor, beat the almond paste, sugar and corn syrup until the mixture has a uniform crumbly texture. Transfer onto a work surface dusted with confectioners' sugar and knead until very smooth, using more sugar as needed to keep from sticking. Divide evenly in 2 portions. Form each half into a flattened ball, wrap them in plastic wrap and refrigerate until needed.

### To make the frosting:

Whip the cream with the sugar and the vanilla until the cream comes to soft peaks that hold their shape. As you frost the cake, the cream will continue to stiffen, so be careful not to overwhip—the cream should hold a shape, but barely.

### To assemble:

Add the vanilla to the Simple Syrup. Using a serrated knife, trim the dome from the top of the cake if you want it to be flat, not rounded. Split the cake in half, keeping the knife level and parallel to the bottom of the cake. Place the bottom cake layer, cut side up, on a flat serving plate or a cardboard circle. Moisten the cake with half of the syrup and spread with half of the raspberry preserves.

On a surface dusted with confectioners' sugar, using a rolling pin, roll one of the marzipan portions into an 8-inch circle about ⅛ inch thick, using as much sugar as needed to keep the marzipan from sticking.

Slip a cardboard circle under the marzipan circle and transfer it onto the top of the moistened cake layer. Spread with a ¼-inch layer of the frosting. Gently flatten the second cake layer on top, brush with the remaining syrup and spread with the remaining raspberry preserves.

Roll a second marzipan circle as you did the first and transfer to the second moistened cake layer. Spread frosting about ½ inch thick on the sides and top of the cake. Press the almonds onto the sides. If desired, spoon the remaining frosting into a pastry bag fitted with a medium star tip and decorate with a shell border.

*Makes 1 (9 x 2-inch) round cake, serves 12.*

▲ High altitude: For the cake, use extra care when whipping the egg whites to soft peaks—as at sea level, they should just fold over; do not beat until stiff and dry.

*Stein Eriksen is Deer Valley's stellar ambassador; he has been director of skiing since our premier season. In the 1950s, representing Norway, he won an Olympic gold medal and many other championships in alpine skiing. He is still an inspirational skier. Each December we make Stein's Favorite Marzipan Cake to celebrate his birthday, which falls at the opening of the ski season.*

# ■ Low-Fat Black Forest Mousse Cake

Black Forest cake is traditionally very rich—a combination of cherries, chocolate and whipped cream. This version has a vivid cherry and cocoa mousse, studded with whole cherries, molded around chocolate cake. The mousse is made with egg whites and cocoa powder instead of cream and chocolate, and, in the cake, prune purée replaces the oil. It is a luscious and light makeover.

Cake:
**1½ cups cake flour**
**1 cup sugar**
**¼ cup cocoa powder**
**½ teaspoon salt**
**1 teaspoon baking soda**
**⅓ cup tightly packed pitted prunes**
**3 tablespoons hot water**
**1 tablespoon apple cider vinegar**
**1 teaspoon vanilla extract**
**1 cup cold water**

Mousse:
**1½ tablespoons (about 2 envelopes) unflavored gelatin**
**⅓ cup *plus* 1 cup black cherry juice**❋
**¾ cup *plus* ½ cup sugar**
**½ cup cocoa powder**
**4 egg whites (about ½ cup)**
**4 teaspoons water**
**¼ teaspoon cream of tartar**
**1 cup pitted sweet cherries, fresh or canned, drained**

❋ 100 percent black cherry juice, without added sugar, is available in health food stores or the specialty section in grocery stores. Blackberry-apple juice, with no added sugar or fructose, is a good substitute or variation.

**To make the cake:**
Preheat the oven to 350°. Generously spray a 9-inch round pan with cooking spray. Line the bottom with a circle of parchment or waxed paper.

Sift the flour, sugar, cocoa powder, salt and baking soda into a mixing bowl. Set aside. Soak the prunes in the 3 tablespoons of hot water for 10 minutes. Purée in a food processor until smooth and no large chunks remain. Transfer to a bowl. Whisk in the vinegar, vanilla and 1 cup cold water. Pour over the dry ingredients and mix for 1 minute, using a hand whisk. Pour into the prepared pan. Bake 30 to 35 minutes, or until the center of the cake springs back when touched with a finger. Cool completely.

**To prepare the cake and make the mousse:**
With a serrated knife, trim the dome from the top of the cake so it is flat, not rounded. Split the cake in half, keeping the knife level and parallel to the bottom of the cake. Trim the cake edges so there will be ¼ to ½ inch of space between the cake and an 8¾-inch

entremet ring. Place the bottom cake layer on a 10-inch cardboard circle or flat serving plate, centering it inside the entremet ring. (If you don't have an entremet ring, substitute the sides of a springform pan, page 247.)

Sprinkle the gelatin over ⅓ cup of the black cherry juice and set aside to soften. Whisk ¾ cup of the sugar, the cocoa powder and remaining 1 cup of juice in a saucepan. Over medium heat, whisking constantly, cook until very hot but not boiling. Stir in the softened gelatin; transfer to a large bowl and set aside.

Whisk the egg whites, the remaining ½ cup of sugar, water and cream of tartar in a bowl. Place over a pan of gently boiling water; the bowl should not touch the water. Cook, whisking constantly, for 3 to 5 minutes, until the mixture reaches 160° on an instant-read thermometer. Remove from heat. With an electric mixer, whip until the meringue is cool and forms stiff peaks.

If the cocoa and gelatin mixture is still warm to the touch, place the bowl over an ice bath of ice cubes and a little water, and stir until the mixture gets syrupy—barely begins to jell. Fold in the egg white meringue, until no streaks of white or cocoa remain.

**To assemble:**
Pour about half of the filling over the bottom cake layer inside the entremet ring, letting it spread to the edge of the ring. Sprinkle three-quarters of the cherries on the filling, pressing them gently into the mousse. Add more filling, if needed, to just cover the cherries.

Place the second cake layer on top. Pour the remaining filling around and over the cake. Arrange the remaining cherries decoratively on top. Carefully, so the filling does not leak out of the ring, place the cake in the refrigerator. Chill until set, at least 6 hours or overnight.

To unmold, warm the sides of the ring with a propane torch or with a hot, wrung-out wet towel. Then lift the ring or springform sides off the cake.

*Makes 1 (9 x 3-inch) cake, serves 12.*

▲ High altitude: For the cake, reduce the sugar by 2 tablespoons. Reduce the baking soda to ¾ teaspoon.

*Less than an hour from Deer Valley, in another canyon of our Wasatch Mountains, lies Snowbird Ski Resort; I sneak away to play there. Snowbird has a hidden run called the Black Forest, where, if you want, you can escape from skier traffic—a little getaway. When I bake, I don't usually worry about calories and diet, but when I need a getaway from high fat, cholesterol and dairy, I make Low-Fat Black Forest Mousse Cake.*

# ◆ Tiramisù Yule Log

Traditional during the holidays, a yule log cake represents the real hearth log burned in celebration on Christmas Eve. This one is delicate chocolate sponge cake filled with mascarpone cheese and spiked with rum and espresso. It's my twist on Italian culinary scholar and author Carol Field's tiramisù recipe. Use a fork to texture the bittersweet chocolate glaze so it looks like tree bark. The chocolate leaves and meringue mushrooms are whimsical garnish and the candied cranberries add seasonal color. Or, enjoy this chocolate-glazed roll without the garnishes any month of the year.

Cake:
**¾ cup sifted cake flour**
**3 tablespoons cocoa powder**
**5 eggs, separated**
**⅛ teaspoon cream of tartar**
**¼ cup *plus* ½ cup sugar**
**1½ teaspoons dark rum**

Moistening syrup:
**2 tablespoons dark rum**
**1 teaspoon instant espresso coffee powder dissolved in 1 teaspoon hot water**
**½ cup Coffee Simple Syrup (page 209)**

Filling:
**8 ounces (1 cup) mascarpone cheese**✺
**¾ cup heavy cream**
**½ cup sugar**
**3 tablespoons dark rum**
**¾ teaspoon vanilla extract**

Assembly and glaze:
**1 teaspoon instant espresso coffee powder**
**1½ cups Chocolate Honey Glaze, warm (page 212)**
**Cocoa powder for dusting**
**6 or 8 Chocolate Leaves (page 216)**
**8 or 10 Meringue Mushrooms (page 227)**
**20 or so Candied Cranberries (page 212)**

✺ Mascarpone is a fresh, soft double cream cheese. It is available in cheese shops and gourmet stores that carry Italian specialty foods.

*Make the yule log decorations such as Chocolate Leaves, Meringue Mushrooms and Candied Cranberries ahead of time to eliminate last-minute pressure.*

**To make the cake:**
Brush the sides of a 12 x 16-inch baking sheet with melted butter and dust lightly with flour or spray with cooking spray. Line the bottom with a rectangle of parchment or waxed paper. Brush with butter or lightly spray the lining paper also. Preheat the oven to 400°.

Sift the flour and cocoa powder together onto a piece of parchment or waxed paper, then sift back into a bowl; set aside. Whip the egg whites and the cream of tartar in a clean bowl using an electric mixer. When the whites are frothy, gradually add ¼ cup of the sugar and whip just until soft peaks form. Gently transfer the whites into another bowl; set aside while you whip the yolks.

Using the same bowl you used for the whites, whip the egg yolks, the remaining ½ cup of sugar, and the rum until very thick and pale yellow, about 5 minutes.

Fold only half of the whipped whites into the yolks. Sift only half of the flour and cocoa mixture over the egg yolk mixture. Add half of the remaining half of the whites and fold to mix. Sift the remaining half of the flour and cocoa mixture over the egg yolk mixture. Add the last of the whites; fold again.

Spread the batter evenly into the prepared pan and bake 10 to 12 minutes, until the center of the cake springs back when touched with a finger. Cool for about 15 minutes, then wrap tightly with plastic wrap. The cake can be frozen at this point for up to a month. Keep wrapped and thaw at room temperature before filling.

**To make the syrup:**
Stir the rum and dissolved espresso powder into the Coffee Simple Syrup.

**To make the filling:**
Put the mascarpone, cream, sugar, rum and vanilla into a bowl and whip by hand or with an electric mixer, until the mixture is smooth and holds a soft shape. Be careful not to overwhip or the filling will curdle.

**To assemble:**
Unwrap the cake. "Rough up" the darker top skin with your fingers and scrape it off, otherwise the filling adheres to the skin and separates from the cake after it is rolled. Place a piece of parchment (or waxed) paper on top of the cake. Put a second baking sheet on the paper. Invert so the cake is upside down, on top of the parchment and the second baking sheet. Carefully peel off the original baked parchment paper.

Place a new piece of parchment on top of the cake bottom. Put the original baking sheet, bottom down, on the new parchment; invert again. The cake will be right side up on a clean piece of parchment paper, on the back side of a baking sheet.

Use a pastry brush to moisten the cake with the "spiked" Coffee Simple Syrup. Spread the mascarpone filling over the cake, leaving a ½-inch border of cake on all sides. Sprinkle evenly with the espresso powder.

Starting with the long side of the rectangle, roll up the cake, using the parchment to lift and roll, ending with the seam side down. The cake, filled, rolled and wrapped, can be refrigerated for up to 2 days.

Carefully transfer the cake roll to a flat serving plate or a cardboard rectangle wrapped in foil. Using an icing spatula, apply a thin coat, about ⅓ cup, of warm Chocolate Honey Glaze. Cut the ends of the roll on an angle. Place these cut ends on top, a couple of inches from each end, to imitate cut branches on a tree. By applying another ⅓ cup of glaze with an icing spatula, seal all the cut edges, including the "branches." Refrigerate about 10 minutes to let the first coat harden.

Frost the roll with the remaining glaze. With the tines of a fork, draw wavy lines down the length of the cake to resemble bark, and in circles on the cut ends, to resemble the rings on a cut tree. Sift cocoa powder lightly over the entire log. Garnish with Chocolate Leaves, Meringue Mushrooms, and Candied Cranberries.

*Makes 1 (15-inch) cake, serves 10 to 12.*

▲ High altitude: For the cake, reduce the sugar for the egg whites by 1 tablespoon. Also, use extra care when whipping the egg whites to soft peaks—as at sea level, they should just fold over; do not beat until stiff and dry.

*Tiramisù seems a ubiquitous dessert—you'll find it on the menu in all kinds of American restaurants, especially those of Italian ilk. The word tiramisù translates as "pick-me-up." Tiramisù's countless variations may contain ladyfingers or sponge cake, mascarpone cheese or custard, rum or marsala, and chocolate or not, but espresso coffee is constant. Sometimes tiramisù is spooned out of a bowl or pan; at other times it is layered and served as a cake.*

# ◆ Lemon and Strawberry Dacquoise

Dacquoise (da-KWAHZ) is a traditional gâteau of southwestern France. The flavors vary and fruit is optional, but dacquoise always has crunchy nut meringue layers sandwiched together with some sort of flavored cream. This cake is molded in a straight-sided ring, which you remove to reveal a border of strawberries nesting in pale lemon cream. Make the meringue, the curd and the candied lemon ahead of time, but put this dessert together the day you serve it; it takes an hour or less to assemble and you want the meringue to be crisp and the strawberries to be fresh and bright.

Meringue:
**1 cup (about 5 ounces) toasted hazelnuts, skins removed, cooled (page 256)**
**⅓ cup *plus* ¼ cup sugar**
**1 tablespoon cornstarch**
**3 egg whites (a little more than ⅓ cup)**
**⅛ teaspoon cream of tartar**

Assembly and lemon cream:
**1 pound fresh strawberries, stems removed**
**1½ cups Lemon Curd, room temperature (page 220)**
**3 tablespoons orange-flavored liqueur**
**2½ teaspoons (about 1 envelope) powdered gelatin**
**1 cup heavy cream**

**Candied Lemon Peel, optional (page 213)**
**12 toasted hazelnuts, skins removed, optional**
**1 cup Strawberry Sauce, optional (page 210)**

**To make the meringue:**
With a pencil, trace 2 (8-inch) circles onto pieces of parchment paper cut to fit 2 baking sheets. Turn over the parchment so the pencil marks won't transfer to the meringue but you can see the tracing. Preheat the oven to 200°.

Grind the cooled nuts in a food processor with ⅓ cup of the sugar and the cornstarch.

Whisk the egg whites, cream of tartar and remaining ¼ cup of sugar in a heat-proof bowl. Place over a pan of gently boiling water; the bowl should not touch the water. Whisk until the egg whites are warm to the touch, about 30 seconds. Remove from heat. With an electric mixer at medium-high speed, whip until stiff peaks form. Whip only to glossy, smooth peaks that are just stiff enough to pipe and hold a shape, or the meringue will be dry and fragile.

Gently fold the nut mixture into the egg whites. Scrape the meringue into a pastry bag fitted with a ½-inch plain tip and pipe in spirals, filling inside the marked circles on the parchment paper. Or spread the meringue into the circles using the back of a spoon. Bake for 1½ to 2 hours. Perfectly baked meringues are soft when warm in the oven and turn crisp as they cool. To decide if they are done, remove from the oven and let cool

*Several times a year, Deer Valley's food and beverage team designs a multi-course banquet for local food and wine enthusiasts. I take the time to perfect new menu ideas for these parties; they are a wellspring of my best and favorite desserts. I made individual Caramel and Blood Orange Dacquoise for one of these parties—with caramel buttercream and blood orange curd encased in hazelnut meringues.*

*Opposite: Lemon and Strawberry Dacquoise, topped with Candied Lemon Peel*

5 minutes. If the meringues feel crisp and dry, they are done; if they are still a bit soft, continue baking another 10 to 15 minutes at 200°. Cool.

**To assemble the cake and make the lemon cream:**
Place an 8¾-inch entremet ring on a 10-inch cardboard circle. (If you don't have an entremet ring, substitute a springform ring, page 247.) If necessary, with a serrated knife, carefully trim one meringue round so there will be ½ to ¾ inch of space between the meringue and the ring. Place the meringue on the cardboard inside the ring. Sort through the strawberries and pick out 10 or so that are fairly close in size. Cut them in equal halves vertically. Stand a border of strawberry halves, the wide end down, the cut side out and touching the inside of the ring. Cut the remaining strawberries in half and set aside.

With a serrated knife, carefully trim the second meringue disk to about 7 inches, so it will fit inside the border of strawberries and actually hold the strawberries up. Set aside.

Put the Lemon Curd in a large bowl and whisk until smooth.❋ If the Lemon Curd is very cold, let it sit at room temperature for about 30 minutes, so the warmed gelatin will incorporate easily into the curd, without seizing.

Pour the liqueur into a small bowl, sprinkle the gelatin over it and allow to soften, about 5 minutes. Meanwhile, whip the cream until it comes to soft peaks that hold their shape. Set aside.

Place the bowl of softened gelatin over barely simmering water and stir until the gelatin melts, about a minute.

Whisk the liquid gelatin into the Lemon Curd. Immediately whisk in a third of the whipped cream, then fold in the rest.

Spread half of the lemon cream about ½ inch thick over the meringue and up against the standing strawberries. Scatter the reserved strawberry halves over the lemon cream, keeping them away from the edges. Spread a thin layer of lemon cream on top of the berries, to adhere the next meringue.

Press the second meringue into the lemon cream, gently pushing a little cream up around the berries. Spread the remaining cream on top of the meringue using an icing spatula. Arrange any leftover strawberry halves on top. Decorate with toasted hazelnuts and strips of Candied Lemon Peel, if you wish. Refrigerate until set, about 2 hours.
To unmold, warm the sides of the ring with a propane torch or with a hot, wrung-out wet towel, then lift the ring or springform sides off the cake. Serve with Strawberry Sauce, if desired.

*Makes 1 (9-inch) cake, serves 12.*

▲ High altitude: Reduce the ⅓ cup sugar in the meringue by 1½ tablespoons.

**Variation:** For a simpler version of this cake, don't bother to line the ring mold with strawberries or scatter them between the layers; assemble the cake with just hazelnut meringue and lemon cream, and accompany the cake with sliced strawberries. Or, replace the meringues with yellow cake layers, moistening the layers with plain Simple Syrup (page 209) flavored to taste with fresh-squeezed lemon juice.

❋ The lemon cream sets quickly, so have all of the ingredients ready and at hand before adding the gelatin.

*Hazelnuts are also known as filberts—they are one and the same nut. They have a mild, sweet flavor that makes them ideal for delicate cakes and desserts. Most hazelnuts are imported from Turkey, Italy and Spain. Oregon is the chief producer in the United States, although the state's commercial crop is less than 3 percent of the world's.*

# ◆ Gâteau Opéra

Namesake of the Paris Opéra, this mocha cake is found in pâtisseries and restaurants all over Paris. It consists of almond sponge cake soaked in strong sweet coffee, with thin layers of coffee buttercream and chocolate mousse, and a bittersweet chocolate glaze. I believe the original version was created by Gaston Lenôtre, of the eponymous pastry school, Ecole-Lenôtre. Former Deer Valley chef Franklin Biggs, who, before opening Deer Valley's kitchens, attended L'Ecole de Cuisine La Varenne, another renowned French cooking school, gave me this recipe.

Cake:
**¼ cup (about 2 ounces) almond paste**
**¼ cup *plus* ¼ cup sugar**
**10 tablespoons (1¼ sticks) unsalted butter, softened**
**5 eggs, separated**
**⅛ teaspoon cream of tartar**
**¾ cup cake flour**

Chocolate mousse:
**5 ounces semisweet chocolate, chopped in ½-inch pieces**
**5 tablespoons whole milk**
**⅔ cup heavy cream**

Moistening syrup:
**¾ cup Coffee Simple Syrup (page 209)**
**2 teaspoons instant espresso coffee powder dissolved in 2 teaspoons hot water**

Coffee buttercream:
**2 tablespoons instant espresso coffee powder dissolved in 2 tablespoons hot water**
**1 tablespoon coffee-flavored liqueur**
**2 cups Meringue Buttercream (page 228)**

**⅓ cup Chocolate Honey Glaze, warm (page 212)**
**White chocolate, melted, for optional inscription garnish**

**To make the cake:**
Brush the sides of a 12 x 16-inch sheet pan with melted butter and dust lightly with flour or spray with cooking spray. Line the bottom with a rectangle of parchment or waxed paper. Preheat the oven to 375°.

Put the almond paste and ¼ cup of the sugar into a food processor work bowl; process until the almond paste has broken down and mixed with the sugar. With the processor running, drop in the butter, 2 tablespoons at a time; mix well. If you don't have a food processor, cream the almond paste, sugar and butter in a bowl using an electric mixer, until the mixture is very light and aerated. Add the egg yolks one at a time and process until the batter is very smooth, stopping to scrape the bowl. Transfer to a large bowl.

*One time Chef Biggs dipped a slice of my Gâteau Opéra into his coffee and held it up, showing how saturated it should be. He admonished me—I hadn't put enough coffee syrup on the cake. Remember, the coffee flavor is essential; be generous when you moisten.*

Whip the egg whites and cream of tartar in a clean bowl, using an electric mixer. When they are frothy, gradually add the remaining ¼ cup of the sugar, whipping until soft peaks form. Fold the whites into the yolk mixture.

Sift the flour onto the batter and gently fold it in. Spread evenly into the prepared pan; it will be a thin layer, about ¼ inch thick. Bake 10 to 15 minutes, until the center of the cake springs back when touched with a finger. Cool. Keep the sponge cake in the pan until you are ready to assemble the cake. The sponge sheet cake, well wrapped, can be kept at room temperature for a day, or frozen up to a month.

**To make the mousse:**

Put the chocolate and milk in the top of a double boiler. Place over gently boiling water; the upper pan should not touch the water. Stir occasionally, until the chocolate melts and the mixture is smooth. Allow to cool at room temperature. Whip the cream until it comes to soft peaks that hold their shape. When the chocolate is cool to touch but still soft, fold in the whipped cream.❄ Refrigerate.

**To assemble:**

Stir together the Coffee Simple Syrup and the dissolved espresso powder. Invert the sponge sheet cake onto a clean cutting board at least the size of the sheet pan. Carefully peel the parchment paper off the cake. Cut the cake lengthwise into three equal lengths, approximately 3x16 inches each. Place one of the sponge cake lengths, with the original bottom of the cake down, on a flat serving plate or a cardboard rectangle covered with foil. Use a pastry brush to moisten it generously with a third of the syrup.

Stir the 2 tablespoons dissolved espresso powder mixture and the liqueur into the Meringue Buttercream, mixing until smooth. Using an icing spatula, spread half of the buttercream on the cake, working to keep the buttercream even and flat and the edge square. Place the second cake length on top and brush it with another third of the syrup. The cake layers should be well soaked, so the cake almost seems brown in color.

Spread the chocolate mousse evenly onto the second moistened cake layer. Place the last cake layer on top and brush with the remaining syrup. Spread with the remaining half of the buttercream, striving again for a level top. Refrigerate until the buttercream hardens, at least 1 hour. The assembled cake can be kept, well wrapped, in the refrigerator for several days, or frozen up to a month. Thaw in the refrigerator before finishing the cake.

**To finish the cake:**

Working quickly, pour the Chocolate Honey Glaze on top of the buttercream layer. Using an icing spatula, spread the glaze evenly; it should be about ⅛ inch thick. Don't worry if the glaze drips over the sides; they will be trimmed. Refrigerate 5 minutes to set the glaze.

With a hot, dry knife, trim all 4 sides of the cake to square up the edges, trimming off the overdripped glaze. If you wish, write "Opéra" fancifully across the top of the cake with melted white chocolate.

*Makes 1 cake, serves 16 to 20.*

▲ High altitude: For the cake, use extra care when whipping the egg whites to soft peaks—as at sea level, they should just fold over; do not beat until stiff and dry.

❄ Whipped cream mixed into warm chocolate can curdle—when you make the chocolate mousse, be sure the melted chocolate and milk are cool before folding in the cream.

# ◆◆ Orange Almond Wedding Cake

Almost every time I make a wedding cake I get a little nervous, because I want the cake to be perfect. I take a few deep breaths and transform the butterflies in my stomach into loving wishes for the bride and groom—my positive thoughts give extra nourishment to the cake. This orange-scented almond cake with orange cream filling and Grand Marnier buttercream is three tiers of celebratory lusciousness. Infuse your love in every step; you'll turn what could be an intimidating endeavor into a beautiful and delicious masterpiece.

Divide the work into stages, over a minimum of 3 days, allowing plenty of time. The First Day must be at least 3 days before the wedding day. You can bake the cakes even earlier and freeze them for up to a month. Make the Orange Curd and Meringue Buttercream ahead too; they can be frozen as well. The Second Day, 2 days before the wedding, will be your busiest day; you'll make the orange flavoring syrup and the cream filling, and assemble and crumb coat the cakes. The Third Day, or the day before the wedding, finish frosting and assembling the tiers. You can enjoy yourself on the wedding day; all you have to do is transport the cake to its display table and decorate it with flowers.

You will need some special equipment. Beg, borrow or buy a 15-inch stainless steel bowl so you can make the cake in one batch. The batter, once all the egg whites are whipped, will overflow a smaller bowl. Have ready 3 wedding cake pans, at least 2 inches deep: a 12-inch, a 9-inch and a 6-inch round. Make sure your oven will fit all 3 cake pans at the same time—otherwise you will need to divide the recipe and make the batter in 2 separate batches.

I strongly recommend using a 4½- or 5-quart free-standing mixer and a large-capacity food processor. To cut the cake layers evenly, you need a long-bladed serrated knife. A cake turntable is essential for efficient cake frosting. To decorate the sides of the cake and pipe the borders, you will need a pastry bag (about 12 inches), a plastic 2-piece coupler, a #3 plain tip, a #67 leaf tip and a #16 or #18 star tip for the borders. Make room in your refrigerator. The space needs to be wide enough to hold the platter on which the finished cake is placed, and tall enough to accommodate a cake at least 9 inches high.

Cakes:
**1 cup (about 9 ounces) almond paste**
**1½ cups *plus* 1½ cups sugar**
**5 teaspoons grated orange zest**
**1⅞ pounds (7½ sticks) unsalted butter, softened**
**28 eggs, separated**
**1 teaspoon orange extract**
**¾ teaspoon cream of tartar**
**2⅔ cups cake flour**
**1¾ cups ground toasted almonds**

Orange cream filling:
⅓ cup orange-flavored liqueur
3¾ teaspoons (about 2 envelopes) powdered gelatin
2½ cups heavy cream
2¼ cups Orange Curd (page 221)

Assembly:
2¼ cups Orange Simple Syrup (page 209)
8 cups Meringue Buttercream, room temperature (page 228)
½ cup orange-flavored liqueur
½ teaspoon orange extract

8 straight plastic straws
3 (12-inch) cardboard circles
3 (9-inch) cardboard circles
3 (6-inch) cardboard circles
14-inch (or wider) serving platter ❊

**First day**
**To make the cakes:**
Brush the sides of a 12-inch round pan, a 9-inch round pan and a 6-inch round pan with melted butter and dust with flour or spray with cooking spray. Line the bottoms with circles of parchment or waxed paper. Preheat the oven to 350°.

Put the almond paste and 1½ cups of the sugar into a food processor work bowl; process until the almond paste has broken down and mixed with the sugar. Add the orange zest. With the processor running, add the butter, 2 tablespoons at a time; mix well. If you don't have a food processor, cream the almond paste, sugar and butter in a bowl using an electric mixer until the mixture is very light and aerated. If your food processor is small, transfer the almond paste and sugar mixture to a bowl and, using an electric mixer, cream with the butter about 10 minutes, until the mixture is very light and aerated.

Slowly add the egg yolks to the almond paste mixture and process or beat well with an electric mixer, until the batter is very smooth. Mix in the orange extract. Transfer to a very large (15 inch) bowl.

Whip the egg whites in 3 batches, so they don't overflow the mixing bowl. Use a clean bowl and whisk for the first batch, but don't clean the bowl or whisk in between each batch. Begin whipping a third of the egg whites (about 1¼ cups) and ¼ teaspoon of the cream of tartar. When they are frothy, gradually add ½ cup of the remaining sugar and whip until soft peaks form. Gently scrape into the large bowl of yolk batter, depositing the whites on top. Repeat the procedure of whipping a third of the egg whites, ¼ teaspoon of cream of tartar and ½ cup of the sugar twice more. When all the whites are whipped, fold them into the yolk mixture.

Stir the flour and the ground nuts together. Sprinkle onto the batter in 3 parts, folding in each time.

❊ If you don't have a large enough serving platter, make one out of cardboard circles. Tape 2 (16-inch) cardboard circles on top of each other, then arrange paper doilies, attached with tape, on the top cardboard.

Pour the batter to equal depths into the prepared pans. Bake 45 to 70 minutes, depending on the cake pan size, or until the cakes are light golden brown and the centers spring back when touched with a finger. Cool completely. Invert onto cardboard circles, remove the paper and re-invert onto other circles the size of each cake. Wrap tightly with plastic wrap.

The cakes can be made ahead, cooled, wrapped in plastic wrap and frozen; they take about 4 hours to thaw at room temperature. The Orange Curd and Meringue Buttercream also need to be made on or earlier than the First Day. If you have made it ahead, thaw the Orange Curd in the refrigerator.

### Second day
### To make the filling:
Pour the liqueur into a small bowl, sprinkle the gelatin over it and set aside to soften, about 5 minutes. Meanwhile, whip the cream until it comes to soft peaks that hold their shape.

Place the bowl of softened gelatin over barely simmering water and stir until the gelatin melts.

Whisk the Orange Curd until smooth. Whisk in the liquid gelatin. Immediately whisk in a third of the whipped cream, then fold in the rest. Set aside.

### To assemble the cakes:
If you made the Meringue Buttercream ahead, bring it to room temperature.

With a serrated knife, trim the "skin" and make level the top of each of the 3 cakes. Also, carefully trim the sides to remove the dry, darker edges. Keeping the knife level and parallel to the bottom of the cake, split each cake in 3 equal and even layers, about ½ inch thick. Set aside about 1 tablespoon of cake crumbs to use when stacking the tiers on the Third Day. Slide cardboard circles the size of the cake under the top layer of each cake. Cover with plastic wrap and set aside. Slide another set of cardboard circles under the middle layer of each cake. Cover with plastic wrap and set aside.

Put the bottom layer of each cake size, 12-inch, 9-inch and 6-inch, sitting on cardboard, on a work surface, forming an assembly line. Use a pastry brush to moisten each bottom layer with Orange Simple Syrup, using ¾ cup total for the 3 bottoms.

Divide the filling in two. Distribute half of the filling among the 3 moistened bottom cake layers, reserving the remaining half for another layer. Spread the filling evenly, ⅜ to ½ inch thick on each bottom layer.

Slide the second cake layers off the cardboard circles onto the filling. Press gently to flatten the cakes. Brush these middle cake layers using ¾ cup total of the Orange Simple Syrup. Distribute the remaining filling, and spread it on the cakes, ⅜ to ½ inch thick.

Slide the last cake layers off the cardboard circles onto the filling; press to flatten. Brush with the remaining Orange Simple Syrup. You should have 3 assemblies of cake and filling, a 12-inch, a 9-inch and a 6-inch, each about 2½ inches high.

For support, slip a second cardboard circle under the bottom cardboards. Wrap each assembled cake and refrigerate for about 1 hour, to let the gelatin filling set.

**To crumb coat the cakes:**

Using an electric mixer, beat the Meringue Buttercream with the liqueur and orange extract until smooth. Divide in two; cover and refrigerate half for the Third Day finish coat.

Remove the 12-inch cake from the refrigerator. Place it on a cake turntable. With a sharp serrated knife, trim the sides of the cake just enough to even any sharp angles, brushing off any loose crumbs.

With an icing spatula, thinly frost the sides and the top of the cake with buttercream (⅛ inch thick) to seal in the crumbs and orange filling. (Review the technique for frosting cakes at the beginning of this chapter.) Use gentle pressure to spread the buttercream and to take away the excess. If you pick up crumbs with the buttercream, keep the "crumby" buttercream separate for crumb coating only—no crumbs allowed in the finish coat. For square edges, always keep the icing spatula in a horizontal plane, parallel to the turntable for the top of the cake and at a right angle for the sides of the cake. Return the crumb-coated 12-inch cake to the refrigerator.

Trim and crumb coat the 9-inch and 6-inch cakes in the same manner. Refrigerate overnight. If you wish, wrap the cakes in plastic wrap after 20 minutes, when the buttercream hardens. This is not necessary unless your refrigerator contains strong-smelling, unwrapped foods.

**Third day**

**To finish coat and stack the tiers:**

Bring the remaining flavored buttercream to room temperature. Remove the 12-inch cake from the refrigerator. Place the cake on the turntable and carefully trim the cardboard so it is the same diameter as the cake. You'll want to keep the support of 2 cardboard circles, but it is hard to trim both at the same time. So, one cardboard at a time, using scissors, trim both cardboards even with the sides of the cake. Tape the cardboards together with a couple of pieces of double-sided tape. Center the cake on the turntable.

Beat the remaining flavored room temperature buttercream until smooth. Apply a finish coat of buttercream, frosting the trimmed cardboard supports, pretending they are part of the cake. Remember to use gentle pressure to spread buttercream, rotating the turntable with your other hand, coaxing the sides and then the top into a smooth finish. Carefully transfer the 12-inch cake to the serving platter.

Cut and position the plastic straw supports. First, lightly trace an 8-inch circle in the middle of the 12-inch cake. Then, poke a straw in the center of the cake, mark the straw exactly the height of the cake and remove it. Cut the straw at the mark. Cut 8 more lengths of straw to match the first one. At even intervals, just inside the traced circle, push the straws completely into the cake. Sprinkle about 2 teaspoons of the reserved cake crumbs inside the traced circle, so the cardboard bottom of the next tier won't stick when you separate them for serving. Refrigerate.

Remove the 9-inch cake from the refrigerator. Place the cake on the turntable and carefully trim the cardboard supports, one at a time, so they are the same diameter as the cake. Tape together the cardboards. Apply a finish coat of buttercream to the cake and its cardboard supports. Remove the 12-inch cake from the refrigerator. Carefully place the

9-inch cake on top of the straws, centered over the 12-inch cake.

Trace a 5-inch circle in the middle of the 9-inch cake. Measure, cut and position 6 plastic straw supports. Sprinkle cake crumbs inside the traced circle. Refrigerate the stacked 12-inch and 9-inch cakes.

Remove the 6-inch cake from the refrigerator. Place the cake on the turntable and carefully trim the cardboard supports one at a time, so they are the same diameter as the cake. Tape together the cardboards. Apply a finish coat of buttercream to the cake and its cardboard supports. Remove the stacked tiers from the refrigerator. Center the 6-inch cake on top of the 9-inch tier.

### To decorate the sides and border:

Spoon about ½ cup of the remaining buttercream into a pastry bag fitted with a small (⅟₁₆ inch) plain tip. On the side of the bottom tier, with a plain tip, pipe a wavy line all around. Pipe branches off the center of each wave undulation. With a small leaf tip, pipe leaves at the end of each branch and occasionally on the wavy line. Moving up the tiers, pipe wavy lines, branches and leaves on the 9-inch and 6-inch cakes.

Spoon more buttercream into the pastry bag, as needed. With a small star tip, pipe a border around the bottom edge of all three cakes, starting with the 12-inch. Finally, pipe a border around the top edge of each cake, working up the tiers from the bottom. Refrigerate the finished cake.

### Fourth day, the wedding day

Decoratively arrange the bride's choice of flowers on top and around the tiers. Display the cake 2 hours at room temperature (not in direct sunlight) before serving. Separate the tiers before cutting each layer.

*Serves 75 to 80. The 12-inch cake serves about 50, the 9-inch cake serves 25 to 30; the 6-inch cake is not counted—freeze and save it for the first anniversary celebration.*

▲ High altitude: Reduce the sugar in the cake to 1¼ cups *plus* 1¼ cups. Use extra care when whipping the egg whites to soft peaks—as at sea level, they should just fold over; do not beat until stiff and dry. As you assemble the cakes, keep the layers covered to keep from drying out.

# Pies and Tarts

●

Phyllo Fresh Fruit Tart

■

McHenry's Frozen Lemon Meringue Pie

■

Pear Cranberry Pie with Brown Sugar Cornmeal Streusel

■

Ski Queen Apple Pie with Gjetost Cheese

■

Spicy Pumpkin Pie in a Gingersnap Cookie Crust

■

Raspberry Linzertorte

■

Caramel Cashew Tart

■

Snuggery Chocolate Silk Pie

■

Tarte Tatin Mariposa

■

Margarita Tart with Fresh Blueberries

■

Zinfandel Pear Tart with Maytag Blue Cheese Crust

■

Fresh Blackberry Pie

◆

White Chocolate Banana Cream Pie

◆

Gingered Peach Pie with a Pecan Nut Crust

◆

Honey Walnut Tart with Chocolate Glaze

# Pies and Tarts

Utah is famous for light powder snow. Frequent winter storms bless the Wasatch Mountains with abundant snow that, once the "freshies" are skied out, compacts into first-rate carving surfaces. I love the snowy months, but I live here year-round and I am grateful for the other seasons. Autumn especially holds a place in my heart. I make a point to get outside on the trails and enjoy the crisp fall days. The hiking and biking are superb; it's not too hot, and the foliage has its fall palette. My favorite days come with a vivid blue sky, and fluffy clouds moving around, constantly changing the sun's lighting. Patches of brilliant orange-red oak dot the canopy of aspen trees, ranging from soft green to bright yellow. A slight breeze from the north brings the promise of winter and blows the leaves to the forest floor. The fallen leaves remind me of golden pennies, glittering under my feet as I climb. My heart pumps, my lungs fill with air and I rejoice in the beauty of the season.

What's that rustle? It's a cow moose, only 30 feet away, also savoring the Indian summer. We both stop, but after a moment continue on our separate paths.

I treasure the peace. I listen to my breath. I let my mind wander from thought to thought. Inevitably, I think about my work. Should we serve Pear Cranberry Pie with a dollop of whipped cream for Jan's Winter Welcome, the fundraising gala benefiting the Park City Ski Team? Star-shaped cinnamon shortbread cookies would add eye-catching height and shape to the warm dessert.

The Nouveau Beaujolais festival desserts must reflect both the harvest season and the wine-producing areas. The Honey Walnut Tart with Chocolate Glaze would be perfect. I should make something with currants, or what about a country apple Tarte Tatin?

When I devise dessert menus, I try to make them match the season. Pies or tarts often come to mind because they are so variable, and they can be elegant and homey at the same time. It doesn't seem to matter whether the filling is creamy custard or luscious fruit or chewy nuts; I know that a good pie or tart can lure the most resistant soul. In this chapter I offer a mountain range of flavors and textures enclosed in pastry.

Pie and tart making skills come with practice and experience. As a rule, pies and tarts should be prepared and assembled in steps. The project will be less ominous and go more smoothly if you separate the work.

Be sure to let the dough rest before rolling. It also needs to rest in the pan before baking. The dough can be wrapped well and frozen up to a month after either of these steps. Most of these recipes instruct you to "blind bake" the shell before filling; read about blind baking on page 243. I even prebake the bottom crust of a 2-crust pie and mold the top crust to the baked edge with my fingers—the result is more crisp than if the filling and the bottom crust bake at the same time. Pre-baked pie and tart shells can be wrapped and held at room temperature for a day, or frozen up to a week.

Cold, cold, cold. These are the key words when working with pie and tart pastry. Start with cold butter, use cold liquids, and as you work with the dough, keep it cold. If your hands are warm or if you work slowly, use a pastry blender to cut in the butter.

"Thin is in," at least when it comes to pie crust rolling. Roll the dough thinly, less than ⅛ inch. Don't feel that you must use all the dough recipe; it is better to use less, roll it thin and discard the scraps. Or, roll and cut extra dough into shapes, sprinkle with cinnamon sugar and bake until light golden brown for little snacks. For tarts, roll the dough a little thicker, but never more than ¼ inch.

Use enough flour, but as little as possible, to keep the dough from sticking. Train yourself to dust the work surface often, but sparingly, unless a recipe indicates otherwise. If you see pieces or streaks of butter when you roll, that's good. The butter melts in the oven and creates air layers in the pastry—making a flaky crust.

Sweet tart dough can be handled more than pie dough, and it must be worked by hand before rolling. Tarts are made in straight-sided pans with removable bottoms. They are usually removed from the pan before serving. Pies are made in deeper pans with sloping sides and are usually served right from the pan.

With the rolling pin, gently coax both pie and tart dough into a circle, as opposed to pushing it. Roll to the edge but not over, so the edge stays the same thickness as the middle. If the dough becomes unruly or doesn't roll smoothly, you will get a more tender crust if you patch it into the pan as is instead of rerolling— the less handling the better.

I use scissors to trim the crust for pies, leaving just enough to build a fluted edge. A decorative fluted pie edge is easy to form and it will hold the filling inside its standing rim. Make a double edge by tucking the overhanging dough under and pinching it together. Place your left index finger on the dough rim inside the pan. With your right thumb and index finger on the outside, push a "V" shape between the two hands, making flutes about every ½ inch. Go around a second time to make the edge neat.

Follow the seasons by baking pies and tarts. Make White Chocolate Banana Cream Pie to serve after a big snowstorm. Welcome spring with Phyllo Fresh Fruit Tart. Save Fresh Blackberry Pie and the Margarita Tart with Fresh Blueberries for the summer months. Celebrate autumn and the approach of ski season with Spicy Pumpkin Pie in a Gingersnap Cookie Crust.

# ● Phyllo Fresh Fruit Tart

Classically, fruit tarts are made with sweet tart dough, but I like the phyllo crust. It is lighter and more flaky, though not as sturdy. Feel free to use different fruit or one single fruit—just be lavish and generous. Thaw the unopened phyllo package in the refrigerator beforehand so it is easier to work with; when defrosted at room temperature, the sheets absorb unwelcome moisture.

> 4 sheets of phyllo (page 253)
> 2 tablespoons (¼ stick) unsalted butter, melted
> 2 tablespoons confectioners' sugar, or as needed
> 1¼ cups (1 recipe) Vanilla Bean Pastry Cream (page 218)
> 12 fresh strawberries, or as needed
> 2 kiwi fruits
> 1 plum or nectarine
> ¼ to ½ cup blueberries, raspberries or blackberries (or a mixture of all)
> ¼ cup Apricot Glaze (page 208)

Preheat the oven to 350°. Unroll the package of phyllo sheets on a work surface. Cover the sheets with a clean, slightly dampened kitchen towel. Keep them covered while you work so they don't dry out. Pick up 1 sheet of phyllo, place it on a large cutting board and brush it lightly with melted butter. Repeat, stacking and buttering 4 layers.

Using a sharp knife, cut the buttered stack of phyllo into an 11-inch square. Fit into a 9-inch fluted tart pan with a removable bottom. Trim the overhanging phyllo with scissors, keeping about ½ inch standing above the tin. Put an empty 9-inch pie pan on top of the phyllo to keep it from puffing up like a pillow. Or, use parchment paper and pie weights (page 253) and "blind bake" (page 243). Bake until the phyllo is golden brown, 15 to 20 minutes.

Slip the baked shell out of the tin and transfer to a serving plate. If the phyllo has puffed up despite the pie pan weight, gently press to flatten. Don't worry if it breaks since it will be covered with pastry cream and fruit. Sprinkle the edge with confectioners' sugar. Whisk the Vanilla Bean Pastry Cream briefly and spread into the shell.

Hull the strawberries and cut them into 6 slices each. Peel the kiwi fruit, cut in half lengthwise, and with the flat edge down, slice ⅛ inch thick. Remove the stone from the plum or nectarine and cut into thin wedges. Arrange the fruit starting at the outside edge, working toward the center, overlapping the fruit slices to cover all the pastry cream; be generous. Start with the strawberries leaning against the phyllo, then overlap the kiwi fruit and plum slices. Fill the center with the small berries.

Heat the Apricot Glaze in a saucepan until it is liquid. With a pastry brush, apply a thin coat to the fruit just so it glistens like a jewel. There should be glaze left over; save it for another recipe. Serve immediately, or refrigerate and serve within 2 hours.

*Makes 1 (9-inch) tart, serves 8.*

▲ High altitude: This recipe needs no adjustment.

**Variation:**

*Individual Fresh Fruit Tarts:* Cut the buttered stack of full sheets of phyllo in half lengthwise and into thirds widthwise, making 6 rough squares. Center each in a 4-inch tart pan, fitting the phyllo into the corners, and trim as with the 9-inch tart shell. After baking, place each shell on a plate and spread about 3 tablespoons of pastry cream into each. Arrange the fruit generously, in any design you choose, filling in the empty spaces so there is no pastry cream showing. Brush with melted Apricot Glaze.

# ■ McHenry's Frozen
# Lemon Meringue Pie

McHenry's restaurant is one of Park City's busiest summer lunch spots, where mountain bikers and hikers meet family and friends for an alfresco meal on the deck. This gratifying lemon dessert, covered with billowy meringue, has refreshed many a diner. Give the finished pie extra room in your freezer, because anything that touches the topping—frozen peas or your finger—mars it. For contrasting color and flavor, serve with raspberry sauce and fresh raspberries. If you are looking for a dessert with less fat, try the "lighter" variation.

Crust:
**1 cup (about 8 whole crackers) graham cracker crumbs**
**2 tablespoons sugar**
**3 tablespoons unsalted butter, melted**

Filling:
**1 (3-ounce) package cream cheese, softened**
**1 teaspoon grated lemon zest**
**1 (14-ounce) can sweetened condensed milk**
**2 eggs**
**½ cup fresh-squeezed lemon juice**

Meringue topping:
**4 egg whites (about ½ cup)**
**¾ cup sugar**
**4 teaspoons water**
**¼ teaspoon cream of tartar**

**To make the crust:**
Preheat the oven to 350°. Brush a 9-inch pie pan with melted butter or spray with cooking spray. Stir the graham cracker crumbs, sugar and melted butter together in a small bowl. With your fingers, press the mixture into the pie pan. Bake for 5 to 7 minutes to set the crust. Cool.

**To make the filling:**
Beat the cream cheese with an electric mixer or in a food processor until it is light, scraping the sides of the bowl several times. Add the lemon zest. Gradually pour in the milk, scraping the bowl frequently to avoid lumps. Add the eggs one at a time; mix until they are incorporated, scraping again. Beat in the lemon juice. Pour the batter into the prepared pie crust and bake 25 to 30 minutes, until the filling reaches 160° on an instant-read thermometer. Cool. Freeze until the filling is firm, at least 2 hours.

**To make the topping:**

Preheat the oven to 500°.* Whisk the egg whites, sugar, water and cream of tartar in a bowl. Place over a pan of gently boiling water; the bowl should not touch the water. Cook, whisking constantly for 3 to 5 minutes, until the mixture reaches 160° on an instant-read thermometer. Remove from heat. With an electric mixer, whip until the meringue is cool and forms stiff peaks.

Cover the frozen pie with meringue, lifting with the back of a spoon to create decorative swirls. (Or, spread half of the meringue on top of the frozen pie, forming a slight dome in the middle, spoon the remaining meringue into a pastry bag fitted with a star tip, and pipe a decorative design over the pie.) Bake 4 to 6 minutes, until the meringue is a light brown. Return to the freezer for at least another hour. Serve the pie frozen, but allow it to temper 5 to 10 minutes, to ease the cutting.

*Makes 1 (9-inch) pie, serves 8 to 10.*

▲ High altitude: No adjustment is needed.

**Variation:**

*"Lighter in Fat" Frozen Lemon Meringue Pie:* Use fat-free cream cheese and fat-free sweetened condensed milk. Use a fat-free liquid egg substitute in place of the whole eggs in the filling, following the serving recommendation on the box.

✳ I use a propane blowtorch to caramelize meringue, saving time and the energy of heating the oven to 500°. To do this, instead of baking the finished decorated pie for 4 to 6 minutes, adjust the blowtorch flame to low and hold it 3 to 4 inches away from the meringue. Move the torch around until the meringue is golden brown all over.

# ■ Pear Cranberry Pie with Brown Sugar Cornmeal Streusel

This pie speaks of fall and winter—and begs for a snowstorm to keep everyone inside. The cranberries give a red blush, and the cornmeal crust adds a pleasant crunch. Serve with whipped cream or à la mode.

Crust:
**1 cup all-purpose flour**
**⅓ cup yellow cornmeal**
**2 tablespoons brown sugar**
**½ teaspoon salt**
**8 tablespoons (1 stick) cold unsalted butter, cut into ½-inch pieces**
**¼ cup ice-cold water**❉

Streusel:
**⅔ cup all-purpose flour**
**⅓ cup yellow cornmeal**
**½ cup firmly packed brown sugar**
**¼ teaspoon salt**
**8 tablespoons (1 stick) cold unsalted butter, cut into ½-inch pieces**

Filling:
**2 pounds (about 5 medium) firm, ripe Bartlett or D'Anjou pears**
**1½ cups fresh or frozen cranberries, coarsely chopped** ❉❉
**½ cup firmly packed brown sugar**
**2 tablespoons all-purpose flour**
**1 teaspoon grated orange zest**

**To make the crust:**
Mix the flour, cornmeal, brown sugar and salt in a medium bowl. Toss in the butter, coating the pieces with flour. Using your fingertips or a pastry blender, mix the butter and flour together until the mixture resembles coarse meal. Pieces of butter about the size of small peas should still be visible. Pour the water over the flour mixture, stirring with a fork to bring it together. Gather the dough with your hands and gently form it into a flattened ball about 1½ inches thick. Wrap in plastic wrap and refrigerate for at least 30 minutes.

On a lightly floured surface, roll the chilled dough into a 12-inch circle about ⅛ inch thick. Fit into a 9-inch pie pan and trim, if necessary, leaving a 1-inch overlap around the edge of the pie pan. Fold the overlapping dough under and crimp it into a fluted edge (page 124). Refrigerate or freeze until cold.

Preheat the oven to 400°. "Blind bake" (page 243) the pie shell 18 to 20 minutes. Carefully remove the pie weights and parchment paper. If the dough seems raw on the bottom, finish baking without the pie weights for about 5 minutes. Cool.

❉ To make ice-cold water, put several ice cubes in cold water. Wait a minute before removing the ice to measure the water.

❉❉ Cranberries chop easily in a food processor. Turn the machine on and off with the pulse button, checking the cranberries after each pulse. If you are using frozen cranberries, let them thaw about 10 minutes, but chop them before they thaw completely.

**To make the streusel:**
Put the flour, cornmeal, brown sugar, salt and butter in a bowl. Using your fingers or pastry blender, work until the mixture is crumbly. Set aside.

**To make the filling:**
Peel and core the pears. Cut them into ¼-inch slices. Toss with the cranberries, brown sugar, flour and orange zest.

Reduce the oven temperature to 350°. Spoon the pear mixture into the pre-baked pie crust. Cover the fruit evenly with the streusel. Bake 60 to 70 minutes, until the topping is golden brown and the pie juices are seriously bubbling. Serve warm or at room temperature.

*Makes 1 (9-inch) pie, serves 8 to 10.*

▲ High altitude: Be sure to prebake the crust, to keep it flaky. The pie juices may take 10 to 15 minutes longer to cook; watch for the ample evidence of juices bubbling through the streusel to be sure the filling has thickened.

*Carolyn Weil, a professional pie maker in Berkeley, California, always prebakes her pie crust for crispier texture. Shirley Corriher, author of* CookWise, *also believes in the superiority of a blind-baked bottom crust; she also recommends baking a decorative top crust separately and placing it over the baked and filled bottom crust.*

# ■ Ski Queen Apple Pie with Gjetost Cheese

This pie is a skier's turn on the American pairing of Cheddar cheese and apple pie—it's made with Norwegian Ski Queen gjetost cheese. "Gjetost" (YEA-toast) translates as "goat cheese." The unusual caramel color comes from boiling goat's milk during the cheesemaking process. Ski Queen is a mild variety of gjetost and is sold either in little red 8.8-ounce boxes or cut into portions from a large block and wrapped in plastic. This recipe calls for only 5 ounces of the cheese in the topping and crust, so if you have any left over, slice it and serve with thin rye crackers for an uncommon snack.

Crust:
¾ cup all-purpose flour
¼ teaspoon salt
6 tablespoons (¾ stick) cold unsalted butter, cut into ½-inch pieces
¾ cup shredded gjetost cheese (about 2 ounces)
3 tablespoons ice-cold water ❋

Streusel:
1 cup all-purpose flour
½ cup sugar
¼ teaspoon salt
8 tablespoons (1 stick) unsalted butter, cut into ½-inch pieces
1¼ cups shredded gjetost cheese (about 3 ounces)

Filling:
2¾ pounds (about 9 medium) apples
2 tablespoons (¼ stick) unsalted butter
2 tablespoons fresh-squeezed lemon juice
½ cup sugar
2 tablespoons all-purpose flour
½ teaspoon ground cinnamon
⅛ teaspoon ground nutmeg
Pinch ground cloves
1 tablespoon Jack Daniels whiskey, optional

Caramel Sauce, warm, optional (page 222)

❋ To make ice-cold water, put several ice cubes in cold water. Wait a minute before removing the ice to measure the water.

**To make the crust:**
Mix the flour and salt in a medium bowl. Toss in the butter, coating the pieces with flour. Using your fingers or a pastry blender, mix the butter and flour together until it resembles coarse meal. Pieces of butter about the size of small peas should still be visible. Stir in the cheese. Pour the water over the flour mixture, stirring with a fork to bring it together. Gather the dough with your hands and gently form it into a flattened ball about 1½ inches thick. Wrap in plastic wrap and refrigerate for at least 30 minutes.

On a lightly floured surface, roll the chilled dough into a 12-inch circle, about ⅛ inch thick. Fit into a 9-inch pie pan and trim, if necessary, leaving a 1-inch overlap around the edge of the pie pan. Fold the overlapping dough up onto the edge of the pie pan and crimp it into a fluted edge. Refrigerate or freeze until cold.

Preheat the oven to 400°. "Blind bake" (page 243) the pie shell 20 to 25 minutes. Carefully remove the pie weights and parchment paper. If the dough seems raw on the bottom, finish baking without the pie weights for about 5 minutes.

**To make the streusel:**

Put the flour, sugar, salt and butter in a bowl. Using your fingers or a pastry blender, work the butter pieces into the flour until the mixture is crumbly. Toss in the cheese, breaking up any long strands with your fingers. Set aside.

**To make the filling and assemble the pie:**

Peel and core the apples. Cut them into ¼-inch slices. Melt the butter in a large skillet and cook and stir the apples until almost tender, about 8 minutes. Strain some of the juice from the cooked apples. Toss them in a large bowl with the lemon juice, sugar, flour, cinnamon, nutmeg, cloves and whiskey, if using.

Reduce the oven temperature to 350°. Spoon the apple mixture into the pre-baked pie crust. Cover evenly with the streusel, gently pressing it into the fruit. Bake 55 to 65 minutes, until the pie juices are bubbling and the topping is golden brown. The gjetost cheese will turn very dark since it is golden brown to begin with. Cool at least 30 minutes before cutting. Serve warm or at room temperature with warm Caramel Sauce, if desired.

*Makes 1 (9-inch) pie, serves 8 to 10.*

▲ High altitude: Be sure to prebake the crust, to keep it flaky. The pie juices may take longer to cook; watch for the ample evidence of bubbling juices through the streusel, to be sure the filling has thickened.

*In the fall I buy apples at the Park City Farmer's Market from a Utah grower. He has more than 40 acres of trees and 20 varieties of apples. I usually choose Golden Delicious because they keep their shape and texture, but the farmer's favorite baking apple is a Rome Beauty. He also suggests Jonathan or Jonagolds. Neither the farmer nor I like Red Delicious apples for baking; they turn out mushy.*

# ■ Spicy Pumpkin Pie in a Gingersnap Cookie Crust

My sister-in-law, Terry, puts orange zest in her pumpkin pie. I've borrowed her idea and built on it by adding more than the usual ground spices. Roll or press the complementary gingersnap cookie crust into the pie pan. Know that the built-up edge tends to fall off in the oven, though it is initially needed in order for the pie shell to hold all the filling. So the edge will still be intact—able to contain the filling—this crust is not "blind baked." If desired, use a more traditional crust, such as Butter Pie Dough or Cream Cheese Pie Dough.

Crust:
**1 cup all-purpose flour**
**⅓ cup firmly packed brown sugar**
**¾ teaspoon baking powder**
**¾ teaspoon ground ginger**
**½ teaspoon ground cinnamon**
**¼ teaspoon salt**
**¼ teaspoon ground cloves**
**⅛ teaspoon ground nutmeg**
**6 tablespoons (¾ stick) cold unsalted butter, cut into ½-inch pieces**
**1 tablespoon unsulphured mild molasses**
**1 tablespoon ice-cold water**※

Filling:
**2 eggs**
**1 (15-ounce) can pumpkin purée**
**¾ cup sugar**
**1 teaspoon grated orange zest**
**½ teaspoon salt**
**¾ teaspoon ground cinnamon**
**½ teaspoon ground ginger**
**⅛ teaspoon ground nutmeg**
**⅛ teaspoon ground allspice**
**⅛ teaspoon ground mace**
**⅛ teaspoon ground cloves**
**1 (12-ounce) can evaporated milk**

❋ To make ice-cold water, put several ice cubes in cold water. Wait a minute before removing the ice to measure the water.

*It's a busy Deer Valley bakery the day before Thanksgiving— the ovens are full of pumpkin pies. To save time, we pre-mix the filling spices and label it "pumpkin pie spice." Then we don't have to measure the 6 different spices every time we make a batch of pies.*

**To make the crust:**
Stir the flour, brown sugar, baking powder, ginger, cinnamon, salt, cloves and nutmeg together in a medium bowl. Using a pastry blender or your fingers, cut the butter into the flour mixture until the mixture resembles coarse meal. Sprinkle the molasses and cold water over the dough, mixing with a fork. Work the dough with your hands, mixing until the pieces come together in a mass.

On a lightly floured surface, roll the dough into a 12-inch circle, ⅛ to ¼ inch thick, and fit into a 9-inch pie pan, leaving a 1-inch overlap. Fold the overlapping dough up onto the edge of the pie pan and crimp it into a fluted edge. (Or, press the dough onto the bottom and sides of the pie pan, building up a ½-inch edge on the pan rim. Crimp the edge into a fluted design.) Refrigerate or freeze until cold.

**To make the filling and bake the pie:**
Preheat the oven to 400°. Whisk the eggs in a large bowl. Add the pumpkin and whisk until smooth. Add the sugar, orange zest, salt and spices, stirring until well mixed. Whisk in the evaporated milk.

Pour the filling into the cold pie shell. Place on a baking sheet and bake for 15 minutes, then lower the temperature to 350° and bake 60 to 70 minutes, until the filling is set, and a knife inserted in the center comes out clean. Cool. Pumpkin pies should sit at room temperature no longer than 1½ hours. Refrigerate the pie after it cools if you are serving later; let sit at room temperature again 30 minutes before serving. If you wish, serve with whipped cream sweetened with a little maple syrup or sugar.

*Makes 1 (9-inch) pie, serves 8 to 10.*

▲ High altitude: Reduce the baking powder in the crust to ½ teaspoon. The pumpkin custard filling will take 10 to 15 minutes longer to bake.

*Did you know—allspice is not a spice mixture, but a spice in its own right, and before grinding, the allspice berry resembles a peppercorn? Did you know—mace is the outer covering of the nutmeg seed, with a flavor similar to, but less intense than, nutmeg?*

# ■ Raspberry Linzertorte

It looks like a tart, so why is it called a torte—doesn't *torte* mean cake? This dessert, an Austrian specialty, doesn't help our word confusion; the original, traditional Linzertorte is cakelike, but we Americans are familiar with this tartlike Linzer. I add fresh apple to the typical raspberry filling and I prebake the bottom crust, to ensure crispness in the finished pastry.

Dough:
**8 tablespoons (1 stick) unsalted butter, room temperature**
**¼ teaspoon grated lemon zest**
**½ cup (2 ounces) sliced almonds, ground**❊
**¼ cup ground cake trimmings or graham cracker crumbs**❊❊
**⅓ cup sugar**
**1 egg**
**¼ teaspoon vanilla extract**
**1½ cups all-purpose flour**
**½ teaspoon ground cinnamon**
**Pinch ground cloves**
**½ teaspoon baking powder**

Filling:
**1 medium apple, any variety**
**1 cup good-quality raspberry preserves**
**½ teaspoon grated orange zest**
**1 teaspoon grated lemon zest**

Assembly:
**¼ cup Apricot Glaze (page 208)**
**Confectioners' sugar to dust the edge of the tart**

**To make the dough:**
In a large bowl, using an electric mixer, cream the butter and lemon zest until light and fluffy. Mix in the ground nuts, cake crumbs and sugar. Add the egg and vanilla. Scrape the sides and bottom of the bowl and mix well. Sift together the flour, cinnamon, cloves and baking powder. Mix into the creamed butter until the dough comes together, scraping as needed. Wrap in plastic wrap and refrigerate at least 3 hours, until the dough is very cold.

On a floured surface, roll two-thirds of the cold dough into an 11-inch circle, ⅛ to ¼ inch thick. Lift and turn the circle frequently, as often as every other roll of the pin. Dust the work surface and the rolling pin generously with flour to keep the dough from sticking. Transfer the dough to a 9-inch fluted tart pan with a removable bottom by rolling it around the rolling pin and unrolling the dough over the pan. Press the dough into the pan, easing it into the corners and patching any tears or holes. Use your thumb to break off the excess dough at the top edge. Wrap and refrigerate the excess dough with the

❊ Grind the almonds, cake trimmings and sugar all at once in a food processor. The sugar keeps the nuts from getting oily and processing the 3 ingredients together saves time.

❊❊ If you don't have any leftover cake trimmings, substitute graham cracker crumbs or chocolate wafer crumbs. Chocolate cake or wafer crumbs make a darker Linzer dough; yellow cake or graham crackers make lighter dough—I use a mix of both light and dark crumbs.

other third of dough until you are ready to assemble the tart. Refrigerate or freeze the tart shell until it is cold.

Preheat the oven to 350°. If desired, "blind bake" (page 243) the tart shell 20 minutes. Cool. Carefully remove the pie weights and parchment paper.

**To make the filling:**
Core and grate the apple, including the peel. Mix in a small bowl with the raspberry preserves and the orange and lemon zests.

Spread the filling into the prepared tart shell, raw or blind baked.

**To assemble and bake the tart:**
Roll the remaining cold Linzer dough into a rectangle, ⅛ to ¼ inch thick, again dusting with as much flour as needed to keep the dough from sticking. Using a fluted pastry wheel, cut strips of dough ½ to ¾ inch wide and about 9 inches long. Lay a row of the strips parallel to each other, about ¾ inch apart, over the filling. Lay a second row of strips at a 45-degree angle to the first, making a lattice with diamond-shaped open spaces. Break off the excess strips at the pan edge. If you wish, cut cookies (page 75) out of the remaining dough.

Place the tart in the preheated oven and bake until the filling begins to bubble and the pastry is just golden. If the bottom pastry was blind-baked, this will take about 30 more minutes; otherwise the tart will bake 50 to 55 minutes. Cool completely.

Remove the outside ring from the tart pan and place the tart on a serving platter. Heat the Apricot Glaze until it is liquid. With a pastry brush, paint a light glaze over the entire tart. Center a 7-inch plate or a cardboard circle on top of the tart as a stencil and sift confectioners' sugar over the exposed border. Serve at room temperature.

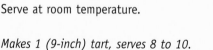

*Makes 1 (9-inch) tart, serves 8 to 10.*

▲ High altitude: Reduce the baking powder to ¼ teaspoon. The tart may take more time to bake to a golden color.

**Variation:**
For the holidays, make Cranberry Linzertorte. Simply add ¼ cup of homemade cranberry sauce to the raspberry and grated apple filling.

# ▪ Caramel Cashew Tart

We change our dessert menu nightly for Snow Park Lodge's Seafood Buffet. We often feature this tart, or one with different nut and chocolate variations. Many years ago I tasted a similar dessert at Greens in San Francisco, a restaurant famous for its vegetarian cuisine. That one was made with macadamia nuts and completely covered with a white chocolate glaze. In this interpretation you can still see the nuts beneath the squiggles of white and dark chocolate.

½ recipe Sweet Tart Dough (page 226)
¾ cup sugar
¼ teaspoon cream of tartar
½ cup water
4 tablespoons (½ stick) unsalted butter
½ cup heavy cream
1¾ cups (about 8 ounces) toasted cashews, cut in ½-inch pieces<sup>⁕</sup>
2 tablespoons (1 ounce) melted semisweet or bittersweet chocolate (page 244)
2 tablespoons (1 ounce) melted white chocolate (page 244)

Prepare the Sweet Tart Dough for rolling. Work it by hand first or it will be too crumbly. Cut the cold dough into ½-cup portions and smear the pieces quickly with the palm of your hand—the motion is similar to kneading but more gentle. Bring the smoothed dough together to form a flattened ball.

On a lightly floured surface, roll the dough into an 11-inch circle, about ⅛ inch thick. Use short coaxing strokes of the rolling pin and lift and turn the circle frequently, as often as every other roll of the pin. Use as little flour as possible, but dust the work surface and the rolling pin as needed to keep the dough from sticking. Transfer the dough to a 9-inch fluted tart pan with a removable bottom by rolling it around the rolling pin and unrolling the dough over the pan. Press the dough into the pan, easing it into the corners and patching any tears or holes. Use your thumb to break off the excess dough at the top edge. Refrigerate or freeze until cold.

Preheat the oven to 400°. "Blind bake" (page 243) the Sweet Tart shell. Cool 5 minutes. Carefully remove the pie weights and parchment paper. If the dough seems raw on the bottom, finish baking without the pie weights for about 5 minutes.

While the shell is cooling, prepare the filling. In a medium saucepan, over low heat, dissolve the sugar and the cream of tartar in the water. Increase the heat to medium-high and cook until the syrup turns a rich golden caramel, 5 to 8 minutes.<sup>⁕⁕</sup> As the syrup cooks, move the pan to swirl the sugar and distribute the heat, but do not stir.

Remove from the heat. Add the butter, about a tablespoon at a time, stirring with a wooden spoon. Be aware of, and protect your face and hands from, splashing hot caramel. Gradually add the cream. Stir in the cashews and pour into the pre-baked shell. Refrigerate until the caramel becomes firm enough to cut, at least 1 hour.

⁕ I start with raw unsalted cashews. To toast cashews, spread them in an ungreased pan. Bake in a preheated 350° oven 5 to 7 minutes, stirring occasionally, or until light golden brown. If you can only find cashews roasted and salted, rinse and dry the nuts thoroughly before using. An 8-ounce bag of salted cashews contains a little more than 1¾ cups.

⁕⁕ You need to cook the caramel to a deep color, so the filling will set nicely, but if you cook it too long, it will have a bitter flavor. The caramel continues to cook off the heat until you add the butter and cream, so make sure these ingredients are ready, near the stove.

Remove the fluted pan rim and transfer the pastry shell to a serving plate. Using the tines of a fork, drizzle the melted dark chocolate over the tart in a random zigzag. Do the same with the melted white chocolate.

*Makes 1 (9-inch) tart, serves 10.*

▲ High altitude: This recipe needs no adjustment.

# ■ Snuggery Chocolate Silk Pie

Dreamy, creamy and rich—this will satisfy your chocolate cravings. Use an instant-read thermometer to check the temperature of the egg mixture; you want to cook the eggs just enough to eliminate the risk of salmonella, but not so much that they scramble. If you've been wanting an excuse to buy one of these thermometers, this is it. I am grateful to Maida Heatter for introducing me to the "silk" genre of chocolate pies in her careful, instructive cookbooks.

Crust:
**Cream Cheese Pie Dough (page 217) or ½ recipe Butter Pie Dough (page 225)**

Filling:
**5 (1-ounce) squares unsweetened chocolate**
**5 eggs**
**1¼ cups firmly packed brown sugar**
**1½ teaspoons vanilla extract**
**½ pound (2 sticks) unsalted butter, softened**

Topping:
**1½ cups heavy cream**
**1 tablespoon sugar**
**¼ teaspoon vanilla extract**
**½ cup chocolate curls**❈

**To bake the crust:**
On a lightly floured surface, roll the Butter Pie Dough or Cream Cheese Pie Dough into a 12-inch circle, about ⅛ inch thick. Fit into a 9-inch pie pan and trim, if necessary, leaving a 1-inch overlap around the edge of the pie pan. Fold the overlapping dough up onto the edge of the pie pan and crimp it into a fluted edge. Refrigerate or freeze until cold.

Preheat the oven to 400°. Place the pie pan on a baking sheet and "blind bake" (page 243) 25 to 30 minutes. Cool 5 minutes. Carefully remove the pie weights and parchment paper. If the dough seems raw on the bottom, finish baking without the pie weights for 5 to 10 minutes, until the bottom is light golden brown. Cool completely.

**To make the filling:**
Cut the chocolate into ½-inch pieces. Set aside.

Whisk the eggs and brown sugar in a large bowl. Place over a pan of gently boiling water; the bowl should not touch the water. Cook, whisking constantly for 4 to 6 minutes, until the mixture reaches 160° on an instant-read thermometer. Remove from the heat. Immediately add the chocolate and stir until the chocolate melts. Stir in the vanilla.

Prepare an ice bath: Fill a large bowl with ice and nest the bowl with the chocolate mixture in it. Stir the mixture until it lowers to 90° on an instant-read thermometer. Remove from the ice bath; set aside.

❈ To make chocolate curls, shave them with a vegetable peeler from the side or back of a bar of dark chocolate. Make sure the chocolate is not cold, but warm room temperature. A melon baller also makes attractive ¼-inch-wide chocolate curls.

Beat the butter with an electric mixer until light and fluffy, about 3 minutes. Add the chocolate mixture and beat to incorporate, scraping the sides and bottom of the bowl. Pour into the pre-baked and cooled pie shell. Refrigerate until firm, at least 3 hours.

**To make the topping:**
Whip the cream with the sugar and the vanilla until the cream comes to soft peaks that hold their shape. Spread the cream over the chilled and firm filling, lifting with the back of a spoon to create swirls. (Or, spoon it into a pastry bag fitted with a medium star tip and pipe shells all over.) Garnish with the chocolate curls or shaved chocolate.

*Makes 1 (9-inch) pie, serves 8 to 10.*

▲ High altitude: The pie crust may take longer to bake to golden brown.

*The Snuggery used to be the name of the Silver Lake Restaurant. When the lodge was built in 1981, it was "snugged" into little Silver Lake Valley, alone in its elegance. Snow Park Restaurant, "hugged" into the small valley at the base of the mountain, was called The Huggery. We changed the names so they are easier to remember, but you can still get a piece of Snuggery Chocolate Silk Pie in either restaurant.*

*Opposite: Snuggery Chocolate Silk Pie*

# ■ Tarte Tatin Mariposa

This is an upside-down apple tart, a rustic French specialty. Apple halves cook stove-top with sugar and butter until the juices turn into caramel, after which they're covered with pastry and baked. When the tart is inverted, the golden pastry becomes the bottom crust. In The Mariposa, we serve Tarte Tatin with housemade Cinnamon Ice Cream or lightly sweetened whipped cream. Vanilla yogurt is a low-calorie alternative that also complements the caramel and apples.

½ cup sugar
8 tablespoons (1 stick) unsalted butter
15 medium (about 5 pounds) Golden Delicious apples
½ recipe Butter Pie Dough (page 225) or
⅓ recipe Classic Puff Pastry Dough (page 229)
Sweetened whipped cream, optional

Put the sugar in a 10-inch oven-proof skillet.❉ Cut the butter into pieces and dot them around on top of the sugar.

Peel, halve, and core the apples.❉❉ Arrange the halves in the pan, standing on end, with the stem end up, the bottoms standing in the sugar. Fit each half into the next, so the outside of each half nestles into the cored center of the apple next to it—like standing stacked spoons. Pack in as many apples as possible, filling the pan. Lay the extra (4 to 5) halves on top; when the apples cook, there will be spaces to tuck these in.

Cook over medium heat. The sugar and butter will melt as the apples begin to cook; after about 15 minutes, they will shrink enough so you can poke the remaining ones in next to the others. When all the apples are nestled in, lower the heat. Cook until the apple juices and sugar thicken into a light caramel. Watch carefully, every so often lifting up an apple to peek, and rotating the pan to avoid hot spots that caramelize quickly. Depending on the heat of your stove burner, this step can take up to 2 hours—long slow cooking will ensure even color and caramelization.

Remove from the heat when the apples are light caramel. These caramelized apples can be set aside for several hours until closer to serving time, when the pastry is baked on top.

Preheat the oven to 400°. On a lightly floured surface, roll the Butter Pie Dough or Classic Puff Pastry into an 11-inch circle, ⅛ inch thick. Discard the extra dough.

Place the pastry over the caramelized apples, tucking the edges down into the pan. Put the pan on a baking sheet to catch any juices bubbling over. Bake 35 to 40 minutes, until the crust is very golden brown.

❉ There are heavy copper pans made especially for Tarte Tatin but I don't own one. I use a cast-iron skillet.

❉❉ I have a system for peeling and coring apples efficiently. First, cut just a little (⅛ inch) off both the top and the bottom of the apples. This reveals an edge of apple skin, a starting and ending point for the vegetable peeler blade. Next, peel all the apples. (You can drop them into a bowl of acidulated water but it is not necessary since the apples will cook until they are brown anyway.) Next, cut the apples in half lengthwise. Finally, remove the core with a small paring knife. So no time is wasted changing tools, complete each step on all the apples before starting the next step: Cut all tops and bottoms, peel them all, cut them all and, lastly, core them all.

Remove from the oven. Run a knife around the edge to make sure the pastry isn't stuck. Immediately, cover with a serving plate and invert the skillet, the tart and the plate in a quick deft motion, taking care not to spatter yourself with the hot caramel. Lift the pan off the plate slowly, to let lingering apples and caramel fall into place. Smooth the apples together with the back of a spoon, and if there is any caramel left in the pan, spoon it back onto the apples.

Serve the tart warm, with a dollop of sweetened whipped cream, if desired.

*Serves 10.*

▲ High altitude: The sugar, butter and apple juices will take longer to caramelize; be patient, watching for overall light golden color.

*Tarte Tatin is named for the Tatin sisters, who, in the early 1900s, ran a small hotel in the Loire Valley of central France. I have heard two stories regarding les mademoiselles Tatin and their tarte. One is that the sisters dropped their apple dessert just before supper and Tarte Tatin is the outcome of a successful salvage. In the other story their father has died. To support themselves, they sell (and make famous) this tart, of which he was particularly fond.*

# ■ Margarita Tart with Fresh Blueberries

This citrus custard filling, enhanced with tequila and orange liqueur, is delightful with its layer of ripe, sweet berries. I thank Madeleine Kamman, consummate teacher, for the idea of combining fresh blueberries and lime, and I raise a toast to Mexico's signature cocktail for further inspiration.

Dough:
**½ recipe Butter Pie Dough (page 225)**
**½ teaspoon grated lime zest**

Filling:
**8 tablespoons (1 stick) unsalted butter, softened**
**1 cup sugar**
**2 teaspoons grated lime zest**
**3 tablespoons all-purpose flour**
**3 eggs**
**3 egg yolks**
**2 tablespoons gold tequila**
**1 tablespoon orange-flavored liqueur**
**⅓ cup fresh-squeezed lime juice**

Topping:
**½ cup Apricot Glaze (page 208)**
**2 tablespoons water**
**1½ cups fresh blueberries**

**To make the crust:**
Place the disk of Butter Pie Dough on a lightly floured surface and sprinkle the dough with the lime zest. Roll the dough into an 11-inch circle, about ⅛ inch thick, rolling in the zest so it becomes part of the crust. Fit the dough into a 9-inch fluted tart pan with a removable bottom, building the edge ¼ inch above the rim to allow for shrinkage. Refrigerate or freeze until cold.

Preheat the oven to 400°. "Blind bake" (page 243) the tart shell 25 to 30 minutes or until the pastry is light golden brown. Cool. Carefully remove the pie weights and parchment paper.

**To make the filling and bake the tart:**
Lower the oven temperature to 350°. Beat the butter and the sugar with the lime zest in a large bowl using an electric mixer or a wire whisk. Add the flour and mix well. Beat in the eggs and egg yolks and the tequila, orange-flavored liqueur and lime juice. Place the bowl over a pan of simmering water and stir with a wire whisk until the filling smoothens and becomes homogenous, 1 to 2 minutes.

Pour the filling into the pre-baked shell and bake until the filling is just set, not liquid in the center, 15 to 20 minutes. Cool completely.

**To finish:**
Remove the fluted pan rim and transfer the pastry shell to a serving plate. Wash the blueberries and sort out any bad ones. Heat the Apricot Glaze with the water in a medium saucepan until it is very hot. Toss in the blueberries and swirl them in the pan until they deepen in hue, about 30 seconds. Immediately strain the berries and spread them evenly on top of the tart. Serve at room temperature or chilled.

*Makes 1 (9-inch) tart, serves 8 to 10.*

▲ High altitude: Reduce sugar by 2 tablespoons. The custard filling will take 5 to 10 more minutes to set.

*The technique of heating blueberries briefly in hot Apricot Glaze or Simple Syrup gives them a wonderful dark color and an attractive shine. It also makes the berries stick to the top of a tart and to each other, so the tart is easy to cut.*

# ■ Zinfandel Pear Tart with Maytag Blue Cheese Crust

Maytag blue cheese is a quality domestic blue-veined cheese, made from Holstein cow's milk, crafted and aged in caves near Newton, Iowa. One Thanksgiving, chef Chuck Wiley made chanterelle mushroom pot pies with a Maytag blue cheese crust. I took the leftover dough and turned it into this surprising dessert. Any decent red wine makes a good poaching syrup for the pears, but the fruity qualities in red Zinfandel marry especially well with this blue cheese. It's best to poach the pears a day or two ahead, giving the red wine time to permeate the pears with rosy pink color.

Pear topping:
**2 cups red Zinfandel or dry red wine**

**1 cup sugar**

**1 cup water**

**1 lemon**

**1 stick cinnamon**

**3 whole cloves**

**4 Bartlett pears, almost ripe**

Crust:
**¾ cup all-purpose flour**

**¼ teaspoon salt**

**5 tablespoons cold unsalted butter, cut into ½-inch pieces**

**2 ounces (about ½ cup) Maytag blue cheese crumbles**❋

**2 tablespoons ice-cold water**❋❋

**1¼ cups (1 recipe) Vanilla Bean Pastry Cream (page 218)**

### To poach the pears:

In a large saucepan, combine the red wine, sugar and water. Cut the lemon in half, squeeze the lemon juice into the pan, and then add the juiced halves. Add the cinnamon and cloves. Over medium heat, bring to a boil, stirring occasionally until the sugar dissolves. Lower the heat, but keep the wine mixture gently boiling.

Peel, halve and core the pears. Drop into a bowl of water as you peel them, so they don't turn brown. Slip the pears into the simmering wine syrup. Cover with a circle of parchment paper and a small plate, to keep the pears submerged in the poaching liquid. Simmer for 7 to 18 minutes, or until the pears are barely tender, being careful not to overcook. The poaching time will depend on the pear's ripeness, with very firm pears taking the full 18 minutes.

Transfer the pears to a bowl, covering with the parchment paper and the plate weight again to keep them submerged in the syrup. Refrigerate the poached pears at least 12 hours or up to 4 days.

❋ Maytag blue cheese has a mild flavor compared to French Roquefort. If you substitute the import, omit the salt and use less cheese. Avoid other domestic blue cheeses; they are salty and astringent, and lack the fine flavor needed for this pastry.

❋❋ To make ice-cold water, put several ice cubes in cold water. Wait a minute before removing the ice to measure the water.

*Opposite: Zinfandel Pear Tart with Maytag Blue Cheese Crust*

**To make the crust:**

Stir the flour and salt together in a medium bowl. Toss in the butter and cheese, coating the pieces with flour. Using your fingers or a pastry blender, mix the butter and cheese into the flour until the mixture resembles coarse meal. Pieces of butter about the size of small peas should still be visible. Pour the water over the flour mixture, stirring with a fork. Gather the dough with your fingers and gently form it into a flattened ball about 1½ inches thick. Wrap in plastic wrap and refrigerate for at least 20 minutes. The dough can be kept in the refrigerator 24 hours or frozen up to a month.

On a lightly floured surface, roll the dough into an 11-inch circle about ¼ inch thick. Fit the dough into a 9-inch fluted tart pan with a removable bottom, building the edge a little above the rim to allow for shrinkage. Refrigerate or freeze until cold.

Preheat the oven to 400°. Place the tart pan on a baking sheet and "blind bake" (page 243) the shell 20 to 25 minutes. Cool 5 minutes. Carefully remove the pie weights and parchment paper. Return the shell to the oven for 5 to 10 minutes more, until the bottom is light golden brown. Cool.

**To assemble:**

Remove the fluted pan rim and transfer the shell to a serving plate. Spread the Vanilla Bean Pastry Cream evenly into the shell.

Place the pears on paper towels to drain. Move them to a cutting board, cut side down, and slice them crosswise into ⅛- to ¼-inch slices.

Strain 1 cup of the poaching liquid into a saucepan and cook over medium heat until reduced to a little less than ¼ cup. Meanwhile, arrange the pear slices on the pastry cream, starting at the outside edge and working toward the center, overlapping, in a flower pattern. Brush the pears lightly with the reduced syrup glaze. Serve within 3 hours.

*Makes 1 (9-inch) tart, serves 8 to 10.*

▲ High altitude: This recipe needs no adjustment.

# ▪ Fresh Blackberry Pie

I am partial to the Pacific Northwest—my mother was born and raised there and it must be in my blood. My favorite summer vacation is a windsurfing trip to the Columbia River Gorge, between Oregon and Washington. Wild blackberry bushes proliferate in the gorge, crowding the woods and the paths to windsurfing launch sites. Between sailing sessions, you can pick and munch on fresh berries to your heart's content. I like to gather a few pints and turn them into pie, a well-earned treat after an active day on the river.

**6 cups fresh blackberries**
**½ teaspoon grated lemon zest**
**1 tablespoon fresh lemon juice**
**1¼ cups sugar**
**½ cup all-purpose flour**
**Butter Pie Dough (page 225)**
**2 tablespoons (¼ stick) unsalted butter, cut into small pieces**
**1 egg beaten with 1 tablespoon milk or water, for glaze**

In a large bowl, stir together the blackberries, lemon zest and juice, sugar and flour. Let stand for at least 15 minutes.

On a lightly floured surface, roll half of the Butter Pie Dough into a 12-inch circle, about ⅛ inch thick. Fit into a 9-inch pie pan and trim, if necessary, leaving a 1-inch overlap around the edge of the pie pan.

Preheat the oven to 400°. Roll the other half of the Butter Pie Dough into an 11-inch circle, about ⅛ inch thick. Reserve the dough trimmings.

Pour the filling into the prepared pie shell. Dot with butter pieces. Lay the 11-inch top crust over the filling. Moisten the edge of the bottom crust with a little water and fold it up over the top, pinching to seal the pastry together. Crimp into a decorative fluted edge.

From the reserved dough trimmings, cut 8 or 10 leaf shapes about 3 inches long and 1 inch wide. Mark veins on the leaves with the back of a small knife.

Brush the pie lightly with the egg glaze. Arrange the leaf decorations on top, one leaf for every wedge of pie. Brush the decorations with egg glaze. Cut 6 slits in the crust so steam can escape as the pie bakes.

Put the pie on a baking sheet to catch overflowing fruit juices. Bake 10 minutes at 400°, then reduce the oven temperature to 375° and bake for another 45 to 60 minutes, until the crust is golden brown and the pie juices are bubbling. Serve at room temperature.

*Makes 1 (9-inch) pie, serves 8 to 10.*

▲ High altitude: More time may be needed for the juices to thicken. If the crust gets too brown before there is ample evidence of bubbling juices, reduce the oven temperature to 350° (or even 325°) and continue to bake.

# ◆ White Chocolate Banana Cream Pie

A heavenly, melt-in-your-mouth rendition of an old favorite, this is the usual vanilla pudding dressed up with white chocolate. Have everything ready and at hand before you begin so you can work quickly when making the filling. Use an extra banana if yours are small or if you want more banana in your pie.

Crust:
**Cream Cheese Pie Dough (page 217)**

Filling:
**1¼ cups (1 recipe) Vanilla Bean Pastry Cream (page 218)**
**1 cup heavy cream**
**5 teaspoons water**
**1 teaspoon fresh-squeezed lemon juice**
**1½ teaspoons powdered gelatin**
**6 ounces white chocolate, melted (page 244)**
**2 or 3 ripe bananas**

Topping:
**1 cup heavy cream**
**1 tablespoon sugar**
**¼ teaspoon vanilla extract**
**⅓ cup toasted macadamia nuts, chopped**❊
**Hot Fudge Sauce, warm (page 214)**

❊ I use raw unsalted macadamia nuts, purchased in bulk. If you can only find them roasted and salted, rinse and dry the nuts thoroughly before using. To toast macadamia nuts, spread them in an ungreased pan. Bake in a preheated 350° oven for 5 to 7 minutes, stirring occasionally, or until light golden brown.

**To make the crust:**
On a lightly floured surface, roll the Cream Cheese Pie Dough into a 12-inch circle. Fit into a 9-inch pie pan and trim, if necessary, leaving a 1-inch overlap around the edge of the pie pan. Fold the overlapping dough up onto the edge of the pie pan and crimp it into a fluted edge. Refrigerate or freeze until cold.

Preheat the oven to 400°. "Blind bake" (page 243) the pie shell 25 to 30 minutes. Cool 5 minutes. Carefully remove the pie weights and parchment paper and return the shell to the oven for 5 minutes, until the bottom is light golden brown. Cool completely.

**To make the filling:**
Put the Vanilla Bean Pastry Cream in a large bowl. If the pastry cream is warm, cool it over an ice bath; fill a larger bowl with ice and nest the bowl of pastry cream in the ice. Bring the pastry cream to at least room temperature or the whipped cream may curdle when added. If the pastry cream is very cold, let it sit at room temperature for 30 minutes, so the white chocolate and gelatin can incorporate easily.

Whip the cream until it comes to soft peaks that hold their shape. Set aside.

Measure the water and lemon juice into a small bowl, sprinkle the gelatin over it, and allow to soften, about 5 minutes. Place the bowl over barely simmering water and stir until the gelatin melts, about a minute.

Whisk the Vanilla Bean Pastry Cream until smooth. Whisk in the melted white chocolate. Whisk in the liquid gelatin. Immediately whisk in a third of the whipped cream, then fold in the rest.

Spread a third of this filling in the baked and cooled pie shell. Peel the bananas and cut them into ¼-inch slices. Arrange half of the slices on top of the filling. Repeat the layers, ending with the filling. Cover and chill at least 2 hours.

**To make the topping and serve:**
Whip the cream with the sugar and the vanilla until the cream comes to soft peaks that hold their shape. Spread the cream over the chilled filling, lifting with the back of a spoon to create swirls. (Or, spoon it into a pastry bag fitted with a medium star tip and pipe shells all over.) Garnish with the chopped nuts. Serve with warm Hot Fudge Sauce.

*Makes 1 (9-inch) pie, serves 8 to 10.*

▲ High altitude: No adjustment is needed.

**Variation:**
Use the Chocolate Cookie Crust from Milk Chocolate Cheesecake (page 94) instead of the Cream Cheese Pie Dough.

# ◆ Gingered Peach Pie with a Pecan Nut Crust

This is not your typical pie crust, as it is really a sugar cookie dough. It is very flaky and tender—I think it goes perfectly with the peaches. The pecans don't overwhelm, and fresh ginger, in both the crust and the filling, ties the flavors together. If you wish, serve this pie with whipped cream or à la mode.

Crust:
**¼ cup toasted pecans, cool**⁎
**¼ cup sugar**
**1⅔ cups all-purpose flour**
**½ teaspoon ground ginger**
**10 tablespoons (1 stick and 2 tablespoons) cold unsalted butter,**
**    cut into ½-inch pieces**
**1 egg yolk**
**1 tablespoon heavy cream**
**1 tablespoon peeled and grated fresh ginger root (about 1-inch piece)**

Filling:
**3 pounds (8 medium) peaches**
**1 tablespoon fresh lemon juice**
**1 tablespoon peeled and grated fresh ginger**
**¼ teaspoon ground cinnamon**
**⅛ teaspoon fresh grated nutmeg**
**⅛ teaspoon salt**
**½ to ¾ cup sugar**⁎⁎
**¼ cup all-purpose flour**

**1 egg beaten with 1 tablespoon milk or water, for glaze**
**Granulated or crystal sugar, optional**

**To make the crust:**
Finely grind the nuts with the sugar; a food processor is the perfect tool. Put in a bowl with the flour and ground ginger and stir to blend. Using your fingers or a pastry blender, cut the butter and flour mixture together until it resembles coarse meal. In a separate bowl, whisk the egg yolk, cream and fresh ginger. Sprinkle over the dough, stirring with a fork to bring it together. Gather the dough with your hands and gently form it into a flattened ball about 1½ inches thick. Wrap in plastic wrap and refrigerate at least 2 hours.

The dough will have a crumbly texture and must be worked by hand before rolling. Cut the cold dough into ½-cup portions and smear the pieces quickly with the palm of your hand—the motion is similar to kneading but more gentle. Bring the smoothed dough together and form two flattened balls, one a bit larger than the other.

Roll the larger piece of dough into an 11-inch circle, about ⅛ inch thick. Use short

⁎ To toast pecans: Spread the nuts in an ungreased pan. Bake in a preheated 350° oven 5 to 7 minutes or until light brown, stirring occasionally.

⁎⁎ Taste the peaches, and if they are sweet, use less sugar; if they are a bit tart, use more.

coaxing strokes of the rolling pin and lift and turn the circle frequently, as often as every other roll of the pin. Use as little flour as possible, but dust the work surface and the rolling pin as needed to keep the dough from sticking. Transfer the dough to a 9-inch pie pan by rolling it around the rolling pin and unrolling the dough over the pan. Ease the dough into the pan, patching any tears or holes. Trim the edges, leaving a ¼-inch over-lap around the edge of the pie pan. Fold the overlapping dough up onto the edge of the pie pan and crimp it into a decorative fluted edge. Keep the border short and toward the inside rim of the pie pan; if the edge is too big, this rich pastry tends to fall off in the oven. (The dough can also be pressed into the bottom and sides of the pie pan, with a built-up fluted edge.) Refrigerate or freeze until cold.

For the top crust, roll the second half of dough into a 10-inch circle, about ⅛ inch thick. (Or press or roll the dough between 2 pieces of parchment paper.) Place on a plate on a piece of parchment paper; cover and refrigerate.

Preheat the oven to 375°. "Blind bake" (page 243) the shell 15 to 20 minutes. Cool 5 minutes. Carefully remove the pie weights and parchment paper.

**To make the filling and assemble the pie:**
Peel the peaches.❀❀❀ Remove the pit and cut into ½-inch slices. Toss the peaches, lemon juice, ginger, cinnamon, nutmeg, salt, sugar and flour in a bowl.

Spoon the peach mixture into the pre-baked pie shell. Remove the rolled top crust from the refrigerator and slide it over the filling. Let the top crust sit on top of the filling about 5 minutes until the dough is pliable, then mold and seal it to the bottom crust with your fingers. Brush the pastry with the egg glaze and sprinkle with sugar, if using. Cut 8 slits in the top crust so steam can escape as the pie bakes.

Place the pie on a baking sheet and return to the 375° oven. Bake until the crust is golden brown and the pie juices are bubbling, 45 to 50 minutes. If the edge of the top crust is browning too quickly, lower the oven to 350°. Cool. Serve warm or at room temperature.

*Makes 1 (9-inch) pie, serves 8 to 10.*

▲ High altitude: Be sure to prebake the crust, to keep it flaky. The pie juices may take longer to cook; watch for the ample evidence of juices bubbling through the slashes, to be sure the filling has thickened.

❀❀❀ To peel peaches, immerse them in a pot of boiling water for about 1 minute, then remove with a slotted spoon and allow to cool until you can handle them. The skins should slip right off, though you may need a knife to help peel less-than-ripe peaches.

# ◆ Honey Walnut Tart with Chocolate Glaze

This tart has a top and bottom crust surrounding the caramel honey filling. Enrobed in chocolate, it looks more like a cake or torte. I serve it in the fall, as one of the desserts at the annual Nouveau Beaujolais wine celebration.

Filling:
**1 cup sugar**
**¼ teaspoon cream of tartar**
**½ cup water**
**½ pound (2 sticks) unsalted butter**
**1 cup heavy cream**
**1½ cups chopped walnuts** *plus* **12 walnut halves to garnish**
**⅓ cup honey**

**Sweet Tart Dough (page 226)**
**¾ cup Chocolate Honey Glaze, warm (page 212)**

**To make the filling:**
In a medium saucepan, over low heat, dissolve the sugar and the cream of tartar in the water. Increase the heat to medium-high. Move the pan to swirl the syrup and distribute the heat, but do not stir. Cook until the syrup turns a deep golden caramel. Remove from heat.

Add the butter, a few tablespoons at a time, stirring with a wooden spoon. Be aware of, and protect your face and hands from, splashing hot caramel. The hot caramel may seize when you add the butter but will melt again as it cooks. Return to medium heat and gradually stir in the cream. Continue to cook about 10 minutes more, letting the caramel thicken and darken slightly in color, stirring occasionally. Transfer to a bowl. Mix in the chopped walnuts and the honey. Stir every so often, until the mixture is cool. The filling may be kept refrigerated up to a week before assembling the tart.

**To assemble the tart:**
Preheat the oven to 400°. Prepare the Sweet Tart Dough for rolling; it must be worked by hand first or it will be too crumbly. Cut the cold dough into ½-cup portions and smear the pieces quickly with the palm of your hand—the motion is similar to kneading but more gentle. Divide into two flattened balls, one a bit larger than the other.

Brush melted butter on the sides and bottom of a 9-inch fluted tart pan with a removable bottom, or spray with cooking spray. On a lightly floured surface, roll the larger portion of dough into a 12-inch circle, ⅛ to ¼ inch thick. Use short coaxing strokes of the rolling pin and lift and turn the circle frequently, as often as every other roll of the pin. Use as little flour as possible, but dust the work surface and the rolling pin as needed to keep the dough from sticking. Transfer to the prepared pan by rolling the dough up onto the rolling pin and laying it over the pan. Ease the dough into the corners of the pan.

*They came from the hills of Burgundy to the cities of Lyon and Paris; fruity, red and young were the wines, still fizzing in their barrels. Thirsty wine lovers rushed to taste the first of the new vintage. The French made it a party— Le Nouveau Beaujolais est arrive!*

Patch any tears by pressing the dough together with your fingers. Trim the edges, leaving 1 inch of the dough standing up above the sides of the pan.

Roll the remaining dough for the top crust. Make it a circle, ⅛ inch thick, a little wider than the pan. Set aside.

Spread the honey walnut filling into the tart shell. Fold the extended inch of pastry over the filling. Brush this edge with water so the top crust will seal to it. Lay the top crust on top of the filling. Use your fingers to pinch off the excess dough and to seal the top and bottom crusts together.

### To bake the tart:

Cut 6 slits in the crust to allow steam to escape. Place on a large baking sheet and bake 35 to 40 minutes, until the top crust is golden brown. Some of the filling may leak; this is typical. Cool at least 1 hour.

Invert the tart onto a flat serving plate or a cardboard cake circle. Remove the fluted pan rim and bottom; you may need to slip a flat knife between the pastry and the pan bottom to release it. If the tart is still difficult to release, return it to a hot oven for 5 to 10 minutes to soften the sticky caramel, then remove the pan rim and bottom. Refrigerate until the filling is firm, 1 or 2 hours.

### To glaze the tart:

Pour half of the warm Chocolate Honey Glaze over the tart. Use a metal spatula to spread a thin base coat, covering all the pastry, including the fluted edges. Refrigerate 5 minutes, so the glaze hardens. Apply the remaining glaze, smoothing the top with the spatula, letting the excess drip down the sides. Press the walnut halves on top, around the edge, marking each portion. Serve the tart cold or at room temperature.

*Makes 1 (9-inch) tart, serves 12 to 18.*

▲ High altitude: The tart may take longer to bake; remove from the oven when the pastry is a rich golden brown.

*We continue the Nouveau Beaujolais tradition at Deer Valley by holding a festival celebrating the new wines on the Sunday before Thanksgiving. We complement the quaffing with lavish buffets, including classic cassoulet and Burgundian cheeses. I make puff pastry bouchées to hold crayfish Nantua, and gougères to pop in one's mouth. Wine country's other bounty inspires my desserts—the array features oranges and lemons and apples and pears, chestnuts, chocolate and cassis, not to mention almonds and walnuts.*

# Ice Creams and Sorbets

● Mocha Chip Ice Cream Pie

● Cranberry Cassis Sorbet

● Blood Orange Sorbet

● Pear Ginger Sorbet

■ Vanilla Bean Ice Cream

■ Tangerine Dream Ice Cream

■ Cinnamon Ice Cream

■ Chocolate Spice Ice Cream

■ Kahlúa Milk Chocolate Ice Cream

■ Blackberry Ice Cream

■ Kadota Fig Ice Cream

■ Julie's Caramel Ice Cream

■ Maple Walnut Ice Cream

# Ice Creams and Sorbets

Bakers deal in mouth-watering creations. The fruits of our labor nourish the eye as well as the tongue. We see the results when we add the last touch to an elegant dessert and when guests exclaim as they approach our pastry displays. Because people in our Western culture love sweets, baking nurtures our self-esteem.

With more than thirty bakers in the winter kitchen, a large part of my job is paperwork and supervision—making sure the bakers have everything they need to do their jobs. Some days I have no time for actual hands-on baking, no time to make tempting desserts. Other days, I roll up the sleeves of my chef's jacket and dig in. Both aspects of the job are rewarding, though I still want that immediate satisfaction from creating a treat with an outstanding look and taste. Making ice creams and sorbets always placates my creative need.

In my role and responsibilities, I alternate between the day lodges, working with the pastry chefs and bakers in each kitchen. Two days a week I work in Silver Lake Bakery where we have the ice cream machine that churns frozen desserts for The Mariposa restaurant. When I walk into the bakery, with my uniform on and tools in hand, I often sign up for ice cream production. The bakers save the job for me because they know I'll work like a mad scientist, concocting and creating new flavors as I go along. I try to use fruit or whatever is on hand for seasonal combinations. Positive feedback comes by tasting a frozen spoonful out of the churning machine.

Ice cream is my favorite accompaniment to a wedge of pie; imagine Julie's Caramel Ice Cream on top of Gingered Peach Pie. As far as I'm concerned, cold and creamy ice cream belongs with warm dessert, such as the perfect pairing of Vanilla Bean Ice Cream and Mariposa Christmas Pudding.

What is the difference between ice cream and sorbet? Both are churned frozen delights, but ice cream is custard-based, made from milk and/or cream, sugar and egg yolks. The ice cream recipes in this book all start with a base of crème anglaise, a stirred custard. If you are making ice cream and have never made a stirred custard, it's a good idea to review the recipe and tips for making Vanilla Bean Crème Anglaise, which is the basis for all of these richer-than-store-bought ice creams. They are very smooth because they contain plenty of emulsifying egg yolks.

Sorbet is made of fruit and sugar, without milk or cream. *Sorbet* is the French word for sherbet, although English dictionaries say that sherbet can include milk or egg white. Since my "fruit ices" contain no dairy products, I call them sorbet. My colleague, pastry chef Lindsey Shere—who, in her book *Chez Panisse Desserts*, offers foolproof recipes for frozen finales—calls her fruit ices sherbet. Sorbet or sherbet—by any name the dessert is a boon for the fat-conscious.

You will need an ice cream machine, either electric or hand crank, to make these frozen desserts. The creamy and fruity bases can be churned with a model that uses ice cubes and salt or one that uses a frozen canister, or if you are really serious, there are some high-tech self-refrigerated models on the home appliance market that cost more than $500. At Deer Valley we use a commercial self-refrigerated batch freezer that churns 2 quarts at a time. For testing the recipes in this book I used a Donvier brand ice cream maker with a frozen canister. All the recipes yield less than a quart; if your machine has a larger capacity and you want to make more, double or triple the recipe.

It is very important to clean and sanitize all machine parts that come in contact with the ice cream. This must be done religiously after each use so bacteria cannot multiply. Clean with soap and hot water, following the manufacturer's instructions. To sanitize, immerse the parts for 1 minute or longer in a bleach solution of 2 tablespoons to 1 gallon of water.

These recipes will acquaint you with techniques and ratios for ice cream making. After that, vary and change the basic recipes with different flavorings and additions. Remember that the ratio of sugar is critical; frozen desserts with excess sugar are almost too soft to scoop, but they will be icy and hard without enough. Let these recipes be the stepping stones for your own creative path.

*Ice cream keeps for several weeks in the freezer if wrapped very well in plastic wrap and covered with an airtight lid. The goal is to prevent moisture crystals from sneaking in and changing the ice cream's texture from smooth to granular.*

# • Mocha Chip Ice Cream Pie

On a hot summer night, this dessert hits the spot. Also try the variation, Vanilla Ice Cream Pie, topped with toasted sliced almonds. You will need to let the ice cream soften before beating it smooth, but don't let it melt too much—just enough so you can scoop it with a heavy-duty spoon from the carton to the mixer.

1 cup chocolate wafer crumbs (about 20 wafers)<sup>※</sup>
2 tablespoons (¼ stick) melted butter
¼ cup Caramel Sauce (page 222), or purchased fine-quality caramel sauce
½ gallon good-quality chocolate ice cream
1 tablespoon instant espresso coffee powder
¾ cup *plus* ¼ cup coarsely grated semisweet chocolate (about 4½ ounces)

Preheat the oven to 350°. Stir the chocolate wafer crumbs and the melted butter together in a small bowl. Use your fingers to spread it evenly up the sides and over the bottom of a 9-inch pie tin; press firmly so there are no loose crumbs. Bake 5 minutes to set the crust. Refrigerate.

Pour the caramel sauce onto the bottom of the prepared crust and spread it with the back of a spoon. If necessary, heat the caramel until it is warm enough to spread.

Remove the ice cream from the freezer and let it soften slightly. Beat the ice cream with an electric mixer until it is soft and smooth but not melted, about 2 minutes. Stir in the espresso powder and ¾ cup of the grated chocolate, reserving the rest for garnish. Spread the ice cream into the crust, mounding it in the middle. Sprinkle the remaining grated chocolate evenly over the top. Cover the pie with plastic wrap and freeze until the ice cream is very firm, at least 3 hours.

Remove from the freezer 5 to 10 minutes before serving to ease cutting. Serve with Hot Fudge Sauce (page 214) or a purchased chocolate sauce.

*Makes 1 (9-inch) pie, serves 8 to 10.*

▲ High altitude: This recipe needs no adjustment.

**Variation:**
*Vanilla Ice Cream Pie:* Substitute vanilla ice cream for the chocolate ice cream. Eliminate the espresso powder and grated chocolate. Sprinkle the top with ¾ cup of toasted sliced almonds.

※ Chocolate wafer crumbs are available in supermarkets, usually in the same aisle as cake mixes.

*You can grate chocolate using a metal cheese grater, but a good bit of the chocolate melts into your hand. I like to use the medium shredding disc of a food processor; it's fast and efficient.*

# ● Cranberry Cassis Sorbet

During the winter holidays, we serve this as one member of The Mariposa's ice cream trio. Its color is brilliant and jewel-like and it has a tangy bite, barely mellowed by the cassis. Lacking cassis, it's fine to substitute any berry eau de vie or flavored liqueur, such as framboise.

> 1½ cups water
> 1 (12-ounce) package fresh or frozen cranberries (about 3 cups)
> 1 cup sugar
> 1 orange
> 3 tablespoons crème de cassis liqueur

Put the water, cranberries and sugar in a stainless steel (noncorrosive) saucepan. Using a vegetable peeler, cut several wide strips of zest off the orange. Squeeze the juice from the orange and add the zest and juice to the cranberries. Over medium heat, bring the mixture to a simmer, stirring occasionally until the sugar dissolves. Cook until the cranberries are soft, 10 to 15 minutes. Remove and discard the orange zest strips. Purée the cranberry mixture in a blender or food processor. Push through a strainer to remove the fibrous cranberry skins. Stir in the crème de cassis liqueur. Refrigerate until cold. Pour into an ice cream maker and churn according to the manufacturer's directions. Transfer to a chilled container, cover and freeze until ready to serve.

*Makes about 2 ½ cups sorbet.*

▲ High altitude: This recipe needs no adjustment.

*Opposite, clockwise from lower left: Pear Ginger Sorbet (page 165),*
*Blood Orange Sorbet (page 164), World's Best Almond Biscotti (page 71),*
*Cranberry Cassis Sorbet*

# • Blood Orange Sorbet

*(See photo on page 162)*

Blood oranges have almost magenta red flesh and juice. When churned into sorbet, the color becomes bright sunset orange. If you can't find blood oranges, which are in season from late November through April, make this refreshing sorbet with pink or white grapefruit, or tangerines or tangelos. Alternatively, substitute other orange varieties, such as navel and Valencia.

> 1½ teaspoons grated zest of blood oranges
> 2 cups fresh-squeezed blood orange juice
> ½ cup sugar
> 1 tablespoon orange-flavored liqueur

Put the grated zest and all but ½ cup of the juice in a bowl. Put the remaining juice and the sugar in a stainless steel (noncorrosive) saucepan. Cook on low heat, stirring until the sugar dissolves. Add to the juice and zest and stir in the liqueur. Refrigerate until cold. Pour into an ice cream maker and churn according to the manufacturer's directions. Transfer to a chilled container, cover and freeze until ready to serve.

*Makes about 2⅓ cups sorbet.*

▲ High altitude: This recipe needs no adjustment.

*To measure the sugar ratio in a liquid, pastry chefs sometimes use an instrument called a Baumé scale or Baumé hydrometer, a slim glass tube marked with a graduated scale ranging from 0° to 50°, resembling a thermometer. A Baumé scale is adjusted so it stands up in cold liquids. When the scale sinks to read 16° to 18°, liquid sugar syrup will freeze into silky smooth sorbet. A lower reading means the sorbet will be icy and grainy; a higher reading indicates the sorbet will be too soft and won't set.*

# ● Pear Ginger Sorbet

*(See photo on page 162)*

To check a pear's ripeness, smell it. Put your nose right to the pear; if you breathe the heady fragrance of fruit, it's ripe. Ripe pears should yield to gentle pressure but have no soft spots; however, if there is any dessert in which to use overripe pears, this sorbet is it. The fresh ginger furnishes a gentle piquant heat.

> **1½ cups water**
> **¾ cup sugar**
> **1½ tablespoons fresh-squeezed lemon juice**
> **3-inch piece fresh ginger, washed, unpeeled**
> **3 Bartlett pears, very ripe**
> **2 tablespoons pear liqueur or brandy**

Put the water, sugar and lemon juice in a stainless steel (noncorrosive) saucepan. Cut the ginger into ¼-inch slices and add to the pan. Bring the mixture to a simmer over medium heat, stirring occasionally until the sugar dissolves.

Meanwhile, peel, core and cut the pears into ½-inch slices. Drop the pear slices in the ginger syrup, cover and cook over medium heat until the pears are tender, about 10 minutes.

Remove and discard the ginger slices. Purée the pears and the syrup in a blender or food processor until smooth. Stir in the pear liqueur. Refrigerate until cold. Pour into an ice cream maker and churn according to the manufacturer's directions. Transfer to a chilled container, cover and freeze until ready to serve.

*Makes about 3 cups sorbet.*

▲ High altitude: This recipe needs no adjustment.

# ■ Vanilla Bean Ice Cream

You know you're getting the real thing when vanilla ice cream is speckled with tiny black flecks from vanilla beans. This recipe is basic Vanilla Bean Crème Anglaise with the addition of heavy cream. Serve as a complement to warm fruit pie, or simply with cookies, fresh fruit or your favorite sauce.

> **2 cups whole milk**
> **Half of a vanilla bean**
> **½ cup sugar**
> **8 egg yolks**
> **½ cup heavy cream**

Put the milk in a heavy-bottomed saucepan. Using a small, sharp-bladed knife, cut a lengthwise split in the half vanilla bean. Scrape the tiny seed pods out of the inside of the bean and add the seeds and the bean itself to the milk. Heat almost to a boil. Remove from heat.

Prepare an ice bath: Fill a large bowl with ice and nest another bowl in it. Place a fine sieve over the top bowl. Set aside.

In a medium bowl, whisk the sugar and the egg yolks until smooth. Slowly whisk in the hot vanilla milk. Transfer to a clean saucepan. Cook over medium-low heat, stirring constantly with a wooden spoon, until the custard thickens slightly and coats the back of a spoon; cooking will take 3 to 5 minutes. Do not let the custard boil or you will end up with grainy pieces of cooked egg suspended in sweet milk.

Immediately strain the custard into the ice-nested bowl. Stir occasionally until cold. Stir in the cream. Pour into an ice cream maker and churn according to the manufacturer's directions. Transfer to a chilled container, cover and freeze until ready to serve.

*Makes about 3 cups ice cream.*

▲ High altitude: This recipe needs no adjustment.

*To see if the custard coats the back of a spoon, remove from the heat, but continue to stir. Quickly dip a spoon into the custard and run your finger through the film of custard that remains on the spoon. If your finger trail remains, the custard is done. If custard flows into the trail, cook it a little more and test again.*

*Opposite: Vanilla Bean Ice Cream and (bottom left) Chocolate Espresso Slice and Bakes (page 66)*

# ▪ Tangerine Dream Ice Cream

Remember the orange-flavored ice cream bars called creamsicles? This homemade ice cream is reminiscent of those bars, with its combination of citrus and vanilla. You can, of course, replace the tangerine zest and juice with the same amounts from regular or blood oranges. Sometimes the grated citrus zest gets caught in one big clump as the churning paddle goes around. Since you want each person's scoop to contain the tiny bits of colored zest, stir the churned ice cream to evenly disperse the zest.

> **2 cups whole milk**
> **Half of a vanilla bean**
> **½ cup sugar**
> **6 egg yolks**
> **1 tablespoon grated tangerine zest**✻
> **½ cup fresh-squeezed tangerine juice**
> **2 teaspoons orange-flavored liqueur**

✻ I find the smallest holes on a box grater the most efficient means of grating citrus zest—easier than a hand zester. However, some tangerines have such a thin peel it is difficult to remove the zest. If that is the case, use a knife to remove a strip of peel, scrape away any white pith, and finely mince the zest.

Put the milk in a heavy-bottomed saucepan. Using a small, sharp-bladed knife, cut a lengthwise split in the half vanilla bean. Scrape the tiny seed pods out of the inside of the bean and add the seeds and the bean itself to the milk. Heat almost to a boil. Remove from heat.

Prepare an ice bath: Fill a large bowl with ice and nest another bowl in it. Place a fine sieve over the top bowl. Set aside.

In a medium bowl, whisk the sugar and the egg yolks until smooth. Slowly whisk in the hot vanilla milk. Transfer to a clean saucepan. Cook over medium-low heat, stirring constantly with a wooden spoon, until the custard thickens slightly and coats the back of a spoon; cooking will take 3 to 5 minutes. Do not let the custard boil or you will end up with grainy pieces of cooked egg suspended in sweet milk.

Immediately strain the custard into the ice-nested bowl. Stir in the tangerine zest. Stir occasionally until cold, then refrigerate for at least 2 hours, giving time for the zest's concentrated bouquet to infuse flavor into the custard. Stir in the juice and liqueur. Pour into an ice cream maker and churn according to the manufacturer's directions. Transfer to a chilled container, cover and freeze until ready to serve.

*Makes about 3 cups ice cream.*

▲ High altitude: This recipe needs no adjustment.

# ▪ Cinnamon Ice Cream

Cinnamon sticks bestow a distinct smooth spiciness when infused into a liquid—this ice cream is a beguiling opposition of cold ice cream and the spice's sweet heat. Don't substitute powdered cinnamon here; it will fall short, imparting a dusty essence. Serve with baked apples in any form or roll this ice cream into Chocolate Crêpes.

**2 cups whole milk**
**5 (3-inch) cinnamon sticks**
**½ cup sugar**
**6 egg yolks**
**½ cup heavy cream**

Put the milk in a heavy-bottomed saucepan. Break the cinnamon sticks in half and add to the milk. Heat almost to a boil. Remove from the heat, cover and let steep for at least 30 minutes.

Prepare an ice bath: Fill a large bowl with ice and nest another bowl in it. Place a fine sieve over the top bowl. Set aside.

Bring the cinnamon milk almost to a boil for a second time. Remove and discard the cinnamon sticks.

In a medium bowl, whisk the sugar and the egg yolks until smooth. Slowly whisk in the hot cinnamon-infused milk. Transfer to a clean saucepan. Cook over medium-low heat, stirring constantly with a wooden spoon, until the custard thickens slightly and coats the back of a spoon; cooking will take 3 to 5 minutes. Do not let the custard boil or you will end up with grainy pieces of cooked egg suspended in sweet milk.

Immediately strain the custard into the ice-nested bowl. Stir occasionally until cold. Stir in the cream. Pour into an ice cream maker and churn according to the manufacturer's directions. Transfer to a chilled container, cover and freeze until ready to serve.

*Makes about 3 cups ice cream.*

▲ High altitude: This recipe needs no adjustment.

# ■ Chocolate Spice Ice Cream

This might be the ultimate chocolate ice cream. The spices are a mere hint—so the taster wonders, "Wow, what is that flavor?" Expect the chocolate custard to be very thick before it is churned into a voluptuous frozen fantasy. If you like texture in your ice cream, sprinkle in ¾ cup of grated chocolate (dark, milk or white) after the ice cream has been churned.

**½ cup heavy cream**
**5 ounces bittersweet chocolate, chopped in ½-inch pieces**
**2 cups whole milk**
**Half of a vanilla bean**
**½ cup sugar**
**8 egg yolks**
**2 tablespoons cocoa powder**
**¼ teaspoon ground cinnamon**
**Pinch ground nutmeg**

Heat the cream in a saucepan on medium-low until very hot (do not boil). Remove from the heat. Whisk in the chocolate until the mixture is smooth and glossy. Transfer to a medium bowl and set aside.

Put the milk in a heavy-bottomed saucepan. Using a small, sharp-bladed knife, cut a lengthwise split in the half vanilla bean. Scrape the tiny seed pods out of the inside of the bean and add the seeds and the bean itself to the milk. Heat almost to a boil. Remove from heat.

Prepare an ice bath: Fill a large bowl with ice and nest another bowl in it. Place a fine sieve over the top bowl. Set aside.

In a medium bowl, whisk the sugar and the egg yolks until smooth. Slowly whisk in the hot vanilla milk. Transfer to a clean saucepan. Cook over medium-low heat, stirring constantly with a wooden spoon, until the custard thickens slightly and coats the back of a spoon; cooking will take 3 to 5 minutes. Do not let the custard boil or you will end up with grainy pieces of cooked egg suspended in sweet milk.

Immediately strain the custard into the ice-nested bowl. Stir occasionally until cold. Whisk the custard into the reserved chocolate mixture. Sift in the cocoa powder, cinnamon and nutmeg and whisk until smooth. Pour into an ice cream maker and churn according to the manufacturer's directions. Transfer to a chilled container, cover and freeze until ready to serve.

*Makes about 3 cups ice cream.*

▲ High altitude: This recipe needs no adjustment.

# ■ Kahlúa Milk Chocolate Ice Cream

The connoisseur in me prefers dark chocolate, but my inner child remembers chocolate malted milk shakes. This ice cream is a throwback to younger years but with an added adult nip.

⅓ cup heavy cream
8 ounces milk chocolate, finely chopped
2 cups whole milk
Half of a vanilla bean
¼ cup sugar
8 egg yolks
2 tablespoons coffee liqueur

Heat the cream in a saucepan on medium-low until very hot (do not boil). Remove from the heat. Whisk in the chocolate until the mixture is smooth and glossy. Transfer to a medium bowl and set aside.

Put the milk in a heavy-bottomed saucepan. Using a small, sharp-bladed knife, cut a lengthwise split in the half vanilla bean. Scrape the tiny seed pods out of the inside of the bean and add the seeds and the bean itself to the milk. Heat almost to a boil. Remove from heat.

Prepare an ice bath: Fill a large bowl with ice and nest another bowl in it. Place a fine sieve over the top bowl. Set aside.

In a medium bowl, whisk the sugar and the egg yolks until smooth. Slowly pour in the hot vanilla milk, whisking. Transfer to a clean saucepan. Cook over medium-low heat, stirring constantly with a wooden spoon, until the custard thickens slightly and coats the back of a spoon; cooking will take 3 to 5 minutes. Do not let the custard boil or you will end up with grainy pieces of cooked egg suspended in sweet milk.

Immediately strain the custard into the ice-nested bowl. Stir occasionally until cold. Whisk the custard into the reserved chocolate mixture. Stir in the coffee liqueur. Pour into an ice cream maker and churn according to the manufacturer's directions. Freeze until ready to serve.

*Makes about 3 cups ice cream.*

▲ High altitude: This recipe needs no adjustment.

# ■ Blackberry Ice Cream

It has the bouquet of summer, but you can make this ice cream year-round, using frozen berries. Furthermore, if you replace the blackberries with raspberries or blueberries, you'll create a different, yet still delicious, bright hue and flavor. Pair this fuchsia-shaded ice cream with dark chocolate Deer Valley Double Chocolate Chip Cookies for a winner in the contest of exotic ice cream sandwiches.

**2 cups (about 10 ounces) fresh or frozen blackberries**
**½ cup sugar**
**2 tablespoons fresh-squeezed orange juice**
**2 cups whole milk**
**Half of a vanilla bean**
**½ cup sugar**
**6 egg yolks**
**1 tablespoon crème de cassis liqueur**

Put the berries, sugar and orange juice in a stainless steel (noncorrosive) saucepan. Bring the mixture to a simmer over low heat, stirring occasionally until the sugar dissolves. Continue cooking until the berries are very soft and have released their juice; this will take about 7 minutes with fresh berries, longer if the berries are frozen. Set aside. You should have a little more than a cup of berries and juice remaining.

Put the milk in a heavy-bottomed saucepan. Using a small, sharp-bladed knife, cut a lengthwise split in the half vanilla bean. Scrape the tiny seed pods out of the inside of the bean and add the seeds and the bean itself to the milk. Heat almost to a boil. Remove from heat.

Prepare an ice bath: Fill a large bowl with ice and nest another bowl in it. Place a fine sieve over the top bowl. Set aside.

In a medium bowl, whisk the sugar and the egg yolks until smooth. Slowly whisk in the hot vanilla milk. Transfer to a clean saucepan. Cook over medium-low heat, stirring constantly with a wooden spoon, until the custard thickens slightly and coats the back of a spoon; cooking will take 3 to 5 minutes. Do not let the custard boil or you will end up with grainy pieces of cooked egg suspended in sweet milk.

Immediately strain the custard into the ice-nested bowl. Stir occasionally until cold. In a blender or a food processor, purée the reserved blackberries and their juice with the cold custard. Push through a strainer to remove the blackberry seeds. Stir in the liqueur. Pour into an ice cream maker and churn according to the manufacturer's directions. Transfer to a chilled container, cover and freeze until ready to serve.

*Makes about 3½ cups ice cream.*

▲ High altitude: This recipe needs no adjustment.

*Ice cream sandwiches are a playful, casual treat. Bake the cookies any size you wish—1½ inches to 4 inches in diameter—and freeze them. Use ice cream that has been frozen for at least 2 hours, but allow it to soften a few minutes before assembling the sandwiches—you want the ice cream very cold (not melting), yet pliable enough that the cookies don't break when you press them around the ice cream. Place a generous scoop onto the bottom of one frozen cookie, spread to cover and top with a second frozen cookie. Wrap in plastic wrap and keep frozen until ready to serve. Ice cream sandwiches are best when made several days ahead, allowing the cookies to soften a bit. Cut jumbo ice cream sandwiches in quarters and serve with a small bowl of warm sauce, such as Hot Fudge Sauce or Caramel Sauce. Perfect for dipping!*

# ■ Kadota Fig Ice Cream

Figs, both fresh and dried, are a delicious, not-to-be-overlooked fruit, cultivated mainly in Mediterranean climates. There are more than 100 varieties; dried Kadota figs are fairly light-colored, but the darker Mission figs are more readily available. Fig ice cream makes a fantastic ice cream sandwich, especially when pressed between gingersnap cookies.

**1 cup dried Kadota or Mission figs**
**¼ cup sugar**
**¾ cup water**
**3 tablespoons dark rum**
**2 cups whole milk**
**Half of a vanilla bean**
**⅓ cup sugar**
**6 egg yolks**
**¼ cup heavy cream**

Trim the stem from the figs and cut the fruit into ½-inch pieces. Put them in a stainless steel (noncorrosive) saucepan with the sugar, water and rum. Bring to a simmer on low heat, stirring occasionally until the sugar dissolves. Cover and cook until the figs are soft, 20 to 25 minutes.

Put the milk in a heavy-bottomed saucepan. Using a small, sharp-bladed knife, cut a lengthwise split in the half vanilla bean. Scrape the tiny seed pods out of the inside of the bean and add the seeds and the bean itself to the milk. Heat almost to a boil. Remove from heat.

Prepare an ice bath: Fill a large bowl with ice and nest another bowl in it. Place a fine sieve over the top bowl. Set aside.

In a medium bowl, whisk the sugar and the egg yolks until smooth. Slowly whisk in the hot vanilla milk. Transfer to a clean saucepan. Cook over medium-low heat, stirring constantly with a wooden spoon, until the custard thickens slightly and coats the back of a spoon; cooking will take 3 to 5 minutes. Do not let the custard boil or you will end up with grainy pieces of cooked egg suspended in sweet milk.

Immediately strain the custard into the ice-nested bowl. Stir occasionally until cold. Purée the figs and their syrup with the cold custard in a blender or the work bowl of a food processor. To remove some of the fig seeds, push half of the mixture through a strainer.❈ Stir in the cream. Pour into an ice cream maker and churn according to the manufacturer's directions. Transfer to a chilled container, cover and freeze until ready to serve.

*Makes about 2¾ cups ice cream.*

▲ High altitude: This recipe needs no adjustment.

❈ Too many seeds overwhelm the tongue; you want just enough seeds to recollect fig sandwich cookies from childhood.

# ■ Julie's Caramel Ice Cream

This chilly but so very creamy confection is named for Julie Wilson, Deer Valley's food and beverage director, who loves caramel in any aspect, from rich molten sauce to fluffy caramel whipped cream. In her honor, we once devised a dessert of roasted caramelized pears and this caramel ice cream, adorned with gossamer caramel stars.

> **2 cups whole milk**
> **Half of a vanilla bean**
> **½ cup sugar**
> **2 tablespoons corn syrup**
> **¼ cup water**
> **8 egg yolks**
> **½ cup heavy cream**

Put the milk in a heavy-bottomed saucepan. Using a small, sharp-bladed knife, cut a lengthwise split in the half vanilla bean. Scrape the tiny seed pods out of the inside of the bean and add the seeds and the bean itself to the milk. Heat almost to a boil. Remove from heat.

Prepare an ice bath: Fill a large bowl with ice and nest another bowl in it. Place a fine sieve over the top bowl. Set aside.

In another heavy-bottomed saucepan, over low heat, dissolve the sugar and the corn syrup in the water. Increase the heat to medium-high and cook until the syrup turns a very deep golden caramel, about 5 minutes. While the sugar cooks, move the pan to swirl the sugar and distribute the heat, but do not stir. Remove from the heat. Slowly whisk in the hot vanilla milk. The hot caramel will seize when you add the milk, so return the pan to low heat and stir to melt and incorporate the caramel from the corners of the pan.

In a medium bowl, whisk the egg yolks to lighten. Pour in the hot caramel milk mixture, whisking. Return to the saucepan. Cook over medium-low heat, stirring constantly with a wooden spoon, until the custard thickens slightly and coats the back of a spoon; cooking will take 3 to 5 minutes. Do not let the custard boil or you will end up with grainy pieces of cooked egg suspended in sweet milk.

Immediately strain the custard into the ice-nested bowl. Stir occasionally until the custard is cold. Stir in the cream. Pour into an ice cream maker and churn according to the manufacturer's directions. Transfer to a chilled container, cover and freeze until ready to serve.

*Makes about 2½ cups ice cream.*

▲ High altitude: Caramelization of the sugar may take a little less time.

# ■ Maple Walnut Ice Cream

The first step for this recipe is making walnut brittle candy from the maple syrup, brown sugar and walnuts. This process intensifies the maple flavor and, by hardening the sugars, preserves the scoopable quality of the finished ice cream. The walnut brittle is ground with vanilla custard and churned with heavy cream for a lip-smacking, memorable ice cream.

½ cup maple syrup
¼ cup brown sugar
½ cup walnut pieces, lightly toasted (page 256)
2 cups whole milk
Half of a vanilla bean
⅓ cup sugar
8 egg yolks
½ cup heavy cream

Lightly coat the bottom of a baking sheet with butter. Put the maple syrup and the brown sugar in a medium saucepan; the pan needs to be large enough so the mixture can bubble high yet remain in the pan (not boil up and over the pan). Over medium heat, bring the sugars to a boil and cook 5 to 7 minutes, until they reach a hard-crack stage (300° on a candy thermometer). Move the pan occasionally, swirling the sugars to distribute the heat, but do not stir. Using a wooden spoon, stir in the toasted walnuts, then immediately pour onto the prepared baking sheet. Cool.

Put the milk in a heavy-bottomed saucepan. Using a small, sharp-bladed knife, cut a lengthwise split in the half vanilla bean. Scrape the tiny seed pods out of the inside of the bean and add the seeds and the bean itself to the milk. Heat almost to a boil. Remove from heat.

Prepare an ice bath: Fill a large bowl with ice and nest another bowl in it. Place a fine sieve over the top bowl. Set aside.

In a medium bowl, whisk the sugar and the egg yolks until smooth. Slowly whisk in the hot vanilla milk. Transfer to a clean saucepan. Cook over medium-low heat, stirring constantly with a wooden spoon, until the custard thickens slightly and coats the back of a spoon; cooking will take 3 to 5 minutes. Do not let the custard boil or you will end up with grainy pieces of cooked egg suspended in sweet milk.

Immediately strain the custard into the ice-nested bowl. Stir occasionally until cold. Using your hands, break the maple-sugared walnuts into 1-inch pieces. In a blender or a food processor purée the pieces with the cold custard until the mixture is very smooth. Stir in the cream. Pour into an ice cream maker and churn according to the manufacturer's directions. Transfer to a chilled container, cover and freeze until ready to serve.

*Makes about 3 cups ice cream.*

▲ High altitude: The maple syrup and brown sugar mixture will reach the hard-crack stage at a lower temperature. Test for hard-crack using the cold water method or calculate the correct temperature for your altitude (page 237).

# Odd Stuff

●

Warm Apple Raspberry Crisp

●

Chocolate and Blueberry Bread Pudding

●

Fresh Nectarine Shortcake with Caramel Whipped Cream

■

Gratin of Oranges "Girardet"

■

Cinnamon Poached Pears with Chocolate Truffle Filling

■

Roasted Banana Panna Cotta

■

Mariposa Christmas Pudding with Pinot Noir Sauce

■

Chocolate Casbah Terrine

■

Apple Phyllo Bundles

■

Cherry Berry Best Summer Pudding

■

Francy's Strawberry Napoleons

■

Chocolate Crêpes filled with Cinnamon Ice Cream

◆

Baked Alaska Ali Babas

# Odd Stuff

## Distinctive Desserts, Puddings and Fruit Specialties

We have a tradition of commemorative T-shirts in the bakery. A few years ago, we turned our white cotton shirts into cool, psychedelic attire at a tie-dye party. We covered the tables with layers of old newspapers and protected the floor with painter's drop cloths. Everyone got to fold and tie their own designs and dye a shirt with their favorite colors. That year the shirts said "Life is uncertain, eat dessert first."

The memento T-shirts are a celebration of the busy ski season. We change the back design depending on our muse, but the front pockets on the annual shirts always say "Deer Valley Bakery" and the year. Once we printed the cheat-sheet of measuring equivalents just as we have it posted in the bakery.

        3 teaspoons = 1 tablespoon
        4 tablespoons = ¼ cup
        16 tablespoons = 1 cup
        2 tablespoons = 1 ounce
        4 cups = 1 quart
        16 cups = 1 gallon

Even former bakers can't forget the measurements, they just look at the keepsake shirt in their closet or drawer.

Another edition had a large caricature happy face wearing a chef's toque. It read "Happy Bakers" because one of the kitchen chefs used to chime out "Happy bakers" every time he walked through the bakery. I think he had a hankering for a particularly cute girl, one who was always smiling. We took his joshing to heart and put it on our T-shirts.

At Deer Valley we file our recipes in three-ring notebooks and keep them handy on a shelf above a wooden work table. One of these dark green binders is labeled "Odd Stuff." It contains the recipes for puddings, seasonal fruit specialties and miscellaneous desserts. This chapter, "Odd Stuff," is where you'll find those same recipes—Warm Apple Raspberry Crisp, Chocolate and Blueberry Bread Pudding and Roasted Banana Panna Cotta—the recipes that don't belong anywhere else.

Life is uncertain, eat dessert first. Of course, this mocks what we've been told, "You can't have dessert until you finish your dinner." It breaks the rules. I enjoy rascality and I am a pastry chef, so it makes sense to me. When life is uncertain, eat *these* desserts first.

# ● Warm Apple Raspberry Crisp

Fresh fruit with a streusel-like topping, baked until the top is crisp and the fruit juices are bubbling, this is a marvelous finish to the meal. Fruit crisp may be simple and casual, but it elicits as many "oohs" and "aahs" as the most elaborate of desserts. You can dress it up by baking in individual bowls or gratin dishes. The topping can cover myriad fruits, from ripe, peeled summer peaches to cherries and apricots and pears—whatever your heart desires.

Filling:
**3½ to 4 pounds Granny Smith apples (7 or 8 apples)**
**3 tablespoons unsalted butter**
**⅔ cup firmly packed brown sugar**
**1¼ teaspoons ground cinnamon**
**¼ teaspoon ground nutmeg**
**1 cup fresh or frozen raspberries**

Topping:
**1¼ cups all-purpose flour**
**1 cup sugar**
**12 tablespoons (1½ sticks) cold unsalted butter, cut into pieces**
**⅔ cup old-fashioned rolled oats**
**½ cup coarsely chopped walnuts, optional**

**To make the filling:**
Preheat the oven to 350°. Brush a 9 x 13-inch baking pan with melted butter or spray generously with cooking spray. Peel, core and slice the apples about ½ inch thick.

In a large skillet on medium-high heat, melt the butter. Add the apples and cook, stirring occasionally, until they are barely tender. If there is any excess liquid, pour it off and discard. Stir in the brown sugar, cinnamon and nutmeg, and then the raspberries. Spoon into the prepared pan and set aside while you make the topping.

**To make the topping:**
In a medium bowl, or in the work bowl of a food processor, mix the flour, sugar, butter and oats until crumbly and no butter pieces are visible. The mixture should resemble coarse sand. Stir in the walnuts, if using. Spread evenly over the fruit in the baking pan.

Bake until the topping is lightly browned, 45 to 60 minutes. Serve warm, in shallow bowls, with vanilla ice cream or softly whipped cream.

*Serves 16 to 20.*

▲ High altitude: The crisp may need more baking time.

# • Chocolate and Blueberry Bread Pudding

Just as blueberries complement and balance the chocolate in this creamy pudding, the dessert itself is a match for fruity red wine. In fact, it made its debut at a Fisher family dinner, paired with Fisher Coach Insignia Cabernet Sauvignon. Go the extra step; first bake a batch of Dark Chocolate Bread. Although delicious when put together with white French bread, this dessert is even better made with cubes from an actual chocolate loaf.

**1 loaf Dark Chocolate Bread (page 53) or white French bread**
**1½ cups heavy cream**
**¾ cup whole milk**
**6 ounces bittersweet chocolate, chopped in ½-inch pieces**
**4 eggs**
**¼ cup sugar**
**1 teaspoon vanilla extract**
**¼ teaspoon salt**
**1 cup fresh or frozen blueberries**

**Blueberry Whiskey Sabayon (page 219)**
**Extra blueberries, for garnish**

Preheat oven to 350°. Brush a 1½-quart soufflé dish with melted butter or spray with cooking spray. Trim the crust off the bread. Cut it into ½-inch cubes, yielding about 4 cups of bread cubes. Cover to keep the bread from drying out; set aside.

Stir the heavy cream, milk and chocolate in a saucepan over medium heat until the chocolate melts, about 5 minutes. In a large bowl, whisk the eggs and sugar until smooth. Stir in the chocolate mixture, vanilla and salt.

Put about a third of the bread in the prepared soufflé dish. Sprinkle half of the blueberries on top. Add another third of the bread and follow with the rest of the blueberries and the final third of the bread. Pour the chocolate custard over. Let stand for 10 to 15 minutes so the custard soaks into the bread. Bake until the pudding is set in the center, 55 to 65 minutes.

Serve warm or at room temperature with Blueberry Whiskey Sabayon and fresh blueberries, if desired.

*Serves 10 to 12.*

▲ High altitude: The custard may take longer to set. Continue baking until the custard in the center is jiggly but not runny.

*Juelle Fisher, of Fisher Vineyards in the Mayacamas Mountains near Santa Rosa, California, was raised in Utah and often returns for family visits and ski vacations. Juelle and her husband, Fred, say the key to serving chocolate with Cabernet Sauvignon is insisting on dark bittersweet chocolate and very little sugar.*

# Fresh Nectarine Shortcake with Caramel Whipped Cream

Nectarine skins have a beautiful red blush, and, unlike fuzzy-skinned peaches, you can use the fruit without peeling. Feel free to substitute peaches, or fresh berries, or even plums. To save time but still have the caramel savoriness, sweeten the whipped cream with fine-quality purchased caramel sauce instead of making it yourself.

Shortcake biscuits:
**1 cup all-purpose flour**
**¾ cup cake flour**
**1 tablespoon sugar**
**2 teaspoons baking powder**
**½ teaspoon kosher salt**
**6 tablespoons (¾ stick) cold unsalted butter, cut into ½-inch pieces**
**¾ teaspoon grated orange zest**
**¾ cup whole milk, *plus* 2 tablespoons for glaze**
**½ teaspoon vanilla extract**
**2 teaspoons crystal sugar or granulated sugar (page 256)**

Nectarines:
**1½ pounds (about 4) ripe nectarines**
**¼ cup sugar**
**1 tablespoon peach schnapps or orange-flavored liqueur**
**2 tablespoons fresh-squeezed lemon juice**

Caramel whipped cream:
**1 cup heavy cream**
**¼ cup Caramel Sauce, cold (page 222)**

**Confectioners' sugar to dust, optional**

**To make the shortcake biscuits:**
Preheat oven to 400°. Line a baking sheet with parchment paper or coat lightly with butter or cooking spray. Into a bowl, sift together the flours, the sugar, baking powder and salt. Toss in the butter and the orange zest. Using your fingertips or a pastry blender, rub the butter and flour together until the mixture resembles coarse meal. Add ¾ cup of the milk and the vanilla; stir with a fork just until the mixture comes together in a sticky dough.

Place rough balls of dough, ¼ cup each, onto the prepared pan, leaving 2 inches between each mound. Brush the tops with the remaining 2 tablespoons milk and sprinkle with the crystal sugar. Bake 20 to 25 minutes, until golden brown. Cool.

*Opposite: Fresh Nectarine Shortcake with Caramel Whipped Cream*

**To make the filling and assemble the shortcakes:**
Cut the nectarines in half lengthwise along their natural indentation and pull the halves apart. Remove the pit; you may have to cut it out with a knife. Cut in ½-inch slices. Put the slices in a bowl; sprinkle with the sugar, liqueur and lemon juice. Set aside.

Whip the cold Caramel Sauce with the cream until the cream comes to soft peaks that just hold their shape.

Split the shortcake biscuits in half horizontally. Place the bottom half of each shortcake on a plate and spoon an eighth of the nectarines on each. Add a dollop of the caramel whipped cream. Lean the biscuit top at an angle on the cream and fruit. Dust with confectioners' sugar, if desired.

*Serves 8.*

▲ High altitude: Reduce the baking powder in the shortcake biscuit to 1½ teaspoons.

*Nectarines are a succulent summer treat, but are not a cross between peaches and plums, as many believe. California nectarines harvest from May to August; the Utah crop ripens in September. Depending on the variety, nectarines and peaches are either freestone (the flesh pulls freely from the pit) or clingstone (the flesh adheres to the pit).*

# ■ Gratin of Oranges "Girardet"

For our wedding rehearsal dinner in The Mariposa, Robbie and I chose this dessert, a pleasing contrast of cool marinated oranges set against warm, smooth custard. The recipe comes from Bill Nassikas, who, as the original food and beverage director, helped establish the standard for Deer Valley's exemplary cuisine. The dessert is named for chef Fredy Girardet, who has been called a genius in the kitchen and with whom Bill trained in Switzerland. For their sweetness and lack of seeds, navel oranges are the best choice, though most fresh fruits are good partners with the broiled vanilla and orange liqueur sauce. Serve with a small cookie, such as miniature World's Best Almond Biscotti.

¾ cup sugar
1 tablespoon lemon juice
¼ cup *plus* ½ cup hot water
1 teaspoon grenadine syrup, optional
8 medium oranges
¼ cup heavy cream
⅔ cup (½ recipe) Vanilla Bean Pastry Cream, cold (page 218)
1 tablespoon orange-flavored liqueur❊
2 tablespoons lightly toasted (page 256) ground pistachio nuts, optional

❊ For the most elegant orange flavor use Grand Marnier.

*A splatter screen, used in cooking to keep sizzling grease in the pan, can also protect hands and face from accidental hot caramel splashes. Place the splatter screen over the saucepan of hot caramel and add the liquid through the screen.*

**To marinate the oranges:**

In a saucepan, over low heat, mix the sugar, lemon juice and ¼ cup of the water. Stir occasionally, until the sugar dissolves into a clear syrup. Cover the pan with a stainless steel bowl; as the syrup cooks, water droplets will condense on the bottom of the bowl and wash down the sides of the pan, preventing crystallization of the sugar.

When the syrup begins to darken (5 to 10 minutes), remove the bowl. Continue to cook the syrup over medium-high heat until it turns a deep amber color. Every so often, move the pan to swirl the sugar and distribute the heat, but do not stir.

Remove from the heat and immediately add the remaining ½ cup of water, keeping your hands and face at a distance. Return to the heat and cook the caramel and water a few minutes to dissolve any lumps. Stir in the grenadine, if using. Transfer to a bowl.

With a sharp knife, slice ¼ inch off the top and bottom of each orange. Remove the peel and white pith: With the orange standing on its cut bottom, slice down the sides, following the orange's contour, completely removing the outside white pith as well as the orange peel.

Section all the oranges: Hold an orange in your hand and remove the segments by cutting between the fruit and the membrane. Lift out each orange segment in one piece and drop into the caramel syrup. Squeeze the juice from what is left of the orange into the caramel. Cover and refrigerate at least 2 hours—the orange sections can marinate in this caramel several days.

**To serve:**

Whip the cream until it comes to soft peaks that hold their shape. In a bowl, whisk the Vanilla Bean Pastry Cream until smooth, then whisk in the liqueur. Fold in the whipped cream using the whisk.

Preheat the broiler with the rack about 4 inches below the burner. Strain the orange sections from the caramel marinade. Divide and arrange the sections in a single layer on the bottoms of 6 individual gratin dishes (page 250). (Or arrange the sections in concentric circles on the bottom of 1 large gratin dish). Pour the cream mixture over the oranges, dividing evenly if in separate servings. Place under the broiler for 1 or 2 minutes, cooking until the top is golden brown.

Sprinkle the pistachios, if using, over the middle of each dessert. Serve at once.

*Serves 6.*

▲ High altitude: This recipe needs no adjustment.

*Deer Valley employs a veteran ski instructor, who goes by the nickname Wheaties. From time to time, he begs an orange from the bakery. I don't go out to watch, but I know what he does with the fruit. He stands at the top of the slope and lets it roll out of his hand and down the hill, following the path of gravity. He uses the orange to demonstrate the natural fall line, the ideal direction of ski travel. If the orange survives its ride, Wheaties's class gets a cool, refreshing bite.*

# ■ Cinnamon Poached Pears with Chocolate Truffle Filling

This is an offspring of the classic French dessert, Belle-Hélène, made with poached pears, vanilla ice cream and hot chocolate sauce. In this version, the hollowed pear cores are filled with velvety chocolate cream, the sauce is a reduction of the white wine poaching syrup and the ice cream is optional. To add crunchy texture, I sometimes dip the bottom of each pear in toasted almond slices.

Pears:
**1 orange**
**4 cups water**
**1 cup white wine**
**2 cups sugar**
**6 cinnamon sticks**
**6 pears, almost ripe, but firm**
**1 lemon, halved**

Filling:
**½ cup heavy cream**
**2 ounces semisweet chocolate, chopped in ½-inch pieces**

### To poach the pears:

Cut a 1-inch wide strip of peel from the orange. Scrape off any white membrane, and cut the peel into ¼-inch strips, 2 inches long; or use a channel knife (page 243) to peel off at least 6 strips. These will be the decorative "stems" of the pears.

Squeeze the orange and put its juice, the water, wine, sugar, cinnamon sticks and the orange strips in a large saucepan. Bring to a boil, stirring occasionally until the sugar dissolves. Lower the heat to a simmer.

Peel the pears, keeping them whole. Rub them immediately with the cut lemon to keep them from turning brown. Carefully remove the core so the pears are hollow all the way through. Squeeze the cut lemon's juice into the simmering syrup.

Slip the whole, cored pears into the hot syrup. Cover them with a circle of parchment paper and a small plate as a weight, to keep the pears submerged in the poaching liquid. The pears will jostle and find their place lying down in the liquid.

Simmer for 10 to 15 minutes, or until the pears are barely tender, being careful not to overcook. The poaching time depends upon the ripeness of the pears; the riper the pear, the shorter the poaching time.

Transfer the pears and liquid, including the cinnamon sticks, to a bowl. Pick out the cooked orange strips and set them aside. Cover the pears with the parchment circle and the plate weight, keeping them fully submerged. Refrigerate until cold. They will keep about 5 days in the poaching liquid, with the cinnamon flavor getting stronger each day.

**To make the filling:**

Heat the cream in a small saucepan until it is very hot, but not boiling. Remove from the heat. Whisk the chocolate into the cream until the mixture is smooth and glossy. Put in a clean bowl and refrigerate. This truffle cream will keep up to 5 days.

**To serve:**

Remove the pears from the liquid. Slice a little piece off the bottom of each pear, if needed, so they will stand up on a plate. Strain the liquid into a saucepan and simmer for 20 to 30 minutes, until reduced to about 1⅔ cups.

Whisk the cold truffle cream just until it holds a soft shape. Fill the cavity of each pear, using a pastry bag fitted with a ½-inch plain or star tip. Place each pear on a plate. Drizzle the reduced syrup over the fruit as a glaze and onto the plate as a sauce. Tuck an orange strip in the chocolate to resemble a pear stem. If desired, serve with vanilla ice cream, homemade or purchased.

*Serves 6.*

▲ High altitude: This recipe needs no adjustment.

# ■ Roasted Banana Panna Cotta

Panna cotta is a gelatin-set dessert of Italian origin; the name literally means "cooked cream." This one is flavored with bananas, roasted for stronger essence, mixed into the heavy cream. A crescent-shaped banana half, warm from the broiler, with a crackly crust of brûléed sugar, accompanies the cold, smooth molded cream. This is a marriage made in heaven, further blessed by warm Hot Fudge Sauce.

2 medium firm but ripe bananas
1 cup (8-ounce carton) sour cream
1½ teaspoons fresh-squeezed lemon juice
½ teaspoon vanilla extract
1 teaspoon powdered gelatin
¼ cup cold water
½ cup heavy cream
½ cup sugar

3 bananas to accompany the panna cottas as garnish
3 tablespoons brown sugar
⅔ cup Hot Fudge Sauce (page 214), warm, or purchased fine-quality chocolate syrup

**To make the panna cottas:**
Preheat oven to 350°. Place the 2 bananas, whole and unpeeled, on a baking sheet and bake 20 minutes. Cool. Peel the bananas and purée the soft pulp in a food processor or mash it in a bowl. Push through a strainer to remove pieces of banana that are not smooth. Whisk the sour cream, lemon juice and vanilla into the smooth banana pulp. Set aside.

In a small bowl, sprinkle the gelatin over the cold water and allow to soften about 5 minutes.

In a saucepan over medium heat, bring the cream and sugar just to a boil, stirring until the sugar dissolves. Remove from the heat. Stir in the softened gelatin until it melts into the cream. Whisk the cream and gelatin mixture into the reserved banana sour cream mixture. Pour into 6 (6-ounce) custard cups or ramekins or other small molds, about ½ cup cream per mold. Chill until set, at least 4 hours or overnight.

**To brûlée or caramelize the banana garnish:**
Preheat broiler with the rack about 3 inches from the heat. With the curve of the banana facing toward you, the banana on its side, keeping the bananas in their peel, slice each banana in half lengthwise—similar to splitting a cake before filling and frosting. Arrange the banana halves still in their skin, cut side up, on a baking sheet. Sprinkle brown sugar evenly, about ½ tablespoon on each half. Place under the broiler until the sugar bubbles and begins to turn brown, about 3 minutes; watch carefully to make sure it doesn't burn. Cool 5 minutes.

**To serve:**

Unmold the panna cottas: Dip each mold briefly in hot water and loosen by running the tip of a small, sharp knife around the inside rim. Invert each mold onto a plate.

Gently peel the skin away from the brûléed banana halves. Arrange one half in front of each panna cotta. Drizzle warm Hot Fudge Sauce over the banana and around the bottom of the panna cotta. Serve immediately.

*Serves 6.*

▲ High altitude: This recipe needs no adjustment.

# ■ Mariposa Christmas Pudding with Pinot Noir Sauce

This recipe comes from one of my baking cohorts, Susan Prieskorn, who discovered the recipe when she worked in a large hotel bakery in Frankfurt, Germany. It is a steamed pudding, quite boozy, and very suitable for the snowy months. Pinot Noir wines, with their red berry hint, are my first choice for the sauce, which can be made with any good-tasting dry red wine.

Pudding:
12 tablespoons (1½ sticks) unsalted butter, softened
9 eggs, separated
4 tablespoons *plus* 5 tablespoons sugar
1½ cups ground almonds (about 6 ounces)
1 cup chocolate wafer crumbs (about 20 wafers) or graham cracker crumbs❄
3 tablespoons kirsch
3 tablespoons dark rum
¼ teaspoon cream of tartar

Sauce:
1½ tablespoons cornstarch
⅓ cup *plus* 1⅔ cups Pinot Noir or other dry red wine
¾ cup sugar
1 teaspoon grated orange zest
¼ cup fresh-squeezed orange juice
½ cup dried cranberries

❄ Chocolate wafer crumbs make a dark pudding; with graham cracker crumbs the pudding comes out much lighter in color. I usually use the chocolate crumbs—they are richer, and, as we all know, there's something about chocolate.

**To make the pudding:**
Preheat oven to 350°. Brush a 6-cup or 9-cup fluted center tube mold with melted butter and sprinkle generously with sugar. In a large bowl, using an electric mixer, cream the butter until it is light and fluffy. Add the egg yolks and 4 tablespoons of the sugar; mix well, stopping to scrape the sides and bottom of the bowl. Mix in the almonds, chocolate wafer crumbs, kirsch and rum.

In a clean bowl, whip the egg whites with an electric mixer until foamy. Add the cream of tartar and continue whipping until the whites hold soft peaks. Gradually beat in the remaining 5 tablespoons of sugar, whipping until they hold soft peaks. Stir a third of the whites into the butter mixture, to lighten it; then gently fold in the rest. Spread the batter into the prepared pan.

Cover the mold tightly with a double layer of aluminum foil. Place in a deep roasting pan; pour in very hot water to reach about 2 inches up the outside of the mold. Bake for 70 to 80 minutes, until the pudding is set and springs back when touched with a finger. Cool at least 20 minutes. To unmold, place a serving plate over the mold and invert it, turning the pudding out onto the plate. Serve the pudding warm or at room temperature, cut into slices, with warm Pinot Noir Sauce.

**To make the sauce:**

In a small bowl, dissolve the cornstarch in ⅓ cup of the wine. Put the remaining 1⅔ cups of wine, the sugar, orange zest, orange juice and cranberries in a saucepan. Bring to a simmer over medium heat, stirring occasionally. Stir in the cornstarch mixture and bring to a boil, stirring constantly. Continue to cook about 3 minutes more, until the sauce is clear and slightly thickened.

*Serves 8 to 10.*

▲ High altitude: The pudding may take longer to bake.

*I forged lasting friendships with the other pastry cooks my first year in Deer Valley's bakery. Not only did we work side by side, we skied and hung out together. My mother would say we were "cohorts in crime." Years later, we still have our hands in the batter, so to speak. We keep in touch, by phone and occasional rendezvous, and it's not surprising that our conversation gravitates to baking. If allowed, we could go on for hours. My husband calls it "talking muffin."*

*Muffin talk is a big reason I fly to San Francisco twice a year, to get together with the group Bakers Dozen and exchange ideas with other pastry artists. The Bay Area group has about 300 members and is open to anyone interested in baking. There is free sharing of information and genuine camaraderie—lots of "talking muffin."*

# ▪ Chocolate Casbah Terrine

Halvah is an exotic candy from the Middle East, a soft confection made with crushed sesame seeds. I think chocolate is the perfect foil for the candy's unique nutty flavor and flaky texture, so I invented this dessert of halvah encased in velvety chocolate mousse. Serve with an amaretto-flavored custard sauce.

Terrine:
**6 (1-ounce) squares unsweetened chocolate, chopped in ½-inch pieces**
**4 ounces semisweet chocolate, chopped in ½-inch pieces**
**½ pound (2 sticks) *plus* 4 tablespoons (½ stick) unsalted butter,**
   **cut into pieces**
**½ cup heavy cream**
**7 eggs**
**¾ cup sugar**
**2 tablespoons water**
**1 teaspoon vanilla extract**
**1 pound vanilla-flavored halvah**❈

Sauce:
**1 cup (1 recipe) Vanilla Bean Crème Anglaise (page 224)**
**¼ cup amaretto liqueur**

**To make the terrine:**
Brush a 12 x 4 x 2¾-inch (approximately) rectangular mold or loaf pan (page 250) with melted butter or spray it with cooking spray. The mold should hold about 8 cups liquid volume. Line the mold with plastic wrap, tucking it into the corners and smoothing it so there are few wrinkles.

Melt the unsweetened and semisweet chocolates and ½ pound of the butter in the top of a double boiler, over gently boiling water; the upper pan should not touch the water. Remove from the double boiler but keep the mixture warm and liquid.

Whip the cream until it comes to soft peaks that hold their shape. Refrigerate the whipped cream until needed.

Whisk the remaining 4 tablespoons of butter with the eggs, sugar and water in a medium bowl. Place over gently boiling water; the bowl should not touch the water. Cook, whisking constantly, for 5 to 10 minutes, until the mixture reaches 160° on an instant-read thermometer. Immediately remove from the heat and, with an electric mixer, whip at high speed for about 5 minutes, until cool to touch. Stir in the vanilla.

Whisk the egg mixture into the melted chocolate and butter. Fold in the whipped cream, mixing until no streaks of white remain.

Spread a third of the chocolate batter into the plastic-lined pan. Crumble half of the halvah in a layer on top. Add another layer of chocolate and one of halvah. Finish with the remaining chocolate, scraping to make the batter level with the top of the pan. Depending on the size of your loaf pan, you may end up with a little extra batter. If you

❈ Halvah comes in vanilla, chocolate and marble flavors. It is available in cans, or sometimes in bulk, at stores that specialize in Mediterranean foods. Health food stores often carry packaged bars of halvah. I prefer the taste of Joyva brand.

have some left, pour it into a small mold and save for a snack. Cover and refrigerate the terrine at least 8 hours, or freeze about 3 hours, until firm. You may keep the terrine wrapped in the refrigerator for up to a week or frozen for up to a month.

To unmold, warm the sides and bottom of the pan by dipping the pan in hot water or heating it with a propane torch. Invert onto a serving platter or a foil-covered cardboard rectangle slightly larger than the pan. If the terrine proves reluctant, warm the sides a little more and tap against the pan to release. Peel off the plastic wrap.

**To make the sauce and serve:**
Flavor the Vanilla Bean Crème Anglaise with liqueur. Cut the cold terrine in slices, ½ to ¾ inch thick, using a hot, clean knife for every cut. For a hot, clean knife, dip a long, thin-bladed knife into a pitcher of very hot water and wipe the knife dry. Place each slice on a dessert plate, and ladle about 1 tablespoon of sauce over the edge of each slice.

*Makes 1 (12 x 4-inch) terrine, serves 16 to 20.*

▲ High altitude: This recipe needs no adjustment.

*We make Chocolate Casbah in individual round molds for The Mariposa. Each dessert gets wrapped in dark chocolate embellished with milk-and white-chocolate squiggles, and each is crowned with a chocolate fan, real gold leaf and a fresh raspberry.*

# ■ Apple Phyllo Bundles

Individual packages like these are sometimes called beggar's purses. They really do resemble a drawstring pouch or a sack of coins. You can adapt the technique of enclosing food in phyllo to different fillings, sweet or savory. Try bundles of pears with candied ginger for dessert or purses of wild mushrooms and balsamic caramelized leeks for appetizers. If you want to prepare the bundles ahead, freeze them unbaked, and bake in a preheated oven directly from the freezer.

> 2 pounds (about 4 large) Golden Delicious apples
> 2 tablespoons (¼ stick) *plus* 8 tablespoons (1 stick) unsalted butter
> ½ cup dried cherries or cranberries
> ¼ cup firmly packed brown sugar
> ½ teaspoon ground cinnamon
> ⅛ teaspoon ground nutmeg
> 8 sheets phyllo (page 253)
>
> Confectioners' sugar, to dust
> 1 cup Caramel Sauce, warm (page 222)

Peel and core the apples. Cut them into ½-inch chunks. Melt 2 tablespoons of the butter in a large skillet. Add the apples and cook and stir over medium heat until they are just tender, 5 to 8 minutes. Remove from heat and pour off and discard any excess liquid. Stir in the dried cherries, brown sugar, cinnamon and nutmeg. Let cool.

Preheat the oven to 375°. Line a baking sheet with parchment paper, or brush it lightly with melted butter, or spray with cooking spray. Melt the remaining 8 tablespoons of butter.

Unroll the package of phyllo sheets on a work surface. Cover the sheets with a dampened kitchen towel. Keep them covered while you work so they don't dry out.

Pick up 1 sheet of phyllo, place it on a large cutting board and brush it lightly with melted butter. Repeat, stacking and buttering 4 layers. Using a sharp knife, cut the buttered stack of phyllo in half, crosswise and lengthwise, making 4 rectangles. Put about ½ cup of the apple mixture in the center of each rectangle. Gather up the corners of the rectangles and gently pinch the dough together just above the apple filling. Butter, stack and cut another 4 rectangles; fill and pinch into bundles.

Place all the bundles on the prepared pan. Bake 45 to 50 minutes or until they are a rich golden brown all over. Keep warm in the turned-off oven with the door ajar.

Dust the phyllo bundles with confectioners' sugar. Place each bundle on a plate and drizzle the warm Caramel Sauce generously over the bundles and on the plates.

*Serves 8.*

▲ High altitude: This recipe needs no adjustment.

# ■ Cherry Berry Best Summer Pudding

A gleaming consolidation of summer fruit, this molded red dome is so impressive it's hard to believe that it consists for the most part of berries and white bread. It's also fat-free, a rarity in edible grand finales. You can substitute other berries or eliminate the cherries; but, to ensure the ruby hue, use at least 1 cup of raspberries.

**1 loaf unsliced white bread**❊
**1 teaspoon gelatin, optional**❊❊
**1 tablespoon orange-flavored liqueur**
**¾ cup fresh sweet cherries, stemmed and pitted**
**5 cups fresh raspberries**
**1 cup sugar**
**2 teaspoons fresh-squeezed lemon juice**
**Extra berries or cherries, for garnish**

Line a 1½-quart bowl or mold with plastic wrap so the finished pudding will invert easily. Trim the brown crust from the bread. Cut the loaf into ¼-inch slices, then cut each slice in half on the diagonal. Arrange the bread triangles, slightly overlapping, to cover the bottom and sides of the mold. Cut smaller pieces to fit in any open spaces, lining the bowl all the way to the rim. Press to flatten the bread, making a seamless casing.

If you are using gelatin, sprinkle it over the liqueur in a small bowl and allow to soften about 5 minutes.

Cut the cherries in half and put them in a stainless-steel (noncorrosive) saucepan with the raspberries and sugar. Cook on low heat 5 to 10 minutes, occasionally swirling the pan, until the sugar dissolves and the berries release some of their juice. Remove from heat.

Stir the liqueur (with or without the gelatin) and lemon juice into the warm berries.

With a slotted spoon, put the fruit mixture into the bread-lined bowl. Arrange bread triangles on top, fitting and filling the spaces where fruit shows. Strain the seeds from the extra juice and drizzle half of the juice over the bread. Cover the bread with plastic wrap.

Put a plate that is slightly smaller than the bowl directly on the plastic on top of the pudding, making sure the plate doesn't catch on the bowl. Put something heavy (at least 5 pounds) on top of the plate so it presses down on the pudding. Refrigerate 6 hours or overnight. Refrigerate the remaining half of the juice.

To unmold, remove the weight, plate and plastic wrap. Place a serving plate over the bowl and invert it, turning the pudding out onto the plate. Peel off the plastic wrap. Spoon reserved juice to cover any unsaturated white bread spots. Decorate with fresh berries and cherries, if you have them. Cut into wedges. Serve with sweetened whipped cream, vanilla ice cream or frozen vanilla yogurt, if desired.

*Makes 1 mold, serves 6 to 8.*

▲ High altitude: This recipe needs no adjustment.

❊ Use a sturdy, dense and flavorful white bread. I like to use Stanford Court Sourdough Bread to keep this dessert fat-free; when I'm not worried about the extra calories, I use butter-rich brioche.

❊❊ The tiny amount of gelatin helps bind the fruit and thickens the juice into a sauce, though the recipe works perfectly fine without gelatin.

*Opposite: Cherry Berry Best Summer Pudding*

# ■ Francy's Strawberry Napoleons

This is ethereal pastry—strawberries and vanilla cream layered with crisp, flaky dough. For a change, or when strawberries are out of season, put diced pears in the filling. I use Zinfandel poached pears (page 147) accented with imported plum spread instead of the strawberry preserves. The pears seem jewel-like suspended in the cream. This recipe is a legacy from Francy Royer, another bakery cohort, who taught me much about the art of baking.

½ recipe (about ¾ pound) Classic Puff Pastry Dough❋ (page 229)
1½ cups fresh strawberries, washed and hulled
⅓ cup good-quality strawberry preserves
3 tablespoons orange-flavored liqueur
2½ teaspoons powdered gelatin
1¼ cups (1 recipe) Vanilla Bean Pastry Cream (page 218)
1 cup heavy cream
Confectioners' sugar, to dust

❋ If you don't have time to make the dough from scratch, substitute 2 sheets of purchased puff pastry.

**To bake the puff pastry:**

Preheat the oven to 375°. Line 2 baking sheets with parchment paper. Have ready a wire cooling rack (page 245) to fit each baking sheet, to place on top of the pastry during baking.

With a sharp knife, cut the ½ recipe of Puff Pastry Dough into 2 equal portions; refrigerate one while you roll the other. On a lightly floured surface, roll one portion into an 8 x 10-inch rectangle, less than ⅛ inch thick. Roll the dough onto the rolling pin and transfer it to a prepared baking sheet. Roll the other piece of dough into a rectangle, and transfer to the second baking sheet.

Using a fork, prick each rectangle all over, about an inch apart. Place the cooling racks, upside down, directly on top of the pricked pastry. Bake 20 to 25 minutes on the upper and middle racks of the oven, watching closely and rotating as needed, until the pastry is an overall golden brown color. The pastry will have risen about ½ inch high under the weight of the cooling racks and there will be grill marks from the racks, but the marks are on the side of the pastry that will be turned upside down. Cool.

**To assemble:**

Slice the strawberries in ⅛-inch slices and set aside. Trim the edges of the baked pastry sheets to make them straight and even. Spread the grill-marked top side of each pastry sheet with a thin coat of the strawberry preserves. Set aside.

Pour the liqueur into a small bowl, sprinkle the gelatin over it, and allow to soften, about 5 minutes. Meanwhile, put the pastry cream in a separate medium-size bowl and whisk until smooth. Whip the cream until it comes to soft peaks that hold their shape. Set aside.

Place the bowl of softened gelatin over barely simmering water, and stir until it melts, about a minute. Whisk the melted gelatin into the pastry cream. Immediately whisk in a third of the whipped cream, then fold in the rest. Spread half of this filling on one of the baked pastry sheets spread with strawberry preserves. Scatter the sliced strawberries evenly over the filling. Spread the remaining filling over the strawberries. Invert the second pastry sheet, grill mark and strawberry jam side down, on top of the filling, pressing gently. Refrigerate at least 15 minutes, to allow the gelatin time to set.

**To serve:**
Cut the assembled dessert with a serrated knife, using a sawing motion. To prevent smashing, cut completely through the top layer first before cutting the bottom pastry. Cut in half lengthwise, then crosswise into 5 rectangles, making 10 individual napoleons. Dust generously with confectioners' sugar. The napoleons will keep several hours, refrigerated, but must be served the same day they are made.

*Makes 10 napoleons, about 1¾ inches by 3½ inches.*

▲ High altitude: This recipe needs no adjustment.

*On occasion, due to the differences in temperature, mixtures of pastry cream and gelatin will seize. You can easily salvage the lumpy or stringy filling by placing the bowl over gently boiling water and stirring until the gelatin pieces melt again, even if you have added some of the whipped cream. Know that the mixture needs very little warmth in order for the gelatin to remelt; watch closely and stir gently but constantly until it becomes smooth.*

# ■ Chocolate Crêpes filled with Cinnamon Ice Cream

Whenever you make crêpes, expect to lose at least the first one. The pan has to "season" and so does the crêpe baker. The first few can be for practice anyway—this recipe yields close to 20 crêpes and you only need to fill 12. Once the heat is adjusted and you have polished your technique, making the crêpes will go smoothly.

Since the crêpes themselves are not very sweet, they become a stage for the cold, creamy ice cream and warm Caramel Sauce. You could use fine-quality purchased vanilla ice cream mixed with ground cinnamon, but, if possible, make your own Cinnamon Ice Cream. Your reward will be a spicy zest, impossible to achieve with the ground flavoring.

Crêpes:
**2 eggs**
**1¼ cups** *plus* **¼ cup whole milk**
**¾ cup all-purpose flour**
**¼ cup cocoa powder**
**3 tablespoons sugar**
**Pinch salt**
**2 tablespoons (¼ stick)** *plus* **2 tablespoons (¼ stick) unsalted butter, melted**
**1 teaspoon vanilla extract**

**2½ cups Cinnamon Ice Cream (page 169)**
**1 cup Caramel Sauce, warm (page 222)**
**¼ cup Hot Fudge Sauce (page 214) or purchased chocolate syrup**
**2 tablespoons chopped toasted pine nuts, macadamia nuts or almonds (page 256)**

### To make the crêpes:

Put the eggs, 1¼ cups of the milk, flour, cocoa powder, sugar, salt, 2 tablespoons of the melted butter, and vanilla in a blender and mix until smooth. (Or, whisk the eggs and milk in a bowl, then whisk in the other ingredients.) Refrigerate and let the batter rest for at least an hour.

Cut waxed or parchment paper into about 20 (5-inch) squares. Set aside. Whisk the remaining ¼ cup of milk into the crêpe batter. Heat a 6-inch crêpe pan or skillet over medium-high heat and brush it lightly with a bit of the remaining 2 tablespoons of melted butter. Pour about 2 tablespoons of batter into the pan and immediately tilt and rotate the pan so the batter spreads evenly on the bottom. Cook 30 to 60 seconds, until the top side of the crêpe is dry, not raw. Lift the crêpe and turn it over with a spatula or your fingers. Cook the other side for about 30 seconds, and slide the crêpe out onto one of the parchment squares. Cook and stack the crêpes until you have used up the batter, layering parchment squares between each crêpe to keep them from sticking. Wrap in plastic and refrigerate until cold. The crêpes can be kept up to a week before filling.

**To fill the crêpes:**

Arrange 12 crêpes, each on a parchment square, in a single layer on a work surface. Peel the crêpes from the parchment so they will be easy to roll when filled, but place them back on the squares. The side that cooks first is usually prettier and should be the outside for serving; with that side down, the crêpes are ready to fill.

Beat the Cinnamon Ice Cream with an electric mixer until it is smooth but still very cold. Dollop 2 spoonfuls of ice cream in a rough line down the center of each crêpe, filling all the crêpes first, so you don't have to set the spoon down in between dollops. Working quickly so the ice cream does not have time to melt excessively, roll each crêpe around the ice cream and place them seam-side down on a large plate or baking sheet. Place the plate with the crêpes in the freezer until the ice cream is again firm. If you are not serving the crêpes the same day, tightly wrap the filled crêpes in plastic wrap, 2 to a package, and freeze up to 2 weeks.

**To serve:**

Ladle 2 heaping tablespoons of the warm Caramel Sauce onto a plate. Place 2 filled crêpes in the center of each plate. Drizzle Hot Fudge Sauce over the crêpes and sprinkle with the toasted nuts.

*Makes 12 crêpes, serves 6.*

▲ High altitude: This recipe needs no adjustment.

*One autumn we served a whimsical dessert for the Park City Cigar and Spirit Society's annual "smoker." Each plate included one Cinnamon Ice Cream–filled chocolate crêpe made to look like a cigar. The crêpe was banded in white chocolate embossed with our deer-head logo and rested in a chocolate "ashtray," with chocolate mousse and chocolate shaving "ashes." Thin caramel structures poked up like smoke and, to complete the fantasy, we made shortbread cookies to imitate matchbooks.*

# ◆ Baked Alaska Ali Babas

Silver Lake pastry chef Wallace Rockwell and I were testing a couple of desserts for The Mariposa when we hit upon this serendipitous combination. Why not crown little rum-soaked baba cakes with ice cream and meringue? The resulting dessert suggests a turbaned head. It is a luscious, showy balance of texture and temperature that we named after Ali Baba, a character in *The Thousand and One Nights*. Allow ample space in the freezer; once the ice cream balls have their meringue topping, they are "ding sensitive." Prepare all the components ahead, but assemble the desserts just before serving.

Babas:
**3 tablespoons dried currants or chopped dark raisins**
**3 tablespoons chopped dried cherries or cranberries**
**3 tablespoons chopped dried apricots**
**3 tablespoons hot water**
**3 tablespoons dark rum**
**1 teaspoon active dry yeast**
**3 tablespoons warm water (105° to 115°)**
**1⅔ cups all-purpose flour**
**1 teaspoon sugar**
**1 teaspoon salt**
**3 eggs, lightly beaten**
**8 tablespoons (1 stick) unsalted butter, softened, cut into 6 pieces**

Rum soaking syrup:
**¾ cup water**
**1 cup sugar**
**¼ cup fresh-squeezed orange juice**
**2 tablespoons fresh-squeezed lemon juice**
**¼ cup dark rum**
**Leftover liquid from the dried fruit marinade (above)**

Meringued ice cream:
**2½ cups Vanilla Bean Ice Cream (page 167) or purchased fine-quality vanilla ice cream**
**4 egg whites (about ½ cup)**
**¾ cup sugar**
**4 teaspoons water**
**¼ teaspoon cream of tartar**

**Sliced fresh fruit or berries and dried cherries, for garnish**

**To make the babas:**
Put the currants, cherries and apricots in a bowl with the hot water and rum; let them macerate while you prepare the dough.

In a large bowl, or in the work bowl of a heavy-duty electric mixer, sprinkle the yeast over the warm water, stirring to dissolve; let stand about 5 minutes.

Add the flour, sugar, salt and eggs. If using a machine, fit the bowl with the paddle attachment, and beat on a low speed. Otherwise, use a wooden spoon and beat for a minute, then turn it out onto a clean surface, and use a scraper to gather the dough up, then slap it down, scraping and slapping to beat the soft and sticky dough. Beat the dough about 5 minutes, stopping to scrape the sides and bottom of the bowl if you are using a machine. Take another 5 minutes to gradually beat in the soft butter, one piece at a time, making sure each piece is absorbed before adding the next. The dough will be very soft, but smooth and elastic.

Place in an oiled bowl at least twice the volume of the dough, cover, and let rise at room temperature until doubled in size, 45 minutes to an hour.

Brush small bucket-shaped "baba" molds or standard-size muffin tins generously with melted butter or spray with cooking spray. Preheat the oven to 350°.

Deflate the dough with your fist. Drain the macerated dried fruit, reserving the liquid to add to the rum soaking syrup. Work the fruit into the dough until it is uniformly distributed. Divide the dough into 8 equal portions. Place 1 portion in each of the prepared molds or tins. Cover and let rise at room temperature until almost doubled in size, 30 to 35 minutes.

Bake until the babas are light golden brown, 30 to 35 minutes. Unmold and let cool. Babas can be kept frozen up to 2 weeks; thaw before soaking in syrup.

**To make the soaking syrup:**
Heat the water and sugar in a small saucepan until the sugar dissolves. Add the orange and lemon juices, rum and reserved macerating liquid. Keep warm.

**To make the meringued ice cream:**
Line a baking sheet with parchment or waxed paper or oil it lightly. Put the baking sheet in the freezer for a few minutes so it is very cold. Scoop 8 portions of Vanilla Bean Ice Cream onto the prepared baking sheet, keeping the scoops at least 3 inches apart. Freeze until the ice cream is very firm.

Whisk the egg whites, sugar, water and cream of tartar in a bowl. Place over a pan of gently boiling water; the bowl should not touch the water. Cook, whisking constantly for 3 to 5 minutes, until the mixture reaches 160° on an instant-read thermometer. Remove from heat. With an electric mixer, whip until the meringue is cool and forms stiff peaks.

Put the meringue into a pastry bag fitted with a medium star tip and pipe the meringue decoratively over the frozen ice cream scoops, covering them completely. (Or, cover the frozen ice cream scoops with the meringue, lifting the meringue with the back of a spoon to create decorative swirls.) Immediately return to the freezer. Make sure the ice cream is as firm as possible before browning the meringue.

Brown the meringue with a propane torch by moving the flame back and forth about 4 inches away until the meringue is golden brown all over. (Or, preheat a broiler and, watching carefully, broil until the meringue is golden brown, 30 to 40 seconds.) Immediately return to the freezer.

**To assemble and serve:**

Cut the rounded dome off the top of each baba. Discard the dome portion. Immerse the babas, a few at a time, in the rum soaking syrup for about a minute, turning them so they can absorb the syrup like a sponge. Strain the leftover soaking syrup; set aside.

Place each baba, cut side up, on a plate. Place a meringued ice cream scoop on top of each and spoon some of the soaking syrup around. Garnish with sliced fresh fruit or berries and dried cherries, if desired.

*Serves 8.*

▲ High altitude: The baba dough will rise faster; check sooner for doubling.

# Fundamental Formulas

- Simple Vanilla Glaze
- Apricot Glaze
- Simple Syrups
- Strawberry Sauce
- Butter Streusel
- Chocolate Ganache
- Chocolate Honey Glaze
- Candied Cranberries
- Candied Citrus Peel
- Hot Fudge Sauce
- Basic Sourdough Starter
- Chocolate Leaves
- Cream Cheese Pie Dough

- Vanilla Bean Pastry Cream
- Blueberry Whiskey Sabayon
- Lemon Curd
- Orange Curd
- Caramel Sauce
- Peanut Brittle
- Vanilla Bean Crème Anglaise
- Butter Pie Dough
- Sweet Tart Dough
- Meringue Mushrooms
- Meringue Buttercream
- Classic Puff Pastry Dough

# Fundamental Formulas

## Letty's Recipe for Skiing

For those who share my appetite for skiing, and for those who bake but don't ski, I include this personal recipe for my favorite winter sport. The formula is rated for all levels of skiers, from never-evers through experts.

**1 or 2 skis or other sliding device with binding attachment for boots**
**1 pair boots**
**2 ski poles, optional**
**1 body, any size**
**Clothing**
**Snow**
**Gravity**
**Relaxation**
**Balance**
**Rhythm**
**Practice**
**Aggressiveness**
**Positive attitude**

Become familiar with the sliding devices, boots and poles, if using. Be sure to understand the basics of how each item will be used.

Dress body in clothing suitable for wintry weather. Fit in boots. Attach boots to sliding device(s), and place poles in hands. Place on snow or other sliding surface with 5- to 50-degree pitch, depending on experience. Apply minimum gravity; more can be added later to taste. Slide in a downward direction.

Relax. Once relaxation takes place, balance follows. Feel the balance on skis from finding the precise body stance that allows relaxation. Add rhythm, moving easily from one turn to the next. Rhythm is necessary in order for sliding to develop into skiing. Blend the body, snow and gravity with relaxation, balance and rhythm. Practice as often as possible.

After abundant practice and on-snow experience, add approximately one part aggressiveness for each part relaxation. Blend relaxation and aggressiveness as needed, appropriate to conditions and level of experience.

Happily seek different snow conditions as skiing expertise develops. Keep a positive attitude—skiing excellence has more to do with the skier than the recipe.

*Yields one skier.*

▲ High altitude: This recipe works very well at high altitudes.

*In skiing, relaxation is the most important ingredient, without which the skiing experience will fail. Just as bread will not rise without yeast, skiing will not occur without relaxation.*

# • Simple Vanilla Glaze

Drizzle this glaze over Beth's Tea Ring or Whole Wheat Cinnamon Brioche Rolls. If you prefer a whiter glaze, replace the water with milk.

**1 cup confectioners' sugar**
**4 teaspoons water**
**½ teaspoon vanilla extract**

Whisk the sugar, water and vanilla in a bowl until smooth.

*Makes about ½ cup.*

▲ High altitude: This recipe needs no adjustment.

# • Apricot Glaze

Apricot Glaze gives a final professional touch to a fruit tart; it brightens the garnish on top of cakes and it dresses up yeasted sweet breads like Beth's Tea Ring. Sometimes I don't strain the melted preserves, so the glaze has a more rustic finish.

**½ cup good-quality apricot jam or preserves**
**2 tablespoons water**

Melt the jam and the water in a small saucepan over medium-high heat, stirring every so often. Strain it through a sieve, then return to the heat and cook just until the glaze begins to bubble. Apply to desserts and breads using a pastry brush.

*Makes about ½ cup.*

▲ High altitude: This recipe needs no adjustment.

# ● Simple Syrups

A dissolved sugar syrup used to moisten cakes, Simple Syrup can be flavored with liqueur, fruit purée or extract to accent or complement the cake. Brush Orange Simple Syrup on orange-flavored cakes and Coffee Simple Syrup on chocolate cakes.

Plain Simple Syrup
**½ cup sugar**
**½ cup water**

Heat the sugar and water in a small saucepan, gently swirling the pan until the sugar dissolves. Cook just until the syrup is clear; do not boil. Cool.

*Makes ¾ cup.*

▲ High altitude: This recipe needs no adjustment.

Orange Simple Syrup
**½ cup fresh-squeezed orange juice**
**½ cup sugar**

Heat the orange juice and sugar in a small saucepan, stirring until the sugar dissolves. Cool.

*Makes ¾ cup.*

▲ High altitude: This recipe needs no adjustment.

Coffee Simple Syrup
**½ cup hot coffee**
**½ cup sugar**

Mix the sugar into the hot coffee, stirring until the heat of the coffee melts the sugar. Cool.

*Makes ¾ cup.*

▲ High altitude: This recipe needs no adjustment.

# • Strawberry Sauce

You may use frozen, thawed strawberries or replace the strawberries with raspberries to make another red fruit sauce.

> **2 cups strawberries, washed, hulled and sliced**
> **¼ cup sugar**
> **2 teaspoons fresh-squeezed lemon juice**
> **1 tablespoon orange-flavored liqueur**

In a blender or a food processor, purée the strawberries with the sugar, lemon juice and liqueur. Strain through a fine sieve to remove the seeds. Refrigerate.

*Makes about 1½ cups.*

▲ High altitude: This recipe needs no adjustment.

# • Butter Streusel

I think all muffins need something sprinkled on top, maybe hinting of what's in the muffins or just to add visual interest. This is a crunchy topping for looks and flavor.

> **¼ cup firmly packed brown sugar**
> **¼ cup all-purpose flour**
> **½ teaspoon cinnamon**
> **2 tablespoons unsalted butter, room temperature**

By hand, with a fork or a pastry blender, mix the brown sugar, flour, cinnamon and butter until crumbly and well blended. Refrigerate and use as needed.

*Makes about ¾ cup.*

▲ High altitude: This recipe needs no adjustment.

# • Chocolate Ganache

Ganache (gah-NOSH) is a bakery basic, a multipurpose cream of French origin. Use it to fill and frost cakes as well as roll into rich chocolate truffles.

**1¼ cups heavy cream**
**3 tablespoons unsalted butter**
**1 pound semisweet or bittersweet chocolate, chopped in ½-inch pieces**

Put the cream and butter in a large saucepan. Heat on medium-low until the butter melts and the cream is very hot (do not boil). Remove from heat. Whisk about one-fourth of the chocolate into the pan until it melts. Add the remaining chocolate and whisk until all of the chocolate has melted and the ganache is smooth and glossy. Transfer to a clean bowl and set aside to cool. You can keep ganache, covered and refrigerated, for up to 3 weeks.

*Makes about 3 cups.*

▲ High altitude: This recipe needs no adjustment.

# ● Chocolate Honey Glaze

Quick and easy to make, this is an attractive finish for cakes and Honey Walnut Tart.

**12 ounces bittersweet chocolate, cut in ½-inch pieces**
**8 tablespoons (1 stick) unsalted butter, cut in ½-inch pieces**
**2 tablespoons honey**
**1 tablespoon fine-quality walnut oil, optional (see note, page 40)**

Place the chocolate, butter and honey in the top of a double boiler, over gently boiling water; the upper pan should not touch the water. When the chocolate and butter are almost melted, remove from the heat. Stir gently with a wooden spoon until smooth. Stir in the walnut oil, if using. This glaze can be made several days ahead and held at room temperature or refrigerated. To reheat, place in the top of a double boiler until almost remelted. Remove from the heat and stir gently.

*Makes about 1 ½ cups.*

▲ High altitude: This recipe needs no adjustment.

# ● Candied Cranberries

Cranberries, of course, are too tart to eat out of hand. And if you cook them with sugar, as for cranberry sauce, they burst and lose their round shape. This method sweetens the cranberries, yet preserves them whole. Use as a holiday garnish on Tiramisù Yule Log or Cranberry Cassis Sorbet.

**⅔ cup sugar**
**½ cup water**
**1 cup cranberries, fresh or frozen**

In a small saucepan, bring the sugar and water to a simmer. Meanwhile, put the cranberries in the top of a double boiler over gently boiling water; the upper pan should not touch the water. Pour the sugar syrup over the cranberries. Cover the cranberries and syrup and cook about 40 minutes, checking to make sure there is always water in the bottom of the double boiler. Remove from the heat. Cool, then refrigerate for at least 3 days. Drain the cranberries just before using. If desired, roll them in granulated sugar and allow to dry.

*Makes about 60 candied cranberries.*

▲ High altitude: This recipe needs no adjustment.

# • Candied Citrus Peel

*(See photo on page 110 for Candied Lemon Peel)*

Easy and elegant. To make bigger pieces of candy, cut the strips wider, ½ inch to 1 inch. For a pleasing contrast of flavors, dip an end of each candied peel in melted chocolate.

**1 whole citrus fruit (lemon, lime, orange or grapefruit)**
**½ cup sugar**
**⅔ cup water**

Peel the rind off the fruit and scrape away any white membrane. Cut into ¼-inch strips. A channel knife (page 243) is the express tool for making these strips.

Put the citrus peel strips in a stainless steel (noncorrosive) saucepan, cover with water, and bring to a boil. Drain. Repeat this blanching procedure once; it takes the bitterness out of the peel. Drain and reserve the blanched peel.

Squeeze the juice from the fruit and strain it into the saucepan.✻ Add the sugar and water. Cook on low heat until the sugar dissolves and the syrup is clear. Add the blanched peel and cook until the strips are tender and translucent, about 30 minutes. Store the candied citrus strips in the syrup, covered and refrigerated. Drain on paper towels just before using.

*Makes 15 to 30 strips, depending on the size of the fruit.*

▲ High altitude: This recipe needs no adjustment.

✻ If you are using the citrus juice for another recipe such as Lemon Curd, candy the peel using only the sugar and water.

# • Hot Fudge Sauce

This chocolate sauce walks down the aisle with anything vanilla and makes a winsome bride in marriage with banana-flavored desserts. We use it for the chocolate drizzle design underneath individually plated Chocolate Snowballs.

> 3 tablespoons unsalted butter
> 2 (1-ounce) squares unsweetened chocolate
> 2 tablespoons cocoa powder
> 1 (5-ounce) can evaporated milk※
> ⅔ cup sugar
> ½ teaspoon vanilla

Melt the butter and chocolate in the top of a double boiler, over gently boiling water; the upper pan should not touch the water. Whisk in the cocoa powder; set aside.

Heat the milk and the sugar in a small saucepan over medium heat, stirring until the sugar dissolves. Bring just to a boil, then whisk into the chocolate mixture. Stir in the vanilla, and whisk until smooth.

Keep the sauce warm if you are serving it in the next hour; otherwise, refrigerate it up to 2 weeks and gently reheat just before serving.

*Makes about 1 cup sauce.*

▲ High altitude: This recipe needs no adjustment.

※ You can replace the evaporated milk with ½ cup of heavy cream; you may prefer the flavor when made with cream. I like the taste of evaporated milk and I keep it in my pantry; I don't always have heavy cream on hand, unless I've purchased it for another recipe.

# • Basic Sourdough Starter

It is sort of a catch-22; in order to make this recipe, you must first obtain some sour-dough starter, from friends or family, wholesale or retail, by hook or by crook.

**2 cups sourdough starter**※
**1 cup chlorine-free water**
**1 cup bread flour**

Stir the sourdough starter, water and flour in a medium glass, ceramic or plastic bowl until smooth. Cover tightly, and let sit at room temperature overnight.

*Makes about 3 ¼ cups starter, enough to make 2 loaves of bread and have some left to replenish.*

▲ High altitude: This recipe needs no adjustment.

※ Sourdough starter is a natural yeast living in a mixture of flour and water. It adds flavor and leavening power to bread and must be kept alive through feeding and care. You can obtain sourdough starter from friends or family. You can often purchase dried and packaged sourdough culture at natural food stores, or King Arthur Flour Baker's Catalog sells a 250-year-old starter by mail (page 257). Fleischmann's has a combo packet of yeast with sourdough starter on the market. It is also possible to make sourdough starter yourself, following instructions in a comprehensive bread baking book.

Once you have obtained a starter, you need to feed it so it stays alive and the natural wild yeasts can multiply. It's a bit like having a pet, but not as demanding. Feed your starter at least every 2 weeks, either when you are using some of it to bake, or if it is just hanging out in your refrigerator.

To feed or replenish your starter, add equal amounts of bread flour and chlorine-free bottled spring or filtered water. Cover with plastic wrap and let sit at room temperature 12 to 24 hours. If you are not using your starter every day, store it, covered, in the refrigerator. Be sure to feed your starter the day before baking to activate flavor and natural yeast, especially if you haven't used it in a while. If you need more than 3 cups of starter (the approximate yield of this basic recipe), increase the amounts of flour and water equally when you feed it.

A few caveats: Use glass, crockery or plastic to store sourdough starter. Do not use a metal container because the sourdough acids can react with the metal. Use clean utensils and bowls. Keep commercial yeast away from your starter—you can add yeast to your sourdough bread, but don't add yeast to the "mother" starter. Dormant, refrigerated starter may have a layer of clear liquid on top; this is normal, just stir the liquid back into the starter.

# • Chocolate Leaves

Make these to accompany Tiramisù Yule Log or any simple frosted cake. You can also make white chocolate leaves following the same procedure.

**4 ounces semisweet chocolate, cut in ½-inch pieces**
**8 to 10 fresh, nontoxic leaves**❋

Wipe the leaves with a damp paper towel and set aside to dry. Melt the chocolate in the top of a double boiler, over gently boiling water; the upper pan should not touch the water.

Hold a leaf by its stem, letting the shiny top of the leaf rest on your palm or other fingers. Carefully, using the back of a spoon, coat the underside of each leaf with chocolate, spreading it about the thickness of the leaf itself or slightly thicker. Take care not to drip chocolate onto the front of the leaf; wipe off any overflow with your fingers. Place the leaves on a baking sheet and refrigerate until the chocolate hardens, about 15 minutes. Working quickly, carefully peel the real leaf away from the chocolate leaf. Refrigerate the chocolate leaves until needed.

*Makes 8 to 10 chocolate leaves.*

▲ High altitude: This recipe needs no adjustment.

❋ Lemon or camellia leaves are good choices. Ask your florist to order them.

# • Cream Cheese Pie Dough

When I say the word "pie" to someone, it often prompts the comment, "That's the one thing I can't do—make a perfect crust." If you feel you can't make a decent pie dough, try this recipe. I think it is one you can depend on.

**6 tablespoons (¾ stick) cold unsalted butter**
**1 (3-ounce) package cream cheese**
**1 teaspoon sugar**
**Pinch salt**
**¾ cup all-purpose flour**

Beat the butter in the bowl of an electric mixer until it is smooth. Add the cream cheese, sugar and salt. Beat well, stopping to scrape the sides and the bottom of the bowl. Add the flour and mix until the dough comes together, scraping again. Gather the dough and form into a flattened 4-inch ball. Wrap in plastic wrap and refrigerate at least 1 hour, or freeze up to 2 months.

*Makes about 9 ounces of dough, enough for 1 (9-inch) pie.*

▲ High altitude: This recipe needs no adjustment.

# ■ Vanilla Bean Pastry Cream

Indispensable in the pastry kitchen, this custard is the basis for countless desserts. We keep it on hand to fill Phyllo Fresh Fruit Tarts, cream pies, eclairs and Francy's Strawberry Napoleons. For a mousse-like sauce, as in Gratin of Oranges Girardet, lighten pastry cream with whipped cream. Add gelatin to pastry cream and whipped cream to make a stable cake filling.

> **1 cup whole milk**
> **Quarter of a vanilla bean**
> **2 egg yolks**
> **⅓ cup sugar**
> **¼ cup all-purpose flour**

Put the milk in a heavy-bottomed saucepan. Using a small sharp-bladed knife, cut a lengthwise split in the quarter vanilla bean. Scrape the tiny seed pods out of the inside of the bean and add the seeds and the bean itself to the milk. Heat almost to a boil. Remove from heat.

In a medium bowl, whisk the egg yolks and sugar. Be sure they are well mixed before adding the flour. Whisk in the flour, making a very thick paste. Slowly whisk in the hot vanilla milk. Strain back into the saucepan. If the pan has a film on the bottom from heating the milk, use a clean pan.

Over medium-low heat, bring the custard to a gentle boil, stirring constantly with a wire whisk. Be sure the whisk scrapes the pan bottom with every stroke, to prevent sticking and scorching. Cook until the cream is very thick, whisking vigorously, about 1 more minute.❋ Transfer to a small, clean bowl. Cover the surface with plastic wrap, so it touches the hot pastry cream, to prevent a skin from forming. Refrigerate. Pastry cream can be kept refrigerated up to 3 days.

*Makes about 1¼ cups.*

▲ High altitude: This recipe needs no adjustment.

**Variations:** For coffee-flavored pastry cream, add 1 teaspoon instant espresso coffee powder dissolved in 1 teaspoon hot water to the hot pastry cream. To make chocolate-flavored pastry cream, stir approximately ⅓ cup of melted dark chocolate into the hot pastry cream.

❋ This makes a very stiff pastry cream, one that holds a shape. The cream should cling to the whisk and fall in a dollop when lifted. If it flows off, it's not cooked enough and will be thin and taste of flour.

# ■ Blueberry Whiskey Sabayon

Sabayon is a mousse-like dessert sauce, the French name for the fluffy Italian zabaglione made with sweet marsala wine. Sabayon has 3 primary ingredients: egg yolks, sugar and alcohol. At Deer Valley we change the basic recipe all the time, begetting flavored sabayons to complement a variety of desserts. In this recipe I've added blueberries to harmonize with Chocolate Blueberry Bread Pudding; I've also turned it into a cold sabay-on by folding whipped cream into the chilled custard base. To accompany chocolate nut torte, make sabayon with dark rum. Or prepare sabayon incorporating white wine or champagne to use as a topping for fresh fruit.

½ cup blueberries, fresh or frozen
2 tablespoons *plus* 2 tablespoons sugar
2 egg yolks
2 tablespoons bourbon whiskey (we use Jack Daniels)
½ cup heavy cream, whipped

Cook the blueberries with 2 tablespoons of the sugar in a stainless steel (noncorrosive) saucepan over low heat, stirring until the sugar dissolves. Continue cooking until the berries are very soft and have released most of their juice, 5 to 8 minutes.

Place the cooked blueberries and juice, the egg yolks, the remaining 2 tablespoons of sugar and the whiskey in the top of a double boiler. Place over gently boiling water; the upper pan should not touch the water. Cook, whisking often, until the custard has thick-ened and reaches 160° on an instant-read thermometer, about 10 minutes.

Prepare an ice bath: Fill a large bowl with ice and nest the bowl of cooked blueberry mixture in it. Whisk the mixture until it is cold. You can refrigerate this sabayon base, covered, for up to 6 days. Before serving, fold in the whipped cream.

*Makes about 1½ cups.*

▲ High altitude: This recipe needs no adjustment.

# ■ Lemon Curd

Lemon Curd is English in origin, served with tea or for breakfast as a spread on toast, biscuits or scones. Be sure to grate the zest before juicing the lemons. If you are planning to make Candied Lemon Zest, which is a fitting garnish for desserts made with Lemon Curd, cut strips of lemon peel also before juicing. You will need 2 to 3 lemons for the curd, depending on the fruit's juiciness.

> **2 teaspoons grated lemon zest**
> **½ cup fresh-squeezed lemon juice**
> **6 egg yolks**
> **⅔ cup sugar**
> **6 tablespoons (¾ stick) unsalted butter, cut into pieces**

Place all ingredients in the top of a double boiler. Place over gently boiling water; the upper pan should not touch the water. Cook, whisking often, until the curd thickens, 10 to 15 minutes. Transfer to a clean container. Cover the surface with plastic wrap, so it touches the hot curd, to prevent a skin from forming. Refrigerate. You can keep Lemon Curd refrigerated for up to a week. It also freezes very well.

*Makes about 1 ½ cups.*

▲ High altitude: The curd may take approximately 5 minutes longer to thicken.

*Always save surplus egg whites—keep them in a (very clean) container in the freezer. Thaw by placing the container in a warm (but not too hot) water bath, until the amount needed has liquefied. For recipes, 1 egg white weighs about 1 ounce and measures about 2 tablespoons.*

# ■ Orange Curd

Orange Curd is a variation of lemon curd and both are Deer Valley bakery staples, almost as important as pastry cream. We fold in whipped cream to lighten and use it to fill miniature tartlets or we stabilize the cream and curd with gelatin for a nectarous cake filling, as for Orange Almond Wedding Cake.

**2 teaspoons grated orange zest**
**½ cup fresh-squeezed orange juice**
**3 tablespoons fresh-squeezed lemon juice**
**9 egg yolks**
**⅔ cup sugar**
**8 tablespoons (1 stick) unsalted butter, cut into pieces**

Place all ingredients in the top of a double boiler. Place over gently boiling water; the upper pan should not touch the water. Cook, whisking often, until the curd thickens, 10 to 15 minutes. Transfer to a clean container. Cover the surface with plastic wrap, so it touches the hot curd, to prevent a skin from forming. Refrigerate. You can keep Orange Curd refrigerated for up to a week. It also freezes very well.

*Makes about 2¼ cups.*

▲ High altitude: The curd may take approximately 5 minutes longer to thicken.

# ■ Caramel Sauce

Caramel Sauce is extremely versatile. It is an ideal accent for many desserts, from ice cream to warm-from-the-oven apple pie. It keeps refrigerated for several weeks, and is easy to reheat. Use it to make caramel whipped cream (page 183), a fashionable change from everyday sweetened whipped cream.

**½ cup sugar**
**1 teaspoon fresh-squeezed lemon juice or water**
**1 cup heavy cream**

Mix the sugar and lemon juice in a heavy saucepan, until it resembles wet sand. Cook, stirring constantly with a wooden spoon, over medium-high heat. After a few minutes, the sugar will begin to melt; continue stirring until any lumps dissolve and the mixture turns a deep caramel color, 4 to 6 minutes. Remove from the heat and immediately stir in a little of the cream. The hot caramel will seize when you add the cold cream but will melt again as it cooks. Return the pan to low heat and gradually stir in the remaining cream. Cook, stirring, until the caramel and cream are homogenous.

*Makes about 1 cup.*

▲ High altitude: This recipe needs no adjustment.

# ■ Peanut Brittle

This can be a basic recipe for any type of nut—almond, cashew, macadamia nut, pecan or hazelnut. Use almonds and hazelnuts with their skins removed. The secret to a delicate nut brittle is continuing to stir the caramel once the nuts have been added. You want to stir until the caramel thins out again, and then stretch the caramel with a spoon after you've poured it onto the baking sheet.

**½ cup sugar**
**1 teaspoon fresh-squeezed lemon juice or water**
**½ cup unsalted dry roasted peanuts**

Lightly coat a baking sheet with butter. Mix the sugar and lemon juice in a heavy saucepan, until it resembles wet sand. Cook over medium-high heat, stirring constantly with a wooden spoon. After a few minutes, the sugar will begin to melt; continue stirring until any lumps dissolve and the mixture turns a clear deep caramel color, 4 to 6 minutes. Immediately stir in the peanuts—their relative coolness will cause the hot caramel to stiffen a bit—and continue to cook and stir until the caramel thins out again and the peanuts move easily in the caramel. Immediately pour the brittle onto the buttered baking sheet. As it cools, spread and stretch it into a thin layer, using the wooden spoon. Cool at least 10 minutes.

*Makes about ¾ cup broken pieces of brittle.*

▲ High altitude: This recipe needs no adjustment.

# ■ Vanilla Bean Crème Anglaise

This velvety stirred custard sauce can be served as is or spiked with liqueur, fruit purée or extract to suit the occasion. The recipe, doubled, is the basic recipe for all of the flavored ice creams in this cookbook.

**1 cup whole milk**
**Quarter of a vanilla bean**
**¼ cup sugar**
**3 egg yolks**

Put the milk in a heavy-bottomed saucepan. Using a small sharp-bladed knife, cut a lengthwise split in the quarter vanilla bean. Scrape the tiny seed pods out of the inside of the bean and add the seeds and the bean itself to the milk. Heat almost to a boil. Remove from heat.

Prepare an ice bath: Fill a large bowl with ice and nest another bowl in it. Place a fine sieve over the top bowl. Set aside.

In a medium bowl, whisk the sugar and the egg yolks until smooth. Slowly whisk in the hot vanilla milk. Transfer to a clean saucepan. Cook over medium-low heat, stirring constantly with a wooden spoon, until the custard thickens slightly and coats the back of a spoon; cooking will take 3 to 5 minutes. Do not let the custard boil or you will end up with grainy pieces of cooked egg suspended in sweet milk.

Immediately strain the custard into the ice-nested bowl. Stir occasionally until cold. Refrigerate. Crème Anglaise can be kept refrigerated up to 6 days.

*Makes a little more than 1 cup.*

▲ High altitude: This recipe needs no adjustment.

*Crème Anglaise tips: Look for the egg foam (from whisking with the sugar) to dissipate, and steam to rise as the custard cooks. At this point the Crème Anglaise will be close to done. If you are unsure, remove from the heat but continue to stir in the saucepan; the custard will keep cooking, but more slowly, and you'll have time to check the consistency. To check if Crème Anglaise coats the back of a spoon, quickly dip a spoon into the custard and run your finger through the film of custard that remains on the spoon. If your finger trail remains, the Crème Anglaise is done. If custard flows into the trail, cook it a little more and test again.*

# ■ Butter Pie Dough

This dough is more tender than some because it has extra fat from the egg and cream. The dough will be flaky if you keep the butter pieces berry-sized. Always work quickly, and keep the dough cold so the butter melts in the oven, not in your hands. For rolling instructions refer to the "Pies and Tarts" chapter introduction (page 123).

**2½ cups all-purpose flour**
**1 teaspoon sugar**
**½ teaspoon salt**
**12 tablespoons (1½ sticks) cold unsalted butter, cut into ½-inch pieces**
**1 egg**
**⅔ cup heavy cream**

Stir the flour, sugar and salt together in a medium bowl. With a pastry blender or 2 forks, cut in the butter, until the pieces are the size of blueberries. In a small bowl, whisk together the egg and cream. Pour this over the flour, stirring with a fork until the mixture mostly holds together. Gather the dough with your fingers, gently incorporating the drier pieces, and divide in 2 equal portions. Form each portion into a 4-inch flattened ball. Wrap in plastic wrap and refrigerate for 1 hour.✽

*Makes 1 ½ pounds of dough, enough for a 2-crust pie or 2 (9-inch) pie shells.*

▲ High altitude: This recipe needs no adjustment.

✽ Because of the fresh egg and cream, this dough spoils quickly—if you are not using it within 24 hours, store it in the freezer. A flattened ball will thaw at room temperature in about 2½ hours. Or, roll the dough, fit it into a pie shell and freeze—you will have a ready-made frozen pie crust.

# ■ Sweet Tart Dough

Sweet Tart Dough is most often used with fluted, straight-sided pans with removable bottoms. Compared to pie dough, Sweet Tart Dough is richer, has a snap to its texture, and, without practice, can be more difficult to handle. Sweet Tart Dough must also be smoothed by hand before rolling; recipes calling for Sweet Tart Dough include directions for smoothing and rolling.

> 1⅔ cups all-purpose flour
> ¼ cup sugar
> 10 tablespoons (1¼ sticks) cold unsalted butter, cut into ½-inch pieces
> 1 egg yolk
> 2 tablespoons heavy cream
> ¼ teaspoon vanilla, optional
> ¼ teaspoon grated lemon zest, optional

Stir the flour and the sugar together in a medium bowl. Using a pastry blender or your fingers, cut the butter into the flour until the mixture resembles coarse meal. In a separate bowl, beat the egg yolk and the cream, and the vanilla and lemon zest, if using. Sprinkle over the dough, stirring with a fork. Mix with your hands until the dough comes together and divide in 2 equal portions. Gently form each portion into a 4-inch flattened ball. Wrap in plastic wrap and refrigerate at least 2 hours.

*Makes 1 pound of dough, enough for 2 (9-inch) tarts.*

▲ High altitude: This recipe needs no adjustment.

# ■ Meringue Mushrooms

Light as a feather and cuter than the button mushrooms they imitate, these candy mushrooms are the fanciful finish to Tiramisù Yule Log. You can also make them for low-calorie Christmas cookies.

> **3 egg whites (about ⅓ cup)**
> **⅛ teaspoon cream of tartar**
> **½ cup sugar**
> **¼ teaspoon vanilla extract**
> **Cocoa powder for dusting**
> **2 ounces bittersweet chocolate, chopped in ½-inch pieces**

Preheat the oven to 200°. Line 2 baking sheets with parchment paper.

Whisk the egg whites, cream of tartar and sugar in a heatproof bowl. Place over a pan of gently boiling water; the bowl should not touch the water. Whisk until the egg whites are warm to the touch, about 30 seconds. Remove from heat. With an electric mixer at medium-high speed, whip until stiff peaks form. Whisk in the vanilla.

Scrape the meringue into a pastry bag fitted with a ½-inch plain tip. On one of the prepared baking sheets, pipe the mushroom stems, straight up, 1 to 1½ inches high and slightly tapered at the top.

On the other baking sheet pipe the caps, in rounded domes, 1 to 1¼ inches wide. Leave at least 1 inch between each dome. Smooth down any points with a wet finger. Sift cocoa powder lightly over the caps, to imitate the brown freckles on savory mushrooms. Bake 1 to 1½ hours, or until the meringue is dry.❋

Melt the chocolate in the top of a double boiler, over gently boiling water; the upper pan should not touch the water.

With the tip of a small knife, carve a tiny hole, less than ¼ inch wide, ¼ inch deep, in the underside of each mushroom cap. Dip the tapered end of a stem in the melted chocolate, then poke the stem into the hole in the cap. Place the assembled mushrooms stem side up on a clean baking sheet. After the chocolate hardens, store the mushrooms in an airtight container at room temperature; do not refrigerate or the meringue will soften.

*Makes 40 to 45 mushrooms.*

▲ High altitude: Reduce the sugar by 1 tablespoon.

❋ To check if the meringue is dry, tear off a square of parchment with a cap or stem on it and remove from the oven. Let it cool a minute, then try to bend it. If it snaps in half, it is done; if it is still soft, continue baking the meringues, checking for the snap every 15 minutes.

# ■ Meringue Buttercream

When a cooked syrup is whipped with egg whites, a fluffy marshmallow-like meringue, called Italian meringue, ensues. This smooth, light-tasting buttercream is made with Italian meringue and is nothing like the buttercream icing from the back of a confectioners' sugar box. Meringue buttercream is a classic European frosting, another bakery essential. We use it to frost and decorate special cakes, especially wedding cakes. If you like, you can flavor the buttercream with any liquer or flavoring extract.

> 1⅓ cups *plus* ⅔ cup sugar
> 1 cup water
> 2 tablespoons corn syrup
> 6 egg whites (⅔ cup)
> 1 pound (4 sticks) unsalted butter, softened
> 2 to 4 tablespoons liqueur or 1 teaspoon extract flavoring, optional

In a saucepan, combine 1⅓ cups of the sugar with the water and corn syrup. Place over low heat and gently swirl the pan until the sugar dissolves into a clear syrup. Raise the heat to medium-high and cook until the syrup reaches the soft-ball stage (240° on a candy thermometer). Do not stir after the syrup begins boiling.

As the syrup boils, whip the egg whites with an electric mixer until they are foamy. Gradually add the remaining ⅔ cup of sugar and whip until soft peaks form. You want the syrup to reach soft-ball stage at the same time the egg whites form soft peaks, so begin whipping the whites when the surface of the boiling syrup is thick with bubbles.

When the syrup reaches soft-ball stage, with the mixer running, pour the syrup in a thin stream over the whites. Aim the syrup between the bowl and the whisk, taking care not to let it run onto the whisk, which spatters the syrup onto the sides of the bowl. Continue beating about 10 minutes, until the egg white and syrup mixture—the Italian meringue—is cool.

With the mixer running, beat the softened butter into the meringue, a little at a time. Scrape the sides of the bowl and continue beating until the mixture becomes a very smooth, spreadable buttercream.❊ Beat in liqueur or extract, if using.

*Makes about 4¾ cups.*

▲ High altitude: The syrup will reach the soft-ball stage at a lower temperature. Test for soft-ball using the cold water method, or calculate the correct temperature for your altitude (page 237).

❊ The butter should incorporate easily into the Italian meringue. If the mixture doesn't come together or appears curdled, continue beating. With time, the mixture homogenizes into smooth buttercream.

# ■ Classic Puff Pastry Dough

This is a delicate, flaky pastry dough made by incorporating butter through a stringent process of rolling, turning and resting the dough. After 6 turns, there will be almost 1,500 layers of butter and dough. In a hot oven, the moisture in the dough creates steam, which "puffs" or raises the dough many times its original thickness. Use Classic Puff Pastry for Francy's Strawberry Napoleons.

1¾ cups *plus* 2 tablespoons all-purpose flour
4 tablespoons (½ stick) *plus* ½ pound (2 sticks) cold, unsalted butter
½ teaspoon salt
1 teaspoon lemon juice
¾ cup ice-cold water

Put the 1¾ cups of flour in a medium bowl. Cut 4 tablespoons of the butter into small pieces and toss into the flour. Using your fingertips or a pastry blender, cut the butter pieces into the flour until the mixture resembles coarse meal. Stir the salt and lemon juice into the water. Pour the liquid all at once into the flour and butter mixture, stirring with a fork. Using your fingers, mix the dough and bring it together into a moist, soft ball with a rough—not smooth—surface. Wrap in plastic wrap and refrigerate 45 minutes.

Cut the remaining ½ pound of butter into 1-inch pieces. Beat with the remaining 2 tablespoons of flour until the butter is smooth and spreadable, but still cold. Put the butter on a sheet of plastic wrap and form it into a 4½-inch square, about ¾ inch thick. You now have 2 components, the dough and the butter; they should be similar in consistency—cool but malleable. The next step is to make a package of dough enclosing the butter.

Unwrap the dough and place it on a lightly floured surface. Using as little flour as needed to keep from sticking, roll the dough into a square, about ⅜ inch thick. Place the butter in the center, with the corners of the butter square pointing towards the sides of the dough square. Fold the dough over the butter, making a package. Use your fingers to seal the edges. Turn the package over onto a lightly floured surface.

*Puff Pastry tips: Roll the rectangles to within ½ inch from the ends—do not take the rolling pin over the top or bottom edge of the dough. Just before you make a fold, square the corner edges. To do this, place the rolling pin perpendicular to your body and gently roll across the top inch.*

Using gentle pressure, so the butter moves evenly between the layers, roll the dough towards and away from you, coaxing it into a rectangle. Make the rectangle 12 x 8 inches. Brush away any excess flour. Fold the rectangle into thirds, like a business letter; fold the bottom up first and then the top down. Rotate the dough so the top flap is to the right, so it might open like a book. You have just completed a "turn."

Roll the dough into a 12 x 8-inch rectangle again, trying to keep the edges aligned and even. Fold again into thirds, like a letter. Make 2 finger indent marks in the top of the dough to remind yourself that you have completed 2 turns. Wrap and refrigerate the dough at least 30 minutes. This is rest time—the gluten needs to relax and the butter needs to cool.

Unwrap the dough and place it on the floured surface so the top flap is on the right. Roll into a 12 x 8-inch rectangle. Fold in thirds, as before, and rotate the flap to the right. Roll into a 12 x 8-inch rectangle and fold in thirds again. Mark with 4 finger indentations, then wrap and refrigerate 30 minutes.

Unwrap the dough and place it on the floured surface, keeping the flap on the right. Roll a 12 x 8-inch rectangle, fold in thirds and turn the flap to the right. Repeat once more. You have now completed 6 turns. Wrap in plastic wrap and refrigerate the dough for at least an hour. Puff Pastry is ready to roll and bake as directed. It can be frozen at this point for up to 2 months.

*Makes about 1 ⅓ pounds of dough.*

▲ High altitude: This recipe needs no adjustment.

*If the butter oozes out as you roll the rectangles, it is too soft. Sprinkle flour on the butter leak, quickly complete the turn and refrigerate. If the room is very warm, you may need to refrigerate the dough between each turn, instead of every other. But beware, if the butter is too cold, it will shatter instead of spread evenly.*

# Baking at
## Celestial Heights

# Baking at Celestial Heights
## About High Altitude Baking

We Deer Valley bakers are used to the peculiarities of high altitude baking. We work in lodges that are nestled into mountain valleys—Snow Park Lodge is situated at 7,200 feet, Silver Lake Lodge snugs in at 8,100 feet, and Empire Canyon pokes out of the woods at a lofty 8,500 feet above sea level. Because our kitchens are at such celestial heights, we adapt. We meet the challenges of thin mountain air by changing formula amounts and taking care with our culinary techniques. In high altitude baking, due to physical laws, some things happen faster, such as bread rising, or slower, as for custard cooking. So, we learn to bake by sight and feel—a blessing because it teaches us to cook with our senses—rather than by a recipe's given cooking times. The variations become normal; we almost forget about habitual compensations for altitude. But the differences are still there. It is not unusual for treasured recipes from our sea level families and colleagues or recipes we glean from magazines and cookbooks to turn out differently. Sometimes this leads to disappointment for the high altitude cook.

The failures and frustrations boil down to the difference in atmospheric pressure—because the air is thinner, the baking process at high altitude is contrary to standard methods. At greater heights there are fewer molecules of air floating around. When these air molecules bump against something, they exert pressure on it—that is, where there is less air, there is less atmospheric pressure.

When a pot of water is heated, the heat on the pan's bottom provides energy, making the liquid water hot enough to turn into water vapor and rise to the top. The water vapor bubbles will collapse and disappear back into the liquid unless the pressure of the water vapor is equal to or exceeds the air pressure weighing down on it. Imagine less push from the air on top of the water, as there is at higher altitudes. As the water gets hotter, and reaches sufficient energy—sufficient pressure—the vapor bubbles survive to break at the surface. In the physical sciences, the temperature at which water vapor bubbles break is called the water's boiling point. At higher altitudes, there is less pressure on the water vapor bubbles, so it takes less energy, pressure and heat for the bubbles to reach the surface. The vapor bubbles break at a lower temperature—the boiling point is lower.

The boiling point of water decreases about 1° for every 500-foot gain in elevation above sea level. The chart below shows the approximate boiling point of water at varying altitude levels.

*The higher the altitude, the lower the boiling point.*

| ALTITUDE | TEMPERATURE |
|---|---|
| Sea level | 212° |
| 2,000 feet | 208° |
| 5,000 feet | 203° |
| 7,500 feet | 198° |
| 10,000 feet | 194° |

If water boils at a lower temperature, foods cooked in or over boiling water will take more time to cook simply because they can never reach the same temperature they do at sea level.

For every 1,000 feet in elevation, atmospheric pressure decreases about ½ pound per square inch of surface. The pressure per square inch at sea level is 14.7 pounds, at 5,000 feet is 12.3 pounds, and at 10,000 feet is 10.2 pounds. As discussed above, because the air pressure is less on a liquid's surface, boiling vapor bubbles break more easily. Since vapor bubbles break more easily, water (and other liquids) evaporates faster—another influence of lessened atmospheric pressure on baking. Rapid evaporation makes sugar more concentrated than it would be at sea level, altering the amount of sugar in proportion to a recipe's other ingredients. Quicker evaporation also changes the ratio of fat in a recipe. The higher concentrations of sugar and fat can weaken the cell structure in batters, causing them to fall.

A third impact of less atmospheric pressure is on the leavening gases in dough and batter—they expand more easily under the thinner blanket of air. The leavening gas for yeast bread—carbon dioxide—is produced by yeast. In quick breads, carbon dioxide results from mixing an acid (lemon juice, cream of tartar, buttermilk) with an alkali (baking soda). Air itself, primarily the gases oxygen and nitrogen, is also a leavener, when beaten into eggs. When leavening gases expand due to lessened air pressure, the dough or batter may rise too much or too quickly. Then the cell structure is stretched, causing a coarse texture, or the cell structure may break, causing the batter to fall.

What does all this science mean for our baking if we live at higher elevations? What do we do to compensate for decreased atmospheric pressure? Unfortunately, there is no set rule for adapting recipes to high altitude. Depending on the ingredients and their quantity and, of course, how high your kitchen is above sea level, recipe conversions will vary. Some recipe categories just need extra attention to technique, such as whipping egg whites to soft peaks rather than stiff peaks. For fragile recipes, you may have to go through trial and error to find the right adaptation.

*Lower boiling point —> Rapid evaporation —> Concentrated sugar*

I have included high altitude adjustments with each recipe—look for the ▲ High Altitude symbol throughout this book. The adjustments are suggestions coming from my experience of baking at 7,000 to 8,500 feet above sea level for the last two decades. Use my suggestions as guidelines; some are reminders that the cooking time will be longer, and some are more exacting, with reductions of sugar or chemical leaveners. The changes will depend on where you live—your altitude. If you live at 3,000 feet or below, you will not need to change your recipe, and if you live higher, do not automatically assume that the sea level recipe will fail. Be sure to record your adaptations as you test and perfect a recipe. In cookbooks, I pencil my high altitude notes in the margins around the recipe. Even in this cookbook, I suggest writing the ingredient amount changes near the printed list of ingredients—a reminder to make the adjustment as you work your way through the recipe. Let this be your workbook for successful high altitude baking.

Wrap all baked goods in plastic wrap as soon as they have cooled—high altitude's dry air quickly draws out moisture. Also, if a baking recipe includes eggs, you can make it more stable by substituting extra large eggs for large eggs. This small change adds extra liquid to the batter, compensating for evaporation, and provides more protein, to help the batter set more quickly in the oven.

For more high altitude information, read the following tips for each baking category. For additional help, Colorado State University Cooperative Extension is an excellent resource for booklets and recipes on high altitude baking and cooking (The Other Bookstore, page 258). Home economists and food science professors at Colorado State University have a long tradition of researching high altitude baking. They are the experts commercial food packagers turn to for developing high altitude adjustments for boxed mixes. The university in Fort Collins has a laboratory chamber that can be pressurized to mimic other altitudes.

▲ **High altitude yeast breads:** Yeast breads are a good example of high altitude baking by sight and feel. When kneading, you will learn to recognize dough as "soft, smooth and elastic" and with experience, your sense of touch will determine how much flour to add. Because of the drier mountain air, you will probably use less flour in the dough than at sea level. Yeast dough rises faster at higher elevations, so check sooner than the time indicated for doubling. You will want to let the cell walls stretch for lightness, but not so far that they break. Test by indenting your finger in the dough near the side of the bowl; if the indentation remains, the dough is ready to deflate. For optimum bread at high altitude, let the dough rise twice in the bowl before shaping; after deflating the dough once, cover, and let rise again. This is an optional step, but the extra rising time allows the bread to develop flavor. You can also use less yeast, to slow the speed of rising. Oven spring, which is the immediate rising of the dough in the hot oven before it begins to brown, is more pronounced with lessened atmospheric pressure. To allow for the extra oven spring, put the shaped, risen loaves in the oven just before they double in size. Some high altitude recommendations suggest increasing the oven temperature to set the cell walls, preventing collapse from too much oven spring, but I find that putting the loaves in the oven a little sooner achieves the same results without the risk of scorched crust.

▲ **High altitude quick breads:** Quick breads include muffins, cornbread, and nut or fruit sweet bread as well as coffee cake and scones. All of these contain chemical leaveners— baking powder and/or baking soda. Without sea level atmospheric pressure, the leavened batters rise higher. If the batter rises too high or too quickly, it will collapse before the oven heat can set the cell walls of baking batter. Therefore, reduce the leaveners by 15 to 75 percent, depending on your altitude. If the leavener is baking soda, be sure to keep enough to react with the acid; 1 cup of sour milk (or yogurt, sour cream or buttermilk) neutralizes ½ teaspoon of baking soda. Quick bread batters have enough sugar in them that, with faster evaporation of the liquids, the sugar becomes more concentrated. Decrease the sugar 1 to 2 tablespoons per cup of sugar to compensate for the liquid evaporation.

▲ **High altitude cookies and bars:** Most sea level cookie recipes will work at high altitude, but can be improved with a few adjustments. Reducing the sugar by 2 tablespoons per cup compensates for sugar concentration from quicker liquid evaporation. At higher elevations, the fat proportion becomes more of a problem; if you are baking at over 9,000 feet above sea level, recipes rich in butter or oil need a reduction of the fat by 1 to 2 tablespoons per cup. In addition, a slight decrease in the leavening can keep cookies from overspreading and bar cookies from overrising and then falling. You will notice that some cookie recipes include baking soda but in my high altitude adjustment I don't reduce the soda amount. Atlanta food scientist Shirley Corriher, author of *CookWise*, explains that the soda is there to neutralize the brown sugar's acidity so the cookies will color to a golden brown.

▲ **High altitude cakes:** Cakes are possibly the trickiest baked item to adjust since they are inherently delicate. First, decrease the sugar by 1 to 2 tablespoons per cup of sugar to compensate for liquid evaporation. A benefit from decreasing the sugar is that the egg protein sets sooner in the oven's heat. That is because sugar interferes with egg protein, raising the temperature at which eggs (and therefore a batter) can set. So, at altitudes where the boiling point is lower, reducing the sugar lowers the temperature needed to set the batter.

It is important to never beat too much air into egg whites, especially at high altitude. Whipped egg whites at high altitude should form peaks that just fold over, versus peaks that are stiff. When egg whites are overbeaten, they are stretched beyond their capacity; there is no room for them to expand in the oven. Where there is less atmospheric pressure, the air bubbles expand even more. You want to leave room for them to expand.

If a cake is chemically leavened, reduce the leavening 15 to 70 percent, depending on your altitude. To strengthen the cell structure of rich cakes, bakers at altitudes over 9,000 feet may need to reduce the fat by 1 or 2 tablespoons per cup of fat.

High altitude recipe adjustment guidelines often suggest increasing the liquid in a recipe by 1 to 4 tablespoons, but I find reducing the sugar alone to be effective. Use cake flour for finer texture. Some guidelines also recommend increasing the flour by 1 to 2 tablespoons per cup; I use this adjustment occasionally, to lend stability to very fragile batters such as angel food cake, and when sugar reduction isn't enough.

Following is the altitude adjustment guide for cake recipes from Colorado State University Cooperative Extension:

| CHANGE | 3,000 feet | 5,000 feet | 7,000 feet |
|---|---|---|---|
| Baking powder: | | | |
| reduce each teaspoon by | ⅛ to ¼ tsp. | ⅛ to ¼ tsp. | ¼ tsp. |
| Sugar: | | | |
| reduce each cup by | up to 1 tbsp. | up to 2 tbsp. | 1 to 3 tbsp. |
| Liquid: | | | |
| increase each cup by | 1 to 2 tbsp. | 2 to 4 tbsp. | 3 to 4 tbsp. |

▲ **High altitude cheesecakes:** Cheesecakes are an example of increased baking time related to high altitude and lowered boiling point. Plan on a sea level cheesecake recipe baking at least 10 to 15 minutes longer at high altitude. Use your sense of sight to recognize when it is done—the batter should have risen slightly and lost its shine, and should not be liquid in the center when you jiggle the pan. Reduce the sugar in the recipe to compensate for liquid evaporation.

▲ **High altitude pies and tarts:** Because of low humidity you may need to add a teaspoon more liquid to pie dough. (Be frugal with extra liquid, particularly if it is water, for water and flour make gluten, which is not conducive to tender pie dough.)

Pie crust takes longer to brown at higher elevations. I always "blind bake" (page 243) the bottom crust without the filling, whether a recipe calls for it or not. That way the crust will be flaky, instead of underbaked and soggy. Since it's difficult to mold an unbaked rolled-top crust to a prebaked bottom, I often use a streusel topping. When blind baking at high altitude, watch for color in the crust instead of relying on the clock.

Fillings such as apple, pear and berry will take longer to bake because the pie juices boil at a lower temperature and therefore need more time to thicken. I precook apple pie fillings even at sea level to give the fruit a head start on the cooking process; precooking is standard procedure at high altitude. When baking fruit pies, keep a sharp eye on the juices bubbling through the slashes or streusel topping. Watch for ample evidence of bubbling juices, to be sure the filling has thickened. Pumpkin pies and other custard pies also take longer to bake, about 15 extra minutes—use the test of "knife inserted near center comes out clean." Some guidelines suggest increasing the baking temperature to compensate for slower cooking, but I choose to practice patience rather than risk burnt pie crust.

▲ **High altitude custards:** Custards such as pastry cream will take longer to cook to proper thickness. Again, this is because of the lower boiling point. Pastry cream needs to boil for several minutes in order for the starch molecules in the flour to thicken; test for doneness by making sure the pastry cream falls off the whisk in a dollop, not a runny flow. Crème Anglaise is similar to pastry cream, but without flour; it must not boil, and thickens into a smooth sauce at about 160°.

Baked custards such as crème brûlée and crème caramel or flan seem to take forever to "set" here in the mountains, sometimes close to double the time at sea level. Resist the urge to turn the oven temperature up—the custard will set eventually. The water bath protecting these custards from the hot oven temperature is simply not as hot as at sea level, since the boiling point is lower.

▲ **High altitude sugar syrup:** Boiling sugar syrup reaches the different stages—thread, soft-ball, hard-crack and caramel—at different temperatures than at sea level. This is due to the water molecules in a sugar syrup vaporizing, eventually resulting in more sugar molecules than water molecules; water evaporates faster at high altitude, so the sugar concentrates faster. The variation is the same as the difference in boiling points—for each

500 foot increase above sea level, the syrup stage temperature should be almost 1° lower. That is, if the boiling point at 7,500 feet is 198°, or 14° less than sea level's 212°, the 240° soft-ball will form at 226°, or 14° less. Likewise, sea level's 300° hard-crack stage will be 286° on a candy thermometer at 7,500 feet in elevation.

I teach bakers to test the stages of syrup using the cold water test, so they don't have to rely on a thermometer or calculate the adjustment for high altitudes. For the cold water test, dip a teaspoon into the boiling syrup, lift a small amount of the syrup with the spoon and dip it into ice-cold water. Quickly press the syrup in the water between your fingers to see how the sugar behaves. (I test without the spoon. Dip thumb and first two fingers into a bowl of iced water. Very quickly dip wet fingers into the boiling syrup to lift a small amount, and then immediately dip back into the iced water. If you test using your fingers, be very careful—hot syrup burns are serious.) At soft-ball stage, syrup dropped into ice-cold water will make a limp ball that flattens when removed from the water. Meringue Buttercream, the frosting in Orange Almond Wedding Cake, is made with soft-ball syrup whipped into egg whites. Since the egg whites for this Italian meringue are not being used as a leavener, whip them until they form firm peaks, just as you would at sea level. Following is a table of the stages of sugar syrup concentration and their sea level temperatures:

| STAGE | TEMPERATURE | FORMS |
|---|---|---|
| Thread | 215° | Fine thread |
| Soft-ball | 234° to 242° | Ball that flattens |
| Firm-ball | 244° to 248° | Ball that holds its shape |
| Hard-ball | 250° to 266° | Harder, pliable ball |
| Soft-crack | 270° to 290° | Firm, bendable thread |
| Hard-crack | 300° to 310° | Brittle thread |
| Caramel | 320° to 350° | Colors light to amber brown |

At high altitude, the sugar stages will look and feel the same as at sea level, but the temperatures on a candy thermometer must be lower—approximately 2° less for every 1,000 foot gain in elevation.

My pastry chef counterparts at a Colorado ski area use the word "altitude" as a verb. Automatically, they "altitude" a sea level recipe for their 9,000-foot elevation; if queried about a failed recipe, their first response is, "Did you altitude it?" The translation: to adjust formulas and/or techniques compensating for decreased atmospheric pressure and humidity at elevated regions 3,000 feet and more above sea level. There are cities and towns in at least 14 of the United States with elevations over 3,000 feet. Some are on the high plateau west of the Mississippi River; others are in distinct mountainous areas. All of us who bake at altitude learn to "altitude" or adapt for the characteristics. Light air is part of the package, the gift of living at celestial heights.

I realize that I naturally choose recipes that will successfully adapt to high altitude. For instance, my favorite sponge cake includes almond paste, which strengthens the batter and adds moisture. Besides that, my recipe is leavened with whipped egg whites; I can control the air bubbles by underbeating the meringue. I also have a predilection for baking with honey, and baked goods with honey are inherently moist. I believe you will find the collection of recipes in this book acclimatable, since these are the recipes we use day in and day out at Deer Valley. Remember that these recipes have been written and tested for sea level and you will need to adjust them, incorporating the information in this chapter and the suggestions that accompany each recipe.

# The Baker's Pantry

## A Glossary of Ingredients, Tools, Terms, Techniques and Resources

*No one who cooks cooks alone. Even at her most solitary, a cook in the kitchen is surrounded by generations of cooks past, the advice and menus of cooks present, the wisdom of cookbook writers.*

—Laurie Colwin

I am inspired by the late writer Laurie Colwin's words, by her essays, articles and cooking memoirs. The quote is from the foreword to one of her books, a delicious collection of writing and recipes, *Home Cooking: A Writer in the Kitchen*. I never feel alone in the bakery, because I have been inspired by the words of other pastry chefs. Their cookbooks wait on my shelf, ready to stir my creativity and answer my questions.

This chapter will keep you from feeling alone in the kitchen. It is an inventory of baking essentials compiled to help you use this cookbook. If you're new to baking, you'll want to read this chapter first and refer to it as you learn. If you want to know the difference between cake flour and bread flour, read about it here. I discuss in detail the basic techniques, such as "blind baking" or whipping egg whites. There are basic utensils necessary for pastry making, and there are helpful but unnecessary tools that save time and give a professional appearance; this chapter lists tools of both kinds. In many recipes, I direct you to these pages for such procedures as melting chocolate or skinning hazelnuts. Refer to the end of this glossary for a list of ingredient and tool suppliers and resources.

**Apple juice concentrate:** Used as a natural sweetener in Healthy Heart Muffins and Low-Fat Honey Jumbo Cookies. Available in the freezer section of supermarkets. To use, thaw and measure with a liquid measuring cup.

**Almond paste and Marzipan:** Both of these products consist of blanched almonds and sugar, causing confusion about their difference. Almond paste has a coarser, more crumbly texture, because it has a higher ratio of nuts. Marzipan is smoother due to its higher sugar content. Almond paste, which is made by grinding almonds with confectioners' sugar and sugar syrup, is usually purchased. In this cookbook, I use almond paste for flavor and moisture in cakes, and to make homemade marzipan. Almond paste is available in well-stocked supermarkets and specialty stores. Marzipan (page 103) is easy to make using almond paste, confectioners' sugar and corn syrup. Purchased marzipan is even sweeter, than homemade and fairly expensive—I don't recommend using it. I roll out marzipan as a layer in Stein's Favorite Marzipan Cake. Both almond paste and marzipan dry out quickly and should be kept well wrapped in the refrigerator.

**Baba molds:** These are very job-specific forms used to make the rum babas, the baba dough bottoms for Baked Alaska Ali Babas. Baba molds are metal, stainless steel or aluminum, about 2¼ inches high. They are bucket or thimble-shaped, a little wider (2¼ inches) across the top than (2 inches) across the bottom. Muffin tins are a fine alternative in case you don't happen to own a set of baba molds.

**Baking pans:** For bar cookies, you'll need a rectangular 9 x 13 x 2-inch baking pan, which is basically a casserole pan for lasagna or enchiladas. The metal ones have sharper corners that make square-edged bar cookies, but glass rectangular baking pans work fine. I use an 8 x 8-inch square pan for some coffee cakes, but a 9-inch round cake pan will substitute.

**Baking powder and Baking soda:** Both produce the gas carbon dioxide, which makes batters rise and expand. Baking powder includes baking soda in its composition. The soda, an alkali, is combined with an acid, such as calcium phosphate or cream of tartar— different brands use different acids. When double-acting baking powder meets the liquid in a batter, the first reaction occurs; then, when the batter is heated, a second occurs. Single-acting baking powder reacts with liquid only. The recipes in this book were tested with double-acting baking powder.

To produce the chemical reaction, baking soda needs to be used with an acidic ingredient, like buttermilk, yogurt, lemon juice, vinegar, honey, molasses, natural cocoa powder or chocolate. Baking soda starts reacting immediately in a batter, so get it in the oven as soon as possible.

Sometimes recipes call for both baking powder and baking soda. The baking powder does most of the leavening work; the baking soda is there to neutralize acids and add rising power. Make sure baking powder and baking soda are well mixed with the other dry ingredients—use a wire whisk to stir all ingredients well, even after sifting. Baking powder loses its power over time and should be replaced if 1 teaspoon mixed in ½ cup of hot water doesn't bubble actively. Baking soda lasts longer. Buy them both in small quantities and replace after a year. At high altitude, the amount of chemical leavening should be decreased (page 236).

**Baking sheets:** You need at least 2 baking sheets. The best choice is the heavy-duty professional aluminum "half-sheet" available at restaurant supply stores. They don't warp or bend and can be used as a jelly roll pan or for sheet cakes. Half-sheet pans are 16 x 12 inches with 1-inch sides. At home I also have several lighter weight "cookie" sheets, which I bought at a secondhand store for less than a dollar—I use them when my half-sheet is already busy. Nonstick and insulated cookie sheets are also suitable.

**Bench scraper:** Sometimes called a dough cutter or a baker's bench knife, this tool is very handy, but not essential. A bench scraper has a thin, rectangular blade and a wooden or plastic handle. Use it to divide bread doughs before shaping, to assist kneading soft dough like brioche and baba dough, and to scrape the excess flour and bits of dough from the work surface.

**Blind baking:** Blind baking is baking an empty tart or pie shell using weights to keep the pastry from puffing. Line the shell with parchment paper or aluminum foil that extends 3 inches beyond the pan. Fill the paper-lined pastry with pie weights (page 253) or dried beans, making sure the paper and beans are tucked into the corners of the dough to make a sharp inside edge. Bake until the edges turn golden brown, 20 to 25 minutes. Allow to cool 5 minutes. Carefully remove the paper and pie weights. If the tart or pie shell still seems raw in the middle, return it to the oven, without the pie weights, for another 5 minutes, until the bottom has finished cooking. It is not necessary to prick the crust with a fork before blind baking. I always blind bake the crust without the filling, whether the recipes call for it or not; that way the crust will be more flaky.

**Box grater:** A 4-sided grater with 4 choices of hole size. I find the smallest holes on a box grater the most efficient means of removing or grating citrus zest or peel—easier than a hand zester.

**Butter:** Recipes in this book call for unsalted butter, which is the same as sweet cream butter and is the choice of professional bakers. Unsalted butter has a subtle, sophisticated taste; salt acts a preservative and can mask off-flavors in butter. At home, I keep unsalted butter well-wrapped in the freezer. Thaw the butter at room temperature for several hours to soften it. If I need soft butter in a hurry, I use the defrost cycle on the microwave, taking care to thaw or soften the butter just enough—microwaves work the butter from the inside out and a few seconds can change the butter from softened to partially melted. When you buy butter, smell the package; rancid butter does not smell sweet.

**Canola oil:** I use canola oil for two reasons. It is has a light taste and research shows that canola oil, like olive oil, is high in monounsaturates, the fat that lowers bad cholesterol without affecting the good cholesterol. I usually bake with butter, but when I use a vegetable oil, I want it to be heart-healthy. You can substitute another liquid oil such as safflower, sunflower, corn, soybean or peanut. Olive oil can also be used, but it does have a strong taste.

**Cake pans:** The recipes in this book call for 9-inch round cake pans. If you buy new cake pans, buy the 2-inch tall, heavy-gauge pans that will last a lifetime. For cheesecakes, you'll also need a 10-inch springform pan with removable 3-inch-high sides.

**Cake turntable:** A revolving cake stand with a heavy base—makes frosting or glazing cakes easier.

**Cardboard cake circles:** Sturdy corrugated cardboard rounds used to store, frost and transport cakes. Available in a range of round sizes and also in rectangles for sheet cakes. Buy them at restaurant or bakery supply stores. You can also cut your own from a cardboard box, but you should cover these with foil before topping with food.

**Channel knife:** A small hand tool used to cut strips of peel from citrus fruit. A notched blade removes ¼-inch-wide pieces and, if cut gently, will remove only the zest, leaving the bitter white pith on the fruit.

**Chocolate:** Chocolate begins in equatorial regions of the world as cacao beans, the fruit of a jungle tree. The manufacturing process includes grinding the dried and roasted beans into a dark paste called chocolate liquor. This liquor (which contains no alcohol) is pressed to make unsweetened baking chocolate. More processing separates the chocolate liquor into cocoa butter and cocoa powder. Chocolate makers add sugar to chocolate liquor to produce bittersweet and semisweet chocolate; they add sugar and milk powder to produce milk chocolate. They remove the dark liquor, but retain the cocoa butter and milk powder to make white chocolate. In this cookbook, I use all forms of chocolate except cocoa butter, which I used when I was a tan-seeking teenager.

**Unsweetened baking chocolate,** sometimes called bitter chocolate, often comes in individually wrapped 1-ounce bars, in 8-ounce packages. Not very pleasant to eat, unsweetened chocolate is mixed with sugar for brownie and cake recipes. At Deer Valley, I use Baker's Champion "naps," from a 5-pound box. At home, I use either Hershey's or Baker's brand. Don't confuse unsweetened bitter chocolate with bittersweet chocolate; they are not interchangeable.

Both **bittersweet** and **semisweet chocolates** are a blend of chocolate liquor, extra cocoa butter, sugar, vanilla and lecithin—with varying amounts and qualities of these ingredients depending on the chocolate manufacturer. If I specify semisweet chocolate in a recipe, feel free to substitute bittersweet if it's what you prefer or have on hand. At Deer Valley we use American-made chocolates—Ghirardelli Queen semisweet chocolate and Merckens Monopol bittersweet chocolate—which come in 10-pound blocks. We keep some Callebaut Belgian bittersweet blocks on hand for extra-special desserts. I try to buy better-quality bulk chocolate for home baking, too—although the semisweet and bittersweet chocolates sold in grocery stores are acceptable, they don't have the smooth taste of good domestic or European chocolate. If you can't find a local source of bulk chocolate, you can mail order or e-mail order (page 257). Buy extra so you'll have it when you need it; bittersweet and semisweet chocolate keep very well, wrapped and stored in a cool, dark place.

**Milk** and **white chocolates** are similar to each other, although officially white chocolate cannot be labeled chocolate, per the U.S. Food and Drug Administration, because it contains no chocolate liquor. Good-quality milk and white chocolate should list cocoa butter as the only fat, not vegetable or palm kernel oil; check the ingredient label. At Deer Valley, we use Merckens Marquis milk and "Ivory" chocolate as well as Callebaut white couverture. Because of the milk solids, these chocolates can become rancid; keep tightly wrapped in a cool, dark place, and buy no more than you can use before it spoils. Milk and white chocolates have a lower melting point; read about melting chocolate below.

**Chocolate morsels** or **chips** should not be substituted for other chocolates; they are made with extra fat so they keep their shape when baked. Look for chocolate and white morsels with cocoa butter in the ingredients, even though other vegetable oils may be added. I use Hershey's semisweet morsels at Deer Valley and at home.

**To melt chocolate:** Chop the chocolate into pieces smaller than 2 inches and put in a heat-proof bowl. With dark chocolates such as bittersweet and semisweet, place the bowl on top of a saucepan of barely simmering water. Never let the bowl sit directly in the hot water, but keep several inches between. Stir the chocolate so it doesn't get too hot (above 120°) as it melts. Milk and white chocolates are even more sensitive to heat; therefore, remove the saucepan of simmering water from the heat before placing the bowl of chocolate on top. Take care that water, or even steam from the hot water, doesn't get into the bowl; the chocolate might seize into a stiff, lumpy and unusable mass.

You can use the microwave oven to melt chocolate. Refer to the manual that came with your oven and use a microwave-safe bowl. Use a medium setting (50 percent power) for dark chocolate; for milk and white chocolates use a low setting (25 to 30 percent power). Only microwave 30 seconds at a time, stirring and checking the chocolate in between.

**Cocoa powder:** There are 2 forms of unsweetened cocoa powder, natural unsweetened and alkalized "Dutch-process." The Dutching process gives the cocoa a darker color and reduces its bitter acidity, but the natural cocoa has a more robust flavor; many times they are interchangeable and it's the baker's choice. I use the natural unsweetened cocoa in this cookbook. For cakes and other batters, I use it with baking soda, which neutralizes some of the acidity and darkens the color.

**Coconut:** Dried shredded coconut is sold both sweetened and unsweetened. In this book, they are interchangeable. At Deer Valley I use sweetened flakes; at home I use unsweetened grated coconut, which I buy at a natural food store. A pastry's ultimate sweetness will depend on which coconut you choose.

**Cooking spray:** Also known as vegetable or food release spray, this very convenient spray is located near the vegetable oils and shortening in supermarkets. Use it to prepare pans for baking, eliminating the step of brushing the pans with melted butter and dusting with flour. I use cooking spray both at Deer Valley and at home. For muffins, I use a heavy-duty spray called Baker's Joy, which has flour in it—the muffins pop right out of the tins. I use either Baker's Joy or a canola oil cooking spray to prepare cake pans. For insurance, I line cake pans with parchment paper after spraying; I want every cake to invert easily from the pan.

**Cooling racks:** Footed wire racks allow air to circulate under and around cooling breads, cakes or other baked goods; they also keep hot pans from damaging countertops. While baking Puff Pastry for Napoleons, turn cooling racks upside down on top of the pastry, so the pastry rises evenly and not too high.

**Corn syrup:** Corn syrup has a chemical structure that keeps sugar from recrystallizing as it boils, so I use it when I make Italian meringue, as in buttercream. Both light and dark corn syrups are available; use the light form for this purpose.

**Cream:** I use heavy whipping cream, which has about 36 percent butterfat. Choose the carton that does not say "ultra-pasteurized" on the label because a) the cream will be fresher and b) the higher temperature reached in ultra-pasteurization imparts a slightly different taste. To whip cream: Ideally, pre-chill the bowl and whisk or beaters. If you whip by hand, nest the bowl into another bowl filled with ice. Use very cold cream right from the refrigerator. Cream is perfectly whipped when it has soft peaks that just hold their shape. With an electric mixer, it's safer to stop whipping early than to overwhip the cream; you can always whip a few extra strokes using a hand whisk. Soft whipped cream is best for spreading on a cake or folding into a mousse, as both processes work the cream even more. Overwhipped cream is stiff and rough-textured—it's on its way to becoming butter—and won't combine smoothly with other ingredients. You can whip cream ahead of time and keep it refrigerated. If it thins before you use it, whisk it by hand to bring it back to soft peaks.

**Creaming:** This is a method of mixing fat and sugar to incorporate air into doughs and batters. You can use a wooden spoon or a hand whisk but it is most easily done with an electric mixer. To cream, beat softened or room temperature butter until it is smooth. Then add the sugar and beat until light and fluffy. Do not use butter that has been melted because it will never take on the creamy texture as softened butter does.

**Cream of tartar:** This is a white powder used to stabilize whipped egg whites. Its acidity can be used to inhibit sugar crystallization in boiling sugar syrup. Cream of tartar is often the acidic component in baking powder.

**Cutting cakes:** To split cakes before filling and frosting, use a long-bladed serrated or bread knife. Hold the knife edge to the cake and rotate the cake on a turntable or on a cardboard circle on a smooth surface. Hold and rotate with one hand and cut into the cake with your other hand. Cut 1 inch all the way around, keeping your elbow into your side so the knife cuts at the same level. Continue to rotate and cut, until you have "inched" the knife all the way to the other side (illustration, page 82). To cut cakes into wedges to serve, use a clean, hot, long-bladed knife. I fill a pitcher with very hot water and dip my knife after each cut. Wipe the excess water and any residual cake on a clean kitchen towel so every piece is neat.

**Double boiler:** A double boiler has 2 elements: a top part for food and a bottom part in which the water simmers. I make my own double boiler with a stainless steel bowl on top, sitting over a saucepan bottom of gently boiling water. The top of the double boiler must be bigger than the bottom, so it doesn't touch the water.

**Dried cranberries and Dried cherries:** Dried cranberries are sold near other dried fruits in the supermarket. Since they are sweetened with sugar, they can be eaten out of hand, just like raisins. Dried cherries are a little harder to find; look for them in specialty stores or by mail (page 257). Both dried fruits have a sweet-tart flavor and you can use them interchangeably.

**Eggs:** The recipes in this book are made with large eggs. At Deer Valley, because of the risk of salmonella, we do not use raw eggs in fillings, mousses and meringues, unless the eggs will be cooked long enough to kill the bacteria. We use a pasteurized egg product, which is not readily available at the retail level. There are liquid egg substitutes available, such as Eggbeaters or Better'n Eggs, but these are 98 percent egg whites with added thickeners, preservatives and color, and they don't substitute well in desserts where the fat of the egg yolk provides texture and emulsification. I use a fat-free liquid egg substitute in the "Lighter in Fat" Frozen Lemon Meringue Pie variation. You can use liquid egg substitute instead of egg whites in the Healthy Heart Muffins.

The recipes for Snuggery Chocolate Silk Pie, Chocolate Casbah Terrine and Black Forest Mousse Cake instruct you to cook eggs over a double boiler to 160° to eliminate the threat of salmonella. Use an instant-read thermometer for accuracy.

Perfectly **whipped egg whites** have a stable, tight structure and lots of volume. Generally, the more sugar, the longer they take to whip and the stronger the foam; plain whites whip quickly and are quite fragile. Exacting bakers use a **balloon whisk** and a copper bowl to whip egg whites because copper ions bond with the egg protein to make very stable whites. I use a **heavy-duty mixer fitted with the whisk attachment.** A **hand-held mixer** can also be used. Make sure there are no specks of egg yolk in the whites, and that the bowl and whisk are scrupulously clean, dry and grease-free, otherwise the whites won't reach full volume. Start with the mixer at medium-low speed. Add the cream of tartar, and as the egg whites whip into a foam, gradually add the sugar. You can increase the mixing speed, but be careful not to overbeat as most of us tend to do; the whites should be smooth, not grainy or resembling soap suds. Lift the whisk to check for the slightly bent peak. If you think they are close, stop. They are probably perfect. If you reconsider and decide they need a little more whipping, play it safe and finish with a hand whisk.

If the whipped egg whites are to be used as a topping, as in McHenry's Frozen Lemon Meringue Pie, I give instructions to eliminate the threat of salmonella. As with whole eggs, again using an instant-read thermometer for accuracy, cook the egg whites with the sugar over a double boiler, whisking constantly, until the mixture is 160°. Remove from heat and whip until the meringue is cool and forms stiff peaks. Meringues that are cooked before whipping are also more stable—not as easy to overbeat.

Safe egg handling should be a habit. Egg safety includes: buying refrigerated eggs and keeping them refrigerated at home, washing your hands before and after handling eggs, washing utensils and work surfaces that come in contact with raw eggs, and discarding cracked eggs.

**Electric mixer:** There are recipes in this book for batters that can be mixed by hand using a wooden spoon or a wire whisk, and hand-held electric mixers will do the job of beating eggs or whipping cream. But if you are serious about baking, you'll want a free-standing mixer with a heavy-duty motor. I use a KitchenAid, which is a miniature version of the huge Hobart mixers we use in the Deer Valley bakery. The KitchenAid mixer comes with 3 attachments and a stainless steel bowl. The flat beater or paddle is for creaming butter and beating stiff cake batters; the wire whip or balloon whisk is for whipping egg batters, egg whites and cream; and the dough hook is for kneading bread dough. When a recipe in this book calls for an electric mixer, it was tested using one of these heavy duty mixers—you'll need to allow more time when working with a less powerful mixer.

**Entremet ring:** Also called dessert rings (*entremet* means "dessert" in French). These are bottomless, straight-sided stainless steel rings available in different sizes, used to construct molded cakes. I use an 8¾-inch diameter ring that is 2⅜ inches high. If you don't have an entremet ring, use the sides of a 9-inch springform pan. Because the springform sides are not as heavy as entremet rings, tape the outside bottom of the springform pan to a 10-inch cardboard circle—this helps prevent the filling from leaking. To unmold a dessert from a metal ring, briefly warm the ring with a propane torch, then slide the ring off the top of the dessert. If you don't own a torch, wrap a hot towel (that you have dipped in very hot water and wrung out) around the ring to loosen it. At Deer Valley we make elegant individual desserts using 3-inch diameter entremet rings.

**Extracts and other flavorings:** Use the best you can buy; if you have a choice between pure and imitation, always choose pure extracts. **Vanilla extracts** vary in strength and quality, depending on the country in which the vanilla beans were grown and the curing and extraction process. **Vanilla beans** are the fruit of a tropical orchid with flowers that look like green beans when they are harvested. As the beans cure, they darken into the aromatic pods we use to flavor desserts and to make vanilla extract. To use a whole vanilla bean, cut it lengthwise and scrape the tiny seeds into the liquid you wish to infuse, adding the bean pod as well. You will remove the bean pod after cooking, but the black flecks remain, giving your custard or ice cream an authentic look, along with quality flavor.

You can make your own vanilla extract with vodka and vanilla beans. Slit 4 beans and steep them in 2 cups vodka in a sealed glass jar for at least 1 month. Use as you would store-bought vanilla extract.

At Deer Valley, we use **coffee extract** in some recipes. At home, I substitute instant espresso coffee powder because the extract is hard to find. Well-stocked supermarkets and specialty stores carry Medaglia D'Oro brand instant espresso coffee powder in 2-ounce jars, usually in the coffee section. Use this powder for rich coffee flavor, alone and to enhance chocolate. You may substitute regular instant coffee—use 1½ times the amount of powder.

**Orange flower water** and **orange extract** add, accent or fortify orange flavor. Both are intense and should be used sparingly. Look for orange flower water in specialty and gourmet shops and, if unavailable, substitute an orange-flavored liqueur. Orange extract is sold in large supermarkets and also in specialty shops; substitute lemon extract if you cannot find orange extract.

**Flour:** The recipes in this cookbook use 4 types of flour: all-purpose flour, bread flour, cake flour and whole wheat flour. When a recipe calls for **all-purpose flour,** you can use either bleached or unbleached. I use unbleached all-purpose at home and bleached at Deer Valley; I find no real difference in the baked product. **Bread flour** is milled from a hard winter wheat and has more protein, which allows the bread to develop a stronger gluten bond and potentially a higher rise. I use unbleached bread flour in both kitchens, but it's not an essential ingredient. You can substitute unbleached all-purpose flour for bread flour in any of these recipes, though you may have to add more all-purpose flour to keep the dough from sticking. **Cake flour** is ground from softer, low-protein wheat kernels. I use it in delicate cakes, where a fine texture is important. You can substitute all-purpose flour for cake flour, though the cake will be slightly more coarse. I use Softasilk brand cake flour at home. **Whole wheat flour** includes the bran and the germ from the wheat kernel; I use it when I'm baking a more nutritious product. It adds a hearty quality and texture to baked goods. Whole wheat pastry flour is made from low-protein wheat and will create a more tender product than regular whole wheat flour, but I don't use it in any of the recipes in this book.

To measure flour, use the "stir, dip and scrape" method. "Stir" the flour to break up any packed clumps, "dip" a dry measuring cup into the container and "scrape" the flour level to the measuring cup using the flat side of any utensil. Don't tap the cup on the counter before scraping or the measurement might change. For cake flour, gently spoon it into the measuring cup before scraping it level. At Deer Valley we measure flour by weight, using a scale; I figure 1 cup of all-purpose flour weighs 4.75 ounces.

**Folding:** Folding helps keep volume in whipped mixtures. It is a method for combining ingredients—especially whipped egg whites into cake batter or whipped cream into pastry cream or flour into an egg ribbon. To fold, place about a third of the mixture to be added on top of the other mixture. Using a rubber spatula, a wire whisk, or your hand with the fingers extended, cut through the two mixtures near the back of the bowl. Scrape the bottom of the bowl and draw toward your body, scraping the side of the bowl and bringing the bottom mixture up to the top. As you draw up, rotate the bowl a quarter turn so the mixture comes up to one side of where you cut in. Continue to cut, scrape and draw up, rotating the bowl, adding the remaining mixture after folding just a few times. The folding technique is gentle repetition of the cutting, drawing up and bowl turning, continued until the mixtures are well blended.

**Food processor:** A well-equipped bakery doesn't really need a food processor but I certainly use mine in both kitchens. It sits on the counter, always ready to chop nuts, grate carrots and chocolate, or mix a streusel dough. You can use a food processor in many recipes to save time, even if I don't suggest it in the recipe directions. Refer to the instruction manual that comes with your machine. A rule of thumb when chopping or mixing with a food processor: turn the machine on and off (pulse) and check the contents of the work bowl after each pulse.

**Gelatin:** When soaked in a liquid and then heated, and then chilled, gelatin will solidify a liquid. I use gelatin to stabilize soft fillings for cakes, so they don't ooze out the sides. I prefer granulated or powdered gelatin, which is sold in small envelopes, each containing a little more than 2 teaspoons. There are two steps to follow with gelatin. First, sprinkle it over cold water or a compatible cold liquid without stirring; there should be 3 to 4 times liquid to gelatin. Let it soften or "bloom" about 5 minutes, until the gelatin has absorbed the liquid. Second, the gelatin needs to be dissolved with heat, one of two ways. Either mix the softened gelatin directly into a hot liquid, or place the softened gelatin in the top of a double boiler to liquefy, then stir it into the other ingredients. Liquefied warm gelatin occasionally seizes when you add it to another ingredient, especially if the ingredient is cold. If this happens, place the mixture in the top of a double boiler and stir until the mucus-like gelatin re-melts and disappears. Let the mixture cool down a little before adding another ingredient, like whipped cream.

**Ginger:** A brisk seasoning from the tropics, ginger complements and accentuates many baking ingredients. We are most familiar with ginger in ground form. Fresh ginger has a vigorous flavor and it keeps for weeks in the refrigerator. To grate, peel the brown skin beforehand and use the smallest holes on a grater. You can freeze fresh ginger; keep it frozen in an airtight plastic bag. Once it has been frozen, grate it when it is just slightly thawed, otherwise it will be too soft to grate. When measuring grated ginger, include the pungent juice, but discard large fibrous hairs. Fresh ginger is available in the produce section of most supermarkets.

**Gratin dishes:** These are heavy ceramic molds used for Gratin of Oranges "Girardet". The ones I use are oval in shape and measure about 5 inches long by 3 inches wide and 1 inch high. A shallow, heat-proof bowl is a good alternative.

**Honey:** I like to bake with honey; it adds moisture, flavor and a certain charm. It is slightly acidic, with a pH of 3.9, and will react with baking soda in a recipe. To measure honey, lightly coat a liquid measuring cup with oil (pour some oil in the clean cup, swirl it as high as you need to measure, and pour it back into the bottle), then pour in the honey—it will slide out of the cup easily. If a recipe calls for both oil and honey, measure the oil first.

**Ice cream scoops:** There are 2 kinds: ice cream dippers and multi-purpose scoops. Dippers are often oval in shape and some have a self-defrosting fluid in the handle for easy release of the ice cream. Multipurpose scoops have a rotating metal bar to help release the food. They can be used to evenly portion cookie dough and muffin batter as well as scoop ice cream. We scoop Deer Valley's jumbo cookies with a #12 scoop, which has ⅓ cup capacity; for small cookies we use a tiny #100 scoop. Look for the number, which tells approximately how many scoops to a quart, engraved on the metal bar that moves inside the scoop.

**Knives:** Use a chef's knife for chopping and slicing; a chef's knife has a wide, stiff blade with a sharp point. Use a paring knife with a narrow, pointed blade for peeling fruit. A long-bladed, serrated knife is the best choice for cutting cake layers and bread. It is important to keep knives sharp.

**Liqueurs and other alcohol:** To accentuate the flavors in many desserts, ice creams and sorbets, I use liqueur or alcohol. For orange and lemon flavor, try Triple Sec, Grand Marnier or another orange-flavored liqueur, such as Cointreau. Amaretto and Frangelico accent nuts and Kahlúa and crème de cacao work well with chocolate. I love complementing fall fruit specialties with French pear alcohol and apple brandy. Dark rum, such as Myer's or Mount Gay, is a good dessert partner; Jack Daniels whiskey makes delicious sabayon sauce. If you cannot use alcohol, substitute the nonalcoholic coffee flavorings they use at espresso stands or use fruit juice.

**Loaf pans:** A metal rectangular baking form for baking breads and molding terrines. The standard size is about 3 inches high, 9 inches long by 5 inches wide, and holds about 7 cups liquid volume. I use a longer loaf pan, approximately 12 inches long by 4 inches wide, for Chocolate Casbah Terrine and sweet breads such as Pumpkin Pecan Bread because I like the "slim" presentation, but the 9 x 5-inch size works just as well. The long loaf pan holds about 8 cups liquid volume.

**Maple syrup:** Use the real thing—pure maple syrup. It's the most natural sweetener available. Maple flavored pancake syrup is not real maple syrup; do not use it as a substitute. Measure with a liquid measuring cup.

**Marzipan:** See Almond paste and Marzipan, page 241. For marzipan recipe, see Stein's Favorite Marzipan Cake, page 103.

**Measuring cups and spoons:** There are two types of measuring cups, dry and liquid, and one should not be used for the other. Measure **dry ingredients** in the dry measuring cups that come nested in each other, ¼ cup to 1 cup. To measure, level off the ingredients (sugar, flour, etc.) using the straight edge of a knife. Measure **liquid ingredients** in the glass heat-proof or plastic pitchers, with the measurements marked on the side, that come in 1-, 2- and 4-cup sizes. To check the mark, bend down and look at eye level. Measuring spoons come in sets of graduated sizes, usually from ¼ teaspoon to 1 tablespoon, though some sets include ⅛ teaspoon and 2 tablespoon sizes.

**Microwave oven:** A convenient tool for defrosting ingredients. It can also be used to melt butter and chocolate (page 244) or heat liquids. Nuke if you are savvy. Review the instructions for your oven. I don't recommend a microwave oven for baking or reheating pastries.

**Mixing bowls:** You need a range of bowl sizes. Some should be metal, to use as the top of a double boiler or to nest on top of ice cubes for an ice bath. At home I have five sizes—6-inch, 8-inch, 10-inch, 13-inch and 15-inch bowls. The 15-inch bowl seems huge, and you need a large cupboard in which to store it, but it comes in handy for mixing big batches of anything, including granola or pasta salad.

**Molasses:** A thick, dark syrup produced in the sugar refining process. Use a high-quality "unsulphured" molasses—I recommend Grandma's brand. I think blackstrap molasses's flavor is too strong for baking. To measure molasses, lightly coat a liquid measuring cup with oil (pour some oil in the clean cup, swirl it as high as you need to measure, and pour it back into the bottle), then pour in the molasses—it will pour out easily.

**Muffin tins:** Metal baking pans with indented cups, they usually come in 12-cup tins. The muffin recipes in this book use standard-size cups—2½ inches across by 1¼ inches deep. Standard muffin cups hold about ⅓ cup of liquid.

**Oven spring:** The accelerated rising of bread loaves in a hot oven during the first 10 to 15 minutes of baking; the final burst of yeast action before the heat sets the cell walls of the dough.

**Oven racks:** A pan of batter or dough should be placed in the middle of the oven for best heat circulation. So that the baked good itself is in the middle, the oven rack will need to be in the lower third of the oven. When you preheat the oven before baking, adjust the oven rack so the baking item will be in the center of the oven.

**Parchment paper:** A time and mess-saving essential. Use it to line baking sheets and cake pans so the batter does not stick and the contents release easily from the pan. Parchment paper is available in rolls at cookware stores and near the waxed paper in well-stocked grocery stores or in large sheets at restaurant supply stores. You can substitute waxed paper, although there will be an odor of melting wax from the oven.

**Pastry bag and tips:** A pastry bag is a cone-shaped bag made of nylon, cloth or plastic. With a pastry tip fit inside, it is used to pipe out batters, whipped cream and decorative frosting borders. I like to have two sizes: a large bag (16- or 18-inch) that fits large and medium tips, and a smaller bag (10- or 12-inch) that fits a plastic 2-piece coupler. The coupler holds the smaller tips and allows you to change the tips without changing the bag. Pastry or piping tips come in many shapes and sizes. A large tip measures about ¾ inch; a medium about ½ inch. I use a medium star tip for borders and a large tip for the stars on the Chocolate Snowball. Small tips are for finer decoration, as on wedding cakes. I use a #3 plain tip for lines, a #16 or #18 star tip for borders and a #67 leaf tip for the leaves on the Orange Almond Wedding Cake. A plastic coupler works as a plain round tip for piping the nut meringue for the Lemon and Strawberry Dacquoise. Some pastry chefs use parchment paper cones for detail work such as piping designs and inscriptions on cakes.

**Using a Pastry Bag:** I follow two rules with pastry bags. First, never fill it more than half full—it's easier to pipe with less filling and you won't have a mess leaking out of the top and all over your hands. Second, use the same hand to twist the top end of the bag taut and press the filling out.

Put the tip or plastic coupler in the pastry bag. You might need to trim a new bag so the pastry tip just pokes out of the end. If you use a coupler, fasten the tip on the out-side. To keep the filling from leaking out the bottom while you fill the bag, tuck some of the bag near the pastry tip into the tip itself. Or pinch a clothespin across the bag right above the pastry tip. Hold the bag in one hand, and fold the top of the bag halfway down over your hand, forming a collar. Use a rubber spatula to fill the bag (but no more than half full) with the batter or frosting. Unroll the collar and twist the bag just at the top of the filling, gently working out any air pockets that would cause the mixture to splatter when you pipe. Hook your thumb and forefinger around the twist, point the bag up and undo the bottom tuck or clothespin. Pipe, applying gentle pressure (with three fingers of the same hand that's twisting the top). Rest your other hand near the tip without squeezing to steady any jitteriness.

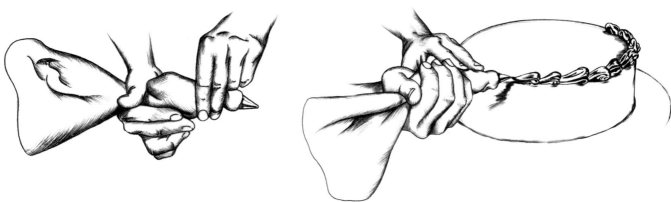

Hold the pastry bag a little above the surface and at an angle as you pipe; this helps control where the filling goes. Continue twisting the bag as it empties, moving your hand down the bag. When there is not enough filling in the bag to keep it flowing, squeeze the remainder back into the mixture and refill the bag as before. When you have finished, turn the bag inside out and remove the tip. Wash in hot soapy water and rinse well. At home, I clean my pastry bags in the dishwasher; a clothespin holds them to the wire rack.

**Pastry blender:** A tool with parallel curved wires attached to a handle. Helps keep the butter cold as you cut or work it into the flour.

**Pastry brush:** Use a pastry brush to apply moistening syrup to cakes, Apricot Glaze to a fruit tart, egg wash to bread dough, or melted butter to phyllo. Get a brush with natural bristles about 1½ inches wide. Don't let anyone use your pastry brush to spread garlic butter on bread or barbecue sauce on chicken—brushes can hold flavors no matter how well you wash them.

**Pastry wheel:** Also called a pizza cutter. This is a rolling sharp wheel attached to a handle. I use one with a fluted or scalloped edge, a ravioli cutter, to cut the dough strips for Raspberry Linzertorte.

**Phyllo:** Often spelled "filo" and sometimes "fillo," this is a delicate flaky pastry dough of Greek origin. The paper-thin rectangular sheets, about 14 x 18 inches, come rolled in boxes of 20 sheets, usually frozen. Many supermarkets carry phyllo, but you can always find it in Greek, Middle Eastern or Mediterranean markets. Sometimes phyllo can be persnickety, but it's really easy to work with; you learn to move the thin leaves comfortably and patch torn sheets together with melted butter. You'll want to brush sparingly with the melted butter or the pastry will be greasy, and start brushing a different edge with each layer. Work quickly, and cover the phyllo you're not using with a slightly damp towel. You can re-roll, wrap tightly and refrigerate any unused sheets—they'll keep about 10 days. You can also refreeze phyllo, but you might lose a few sheets from the extra moisture. I often substitute phyllo for pie and tart dough, creating desserts that seem much lighter.

**Pie pans:** I use a heat-proof 9-inch glass pie plate at home and metal pie tins at Deer Valley. Nine-inch diameter pie pans vary in size; measure from the inside of the top rim. The pie crusts in this book were tested in glass; if you use a metal tin, it may take longer for the crust to bake to a golden brown. Glass pie plates are advantageous also because you can see the color of the crust bottom as it bakes.

**Pie weights:** Used in "blind baking" to weigh down a dough or pastry so it doesn't rise as it bakes. Small metal pellets are sold as pie weights at cookware shops, but dried beans or uncooked rice grains make fine substitutes with negligible cost. We use dried beans at Deer Valley, storing the small black or red beans in a 5-gallon bucket between uses. At home I use short grain brown rice. I keep the rice in a large jar and re-use it as pie weights many times over years.

**Preparing pans:** We prepare the pans so the baked product will release easily. It's a good habit to prepare your pans before starting to mix ingredients so when your batter is ready, your pans are too. At Deer Valley and at home I spray the pans with no-stick cooking spray or food release. I also line my pans with parchment paper, as insurance. If you prefer not to use spray, brush the pans with melted butter and immediately sprinkle about a tablespoon of flour into the pan. Tilt and turn the pan, so a light layer of flour sticks to the butter, then tap the pan upside down so the excess flour falls out. Re-butter the spots where the flour didn't stick.

**Propane torch:** This seems a funny tool for a bakery, but it comes in handy for browning meringue on a pie or for caramelizing sugar on a gratin or crème brûlée. A torch is also the easiest way to remove a molded dessert from an entremet ring. Hardware stores and some kitchen supply stores sell propane torches.

**Prune purée:** Prunes are naturally high in pectin, which adds texture and volume, and sorbitol, which attracts and keeps moisture. These qualities enhance baked goods and allow prunes (the Prune Marketing Board calls them dried plums) to replace fat in recipes. Prunes are the "secret" ingredient that makes Almost Sinless Brownies and Black Forest Mousse Cake fat-free. At Deer Valley we buy large cans of prunes, in their own juice, and purée it all in the food processor. At home, I purée pitted prunes and hot water: Soak 1 cup pitted prunes, tightly packed, in ½ cup hot water for 10 minutes. Purée in a food processor until quite smooth and no large chunks remain. This yields 1 cup prune purée, which can be made ahead and frozen until needed. To replace the fat in a recipe, substitute prune purée one for one, e.g., ½ cup of prune purée replaces ½ cup of oil or butter.

**Ribbon:** This is the term used to describe the stage at which sugar and eggs have been beaten long enough to incorporate air. The batter falls off the lifted beater and back into the bowl in a flowing continuous ribbon and holds that shape for a few seconds before dissolving. At ribbon stage the whipped eggs will be thick and very pale yellow and be almost tripled in volume.

**Rolling pin:** You need a rolling pin for pie and tart dough, rolled cookies, marzipan and cinnamon rolls. My first choice is a wooden rolling pin; mostly I use the American ball-bearing type with handles, but the French handleless type feels better for making puff pastry. Never get water down the handles of a ball-bearing style—the ball bearings will rust and the "pin" will no longer roll smoothly.

**Salt:** The recipes in this book use **table salt** (or **sea salt**) or **kosher salt.** Table salt is the iodized regular salt that we buy in the supermarket. Sea salt may be substituted for table salt; the differences are subtle and these recipes work with either one—my personal choice is sea salt. Kosher salt is coarse-grained; I use it in bread recipes. Coarse kosher salt is the topping of choice for Potato Focaccia with Red Onions and Basil. Neither kosher salt nor sea salt has additives. If a recipe calls for kosher salt and you want to substitute table salt, use a little less, because in a measuring spoon kosher salt takes up more room.

**Saucepans:** I think every home bakery should have at least two saucepans, 4-quart and 6-quart sizes, approximately. Bakers need noncorrosive pans, not aluminum or cast iron, to prevent changes in the color and flavor of the cooked food. I use stainless steel pans with a copper bottom. Other choices include stainless-lined copper or stainless-lined aluminum or enameled iron.

**Scale:** At Deer Valley we use either a balance beam scale or an electronic scale to measure most of our ingredients; scales ensure accuracy. I have a mechanical scale at home that weighs up to 7 pounds in ½-ounce increments and I use it often, to weigh butter and chocolate as well as nuts and dried fruits. Because many home bakers don't own a scale, I have converted Deer Valley's recipes so they measure in tablespoons and cups, not ounces and pounds. If you buy chocolate in bulk, you will need a scale to weigh the chocolate for recipes. Good home-use scales, both mechanical and electronic (battery operated), can be purchased in kitchenware stores, hardware stores and by mail or e-mail order catalogs (page 257).

**Scraping the bowl:** Many recipes in this book call for stopping to scrape the sides and bottom of the bowl. I cannot overemphasize the importance of this step—be in the habit of scraping the bowl and the beater frequently when you mix a batter, especially after you add ingredients.

**Sifters, sieves and strainers:** These items are made for different jobs, but all you really need is a fine-meshed sieve for both sifting and straining. A sifter usually has a rotating wire to push dry ingredients through a screen; you can sift dry ingredients by holding a sieve above a bowl and using your other hand to tap the side of the sieve. A conical strainer is used to strain liquid such as Vanilla Bean Crème Anglaise, or for separating the seeds out of a fruit mixture, although a fine-meshed sieve is also a suitable strainer.

**Skillet:** Sometimes called a fry pan or a sauté pan, this is a shallow, round pan with a long handle used for frying or sautéing food. I use a 10-inch skillet with an oven-proof handle to make Tarte Tatin; I also use a skillet to precook the apples for a pie. Nonstick skillets are valuable for cooking and stirring food without extra butter or oil.

**Spatulas: Rubber or plastic spatulas** are great tools for folding ingredients together and for scraping the batter on the sides and bottom of a mixing bowl. Also used to scrape batter out of the bowl into the baking pan, the best rubber spatulas have wide and flexible blades. A **handleless plastic scraper** gives more leverage for stiff batters and is what we use most in Deer Valley's bakery.

**Icing spatulas** have long, round-ended blades and are used for frosting, glazing and spreading. An **offset spatula** is handy—it's the same as an icing spatula, but with a bend in the blade near the handle, so you can spread a mixture evenly without the edge of the pan getting in the way. I use a small offset spatula to spread filling into tart shells, although the back of a metal teaspoon also works well.

**Sugar:** If a recipe calls for "sugar," use granulated sugar, which is regular white sugar. If a recipe calls for **brown sugar,** you can use either light brown sugar or dark brown sugar. Brown sugar is white sugar with molasses mixed in; dark brown sugar just has more molasses. To measure brown sugar, pack it firmly into a dry measuring cup; when you dump it out it should keep the shape of the cup. For accuracy, I use a scale to measure brown sugar—I figure 1 cup weighs 7 ounces. Over time, brown sugar can harden into an unusable rock. Put a slice of bread in with the sugar; in less than 24 hours it will be soft again. If you are out of brown sugar, you can make your own; 3 tablespoons of molasses and 1 cup of white sugar equal 1 cup of brown sugar.

**Confectioners' sugar** is finely pulverized sugar, mixed with a small amount of cornstarch to prevent caking; it's sold as confectioners' powdered sugar. To measure confectioners' sugar, stir the sugar to lighten, spoon it into a dry measuring cup and level it off with a straight edge. Be sure to sift confectioners' sugar before using, to disperse any lumps.

**Crystal sugar** is a decorative sugar with coarse granules about the size of a pinhead—they add sparkle to pies and cookies. Look for crystal sugar in specialty markets; substitute raw sugar or granulated sugar if crystal sugar is unavailable.

**Raw sugar,** also called turbinado sugar, comes from the first pressing of the sugar cane and has a light brown color because some of the natural molasses has been left in. Raw sugar has a crystal texture and can be used as decorative sugar instead of white crystal sugar.

**Tart pans:** These are metal pans with removable bottoms, with straight, usually fluted, 1-inch sides. They come in different shapes and sizes—in this book I use 9-inch rounds for large tarts and 4-inch rounds for individual fruit tarts.

**Testing for cake doneness:** I use the words "until the center of the cake springs back when touched with a finger." This is a feel that comes with experience, but I find it the most reliable test. The cake should be firm; if your finger leaves an indentation on the surface, the cake is not quite done. Compare with the batter near the pan edge, which bakes faster and will bounce back from your touch sooner. Look for a cake to shrink away from the sides of the pan, which also indicates doneness. Another test is inserting a wire cake tester or a wooden toothpick in the center. If it comes out clean and dry, the cake is done. This test is useful even with very moist cakes, such as the fat-free Black Forest Mousse Cake, or on any cake, as a cross-check for the finger-touch test.

Cool cakes in their pans for 5 to 10 minutes. Invert to remove from the pan, but finish cooling with the cake right side up. Wrap cakes as soon as they are completely cool so they don't dry out.

**Thermometers:** The success of a recipe depends on correct temperatures, with ingredients or in the oven. Use an oven thermometer to be sure your oven is accurate. If necessary, adjust the outside dial to match the real oven temperature.

I strongly recommend an instant-read thermometer as the tool to gauge liquid temperatures for dissolving yeast, and to make certain eggs cook to the salmonella instant-kill temperature of 160°. There are two kinds of instant-read thermometers, both with a stainless steel stem and dial on top. One has a range of 0° to 220°, and the stem must be 1½ to 2 inches into the food for an accurate measure—this is the kind I use at work and at home. The other is a digital battery-operated thermometer with a range of 14° to 392°, and is accurate with ¼ inch of stem in the food. Look for instant-read thermometers in cookware and hardware stores or mail-order kitchenware catalogs.

**Toasting nuts:** Toasting brings out the flavor in all varieties of nuts. Spread nuts in an ungreased pan and toast in a 350° oven for 5 to 7 minutes, until they are slightly browned. Hazelnuts have a papery skin that is somewhat bitter. Remove the skin by rubbing the nuts in a clean towel immediately after toasting. It is almost impossible to get all the skin off hazelnuts; remove as much as you can. You can buy skinned hazelnuts at some specialty or gourmet shops.

**Wire whisk:** A hand tool with wires attached to a handle, used to whip or fold ingredients together. I like to have several whisks handy, in a variety of sizes.

**Yeast:** Yeast is alive; it's a fungus that feeds on sugar and other carbohydrates in grains. It ferments, creating carbon dioxide gas, which makes bread rise. There are several genetic strains of the yeast species used in baking: compressed fresh yeast, active dry yeast, rapid-rise yeast and instant yeast, and each has different characteristics and uses. The recipes in this book were developed and tested using active dry yeast, but you can substitute rapid-rise yeast if that is what you use. Since rapid-rise yeast shortens the fermentation period, the dough has less time to develop flavor and texture.

**Zest:** Zest is the colored part of the peel of citrus fruit. Many recipes with citrus call for grated zest because the essential oil and flavor of the fruit is in the zest. Wash citrus well before grating the peel, to get rid of as much pesticide, fungicide and wax as you can. Grate zest using the smallest holes on a grater tool—I prefer a four-sided box grater. Be careful not to grate any of the white pith off the fruit—it is bitter and should not be used. I estimate the skin of one fruit yields about 1 teaspoon of grated zest. If you are going to candy the zest or use it as decoration, use a zester, a channel knife or a sharp knife to cut the strips.

**Zester:** A small hand tool used to cut threads of zest from citrus fruit. A zester has four to six holes at the top. Choose a high-quality zester, with a sharp, thin blade.

# Resources

### King Arthur Flour: The Baker's Catalog
800-827-6836; P.O. Box 876, Norwich, VT 05055-0876
www.kingarthurflour.com
A comprehensive catalog of tools, ingredients, equipment and books for the home baker. Mail-order source for orange flower water, dried cherries, kitchen scales and instant-read thermometers.

### A Cook's Wares
800-915-9788; 211 37th Street, Beaver Falls, PA 15010-2103
www.cookswares.com
A comprehensive catalog of cookware, gourmet ingredients and cookbooks. Source for knives and other tools, as well as scales and thermometers.

### Chef's Catalog
800-338-3232
Professional restaurant equipment for the home cook.

### Sweet Celebrations

800-328-6722; P.O. Box 39426, Edina, MN 55439-0426
A candy and cake decorating catalog with unusual pans and hard-to-find ingredients like crystallized flowers.

### Williams-Sonoma Mail Order Department

800-541-2233; P.O. Box 7456, San Francisco, CA 94120-7456
A catalog for the home cook.

### Bakers Cash and Carry

801-487-3300; 367 W. Paxton, Salt Lake City, UT 84101
www.bakerscandc.com
Bulk chocolate and cake decorating supplies, including cardboard cake circles.

### The California Press

707-944-0343; Fax: 707-944-0350; 6200 Washington Street, Yountville, CA 94599
Distributors of exceptional first-press virgin walnut, hazelnut, pecan, pistachio and almond oils.

### Bakers Dozen

A group of baking professionals and enthusiasts interested in sharing information and camaraderie. To be included on the Bakers Dozen mailing list for quarterly meetings, send your name, address and telephone number. For the San Francisco Bay Area group, write: Flo Braker, c/o Bakers Dozen, 1550 El Camino Real, Suite 200, Menlo Park, CA 94025. For the East Coast group, write: Nick Malgieri, Bakers Dozen East, c/o James Beard Foundation, 167 West 12th Street, New York, NY 10011.

### The Other Bookstore

970-491-6198; Fax: 970-491-2961; Cooperative Extension Resource Center; 115 General Services Building, Colorado State University, Fort Collins, CO 80523-4061;
e-mail: cerc@vines.colostate.edu
Publications about baking and cooking at high altitudes.

### Penzeys Spices

414-679-7207; P.O. Box 933, Muskego, WI 53150
www.penzeys.com
A catalog of quality spices, herbs and flavorings.

# Deer Valley Resort
## Extraordinary Food and Service

Deer Valley Resort is a premier destination ski area in Utah's Wasatch Mountains; it opened to guests in December of 1981. The resort was conceived and developed by hotelier and businessman Edgar Stern to be a ski area where every customer is treated as a luxury hotel guest. By focusing on personal attention, outstanding customer service and excellent innovative cuisine besides incomparably groomed ski runs, Deer Valley fundamentally changed the ambiance of American ski resorts.

As Deer Valley's executive pastry chef, my job is to make desserts, breads and pastries memorable from first sight to last bite. My goal is elegant, tender cakes or perfectly golden brown and buttery scones—desserts and pastries that "wow." I always ask, "How can I make it better?" We call this resortwide striving for the best "the Deer Valley difference." The difference means attention to every detail, and it includes making all guests feel special and honoring them with genuine consideration and courtesy, along with a welcoming smile. We also try to treat employees and coworkers as the "first guests"—something I believe to be a key to Deer Valley's success.

Deer Valley lies within the city limits of Park City, an old silver mining town. The resort's main buildings are impressive day lodges with sloping roofs that blend into the mountain setting. Inside are massive wood beams and huge Douglas-fir log posts and a diligent mason's stonework. There is a rock fireplace in nearly every public room. Every time the summer trail crew cuts a new path for a ski run, the resultant wood is stacked outside the lodges, ready for winter fires. In the "back of the house," stainless steel and tile are prevalent, spread with sweets and savories in all stages of preparation. Deer Valley is comprised of these day lodges, built for skier comforts as well as evening dining. Guests spend the night in nearby hotels and many privately owned homes and condominiums.

Snow Park Lodge is Deer Valley's base facility. A typical skier's day begins here, with uniformed valets greeting and assisting with ski gear. Snow Park Lodge faces Bald Eagle Mountain and the 2002 Olympic sites, venues for the competitions in slalom, combined slalom, freestyle mogul and aerial skiing.

The Snow Park Restaurant opens for breakfast every day in the winter season, attracting knowing locals as well as hungry skiers. It consists of buffets, with white-toqued cooks at the ready. One buffet offers Belgian waffles with pure Vermont maple syrup, as well as made-to-order omelets with a choice of fillings including goat cheese, fresh basil and house-smoked salmon. Another buffet specializes in house-made Deer Valley Granola, McCann's Irish oatmeal and fresh fruits and juices. The bakery counter tempts guests with Cranberry Orange Bread, enormous Blueberry Corn Muffins, bagels and Banana Maple Nut Coffee Cake.

*Snow Park Lodge*

Before noon, each station in the restaurant switches to lunch mode. The natural breakfast buffet is replaced by a lavish array of composed salads and fresh-baked bread, where guests can walk around the circular polished brass sideboard and pile their plates with healthy fare such as baby spinach, steamed artichokes, fresh mozzarella balls and grilled eggplant. Other stations become the place to ask for homemade soups, grilled-to-order burgers and daily specials. My favorite is the vegetarian enchilada filled with butternut squash, shiitake mushrooms and Anasazi beans, served with tomatillo sauce. At the bakery, Jumbo Chocolate Chip Cookies emerge hot from the oven, and are displayed next to strawberry-topped Deer Valley Cheesecakes and Deep Powder Carrot Cakes.

For après ski, Snow Park Lodge has live music as well as a big-screen television for sports enthusiasts. Parmesan baked pita chips from Snow Park Bakery are on the list of after-ski snacks. The lounge has an outdoor deck, popular for catching the last rays of the sun and watching skiers make their way down the mountain at the end of the day.

Six nights a week, the Snow Park Restaurant food court transforms into a resplendent buffet from the world's oceans, rivers and lakes, called Seafood Buffet. The brass-trimmed "Bakeries" sign hangs above a baker's dozen of scrumptious sweets, an invitation to indulge. This is where you might find White Chocolate Banana Cream Pie or Phyllo and Fresh Fruit Tartlets. Hundreds of miniature cookies and chocolate truffles tempt noshers even as they decide between tiramisù or Mango Cinnamon Trifle. We portion the servings as small as possible so guests can try every dessert they wish. Across the room, the natural buffet presents freshly shucked Quilcene oysters, sushi rolls, house-smoked salmon and Dungeness crab, along with assorted fresh salads. Another station has hot seafood appetizers; one more has seafood entrees such as seared ahi tuna and baked sea bass with a honey soy glaze. For the seafood wary and weary, there is succulent prime rib with roasted garlic mashed potatoes. No wonder Seafood Buffet is listed in *Zagat Restaurant Guide* as one of "America's Top Restaurants."

In the summer, Snow Park Lodge is backdrop for an outdoor concert stage. Besides evenings with the Utah Symphony, there are weekend-long music festivals running the gamut from jazz to bluegrass. Concertgoers arrive early to relax on the lawn with a blanket; some bring gourmet picnics complete with crystal wine glasses.

You can view four chairlifts from Snow Park Lodge. One you can ride all the way to mid-mountain Silver Lake Lodge; another lets you off at the top of Bald Eagle Mountain—you ski the three hundred feet to Silver Lake. When the lifts aren't running at night and in the summer, or if you prefer, drive three miles up the mountain to Silver Lake Lodge.

This lodge matches Snow Park with its rock and wood exterior. Snugged at the bottom of Bald Mountain, Silver Lake Lodge also has a day eatery with separate buffets. Every morning the bakery opens for continental breakfast; possibilities include fresh-baked Sunshine Muffins, Danish pastries and Raspberry Cream Cheese Coffee Cake. At lunch there is the natural salad buffet, every bit as lavish as Snow Park's, with daily-special bread to accompany the smorgasbord of fresh greens, grains and fruits. At the bakery, Snuggery Chocolate Silk Pies and Peanut Butter Lover's Cakes help crowd the shelves. All day long, the baker loads and unloads jumbo cookies from the ovens. He or she bakes these cookies to sell warm at the three ski-day restaurants in the lodge. Oatmeal Raisin, Double Chocolate Chip and Chocolate Chip Jumbos—cookie production keeps the bakers at Silver Lake on their toes.

Bald Mountain Pizza has an excellent view through 30-foot-high windows on its south wall. In the evenings and in summer, when the pizza station is closed, the large room is a favorite for weddings and private parties. McHenry's at Silver Lake Lodge serves gourmet turkey, beef, chicken and garden burgers by day and casual grill meals by night. Dessert persuasions include Warm Apple and Raspberry Crisp and vanilla ice cream sandwiches. We cut the sandwiches in quarters and serve them with a ramekin of Hot Fudge Dipping Sauce.

Tucked in the north corner of the lodge is The Mariposa, Deer Valley's foremost white linen restaurant. On winter evenings, visitors dressed in snow country finery come for the wild mushroom risotto cakes or the roasted loin of venison—to celebrate a special occasion or to enjoy the best of fine dining on their ski vacation. In the foyer, while being escorted to the table, they pass the antique wooden pastry table where the Chocolate Snowball presides. A rich, flourless torte, the Chocolate Snowball has been the culmination of many a Mariposa meal. Mariposa desserts are our most innovative and extravagant finales—each one a seduction.

In summer, the ride up Sterling chairlift just outside Silver Lake Lodge boasts an eye-soothing vista of surrounding mountains and forests. The majority of warm weather chairlift riders are mountain bikers who ride down on their bikes. The resort has become a summer mountain bike mecca. After the snow melts, a network of well-maintained dirt trails becomes navigable, with trails winding through the aspen and evergreen trees. For lunch, hikers and mountain bikers meet family and friends on the deck of McHenry's restaurant. They enjoy a scenic view of the trails and a casual meal of favorites topped off with McHenry's Frozen Lemon Meringue Pie.

Private banquets take place in the lodges year round. Meetings and company parties are an escape from the everyday, especially when Raspberry Granola Bars and Chocolate Truffle Cake are served for dessert. Using the Orange Almond Wedding Cake recipe in this book, you can make your own wedding cake, but if you have your reception at Deer Valley, we'll make the cake for you.

Deer Valley's other mountains are Flagstaff Mountain and Empire Canyon. Tucked into the valley between these mountains is the third day lodge, Empire Canyon Lodge, which opens winter season of the year 2000. Contact Deer Valley Resort at P.O. Box 1525, Park City, Utah 84060; toll-free from the United States and Canada 800-424-3337, or direct 435-649-1000; www.deervalley.com.

# Index

Page numbers in *italics* refer to photo captions

# About the Author

Letty Halloran Flatt has worked at Deer Valley Resort since 1981. She became a baker after ski patrolling for two winters. Executive Pastry Chef since 1988, she supervises more than thirty bakers and the two bakery kitchens supplying Deer Valley's restaurants and banquets.

Flatt was born in California but moved to the mountains when she was twenty, to ski and earn a diploma from the University of Utah. She is a graduate of the French Culinary Institute in New York. She has studied with Madeleine Kamman and attended Ecole-Lenôtre in Plaisir-Grignon in France. She is a member of the Bakers Dozen, a network and idea exchange in the San Francisco Bay Area.

Flatt enjoys the outdoor lifestyle of Park City, Utah. She follows a vegetarian diet and practices yoga. She skis, mountain bikes and windsurfs with her husband, Robbie, whom she met on the ski slopes.